The Middle School:
Humanizing Education for Youth

Donald E. Overly
Centerville City Schools, Centerville, Ohio

Jon Rye Kinghorn
Institute for the Development of Educational Activities
Dayton, Ohio

Richard L. Preston
Centerville City Schools, Centerville, Ohio

Charles A. Jones Publishing Company
Worthington, Ohio

1 2 3 4 5 6 7 8 9 10 / 76 75 74 73 72

Library of Congress Catalog Card Number: 70-150132

International Standard Book Number: 0-8396-0004-6

Printed in the United States of America

Preface

Individualizing and humanizing instruction are emphasized more and more in educational planning. The improved middle school provides preadolescents with a flexible learning environment through which they can flourish and grow more confidently toward maturity. Achieving an effective middle school program has become an increasingly important goal in our education process. And, fortunately for the youngster, many communities are recognizing and meeting the critical needs of the blossoming teenager with new learning approaches inherent in our better middle schools. How to develop a middle school to the fullest potential— for the benefit of the youngster—is what *The Middle School: Humanizing Education for Youth* is all about.

To help the professional arrive at an intelligent understanding of the middle school movement, Part 1 provides a foundation upon which to plan and evaluate school programs. Discussion of various programs in curriculum development in Part 2 lays the framework for the implementation of these programs and answers questions frequently raised by educators. Part 3 presents some alternatives for specific innovations and suggestions for scheduling and staff allocation. In analyzing student outcomes, Part 4 gives direction for student involvement. Part 5 provides specific alternatives for remodeling and designing school facilities with staff and community participation.

Preservice and inservice teachers and educators will find throughout this book ways to increase the learning options available to students and to move toward more humanistic, student-centered learning programs. Parents and community leaders will find ways in which they can become more involved in the planning process and in the implementation of the educational process.

We wish to thank Harold Armstrong, Thomas Curtis, R. L. Featherstone, Roy Larmee, and Louis Romano for their helpful comments and suggestions. We are also indebted to Judy Baker, editor; J. C. Whitman and Susan Lindsey, artists; Rose Brown, Pat Nosil, and Lois Parker, typists; and our families for their understanding and encouragement.

Donald E. Overly
Jon Rye Kinghorn
Richard L. Preston

Contents

Part 1

Rationale for
the Middle School

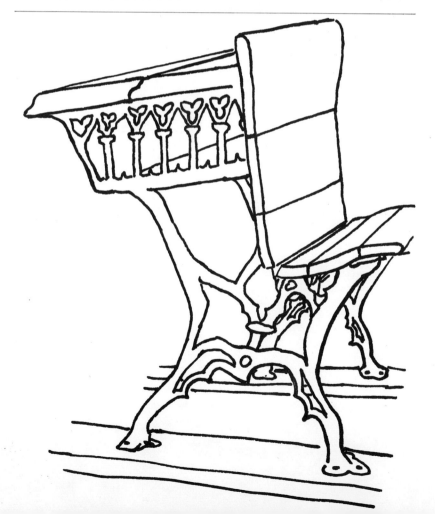

Chapter 1

Humanizing Aspects

Humanizing education — that is what the middle school is all about. Precisely what does one mean by humanizing education? When one deeply cares about the reasons a student has for being in school, how he values himself, what his home life is like, what goals he has, and how he is viewed by other students — and places these things first — then one humanizes education for the student. Indeed, why have a middle school? What are the unique needs of middle school students? Humanizing education in a middle school requires an instructional program that takes into consideration the extreme range of individual differences. The middle school with an individualized program can meet the needs of middle school youth.

Physical and Self-Concept Development

If a person enjoys young adults, then working in a middle school is a delightful experience. One is able to interact with students of varying physical development. Some students are so small in physical development that their feet will not touch the floor when they sit in a normal-sized chair. Other students may have difficulty finding a chair big enough in which to sit.

Many students are unsure of themselves and of how fellow students view them. This lack of self-concept is exhibited in many ways. For example, a shy student may be very hesitant to talk to fellow students and may stand in awe of a teacher. He may seem to be cowed in a chair or in the corner and may need the attention of the professional staff in order to be involved to any extent in the instructional program. This shy student can be contrasted with the student who seems to always be talking, who is boisterous and feels a need to be the center of attention. In the middle school some young girls, 10 or 11 years old, seem to spend the year giggling. These various kinds of behavior are most delightful if one realizes that they represent normal behavior, not overt acts designed to test the teacher's authority.

The sheer physical energy exhibited by middle school students is enormous. They are enthusiastic, eager to learn, and will exhibit this enthusiasm not only in their physical manifestations, but in their intellectual curiosity as well. Certainly, students are not always exuberant and excited about learning what teachers might want them to learn, but they are excited about learning. For example, a student in his eighth year of school may not exhibit much enthusiasm or excitement about sentence structure. However, if that boy becomes involved in such activities outside of the school setting as working on an automobile or doing something else that he feels is important, his tremendous energy and enthusiasm are brought forth.

Many books have been written describing and categorizing the physical characteristics of the middle school student. However, merely reviewing a list of physical characteristics typical of this age group is not sufficient. What is important is that the middle school staff learn to appreciate, enjoy, and capitalize on these physical differences expressed by middle school students. The young man who is so clumsy that he is constantly falling out of his seat and stumbling over his own feet is not being bad, but is in the growth process of becoming a man. This young man can accept physical changes in an understanding and nonthreatening environment, rather than in an environment in which he does

not feel free to express himself and is constantly embarrassed.
The student thrives in the environment in which he feels secure.
The middle school staff should seek to provide an educational set-
ting that does not threaten the dignity of each individual.

Goals

Middle school students are no different from other students in
that they enter school with different personal needs. They have
different backgrounds, different values, and different abilities.
Middle school students are in the process of establishing goals for
themselves. One of these goals is to establish their adult life pattern. In doing this they are moving out of the domination of the
home and attempting to acquire more freedom to go where they
are not always supervised by adults. Often students are experi-
menting with certain behaviors to see what effect they have on
the adult world, and, indeed, what effect their behaviors have on
themselves.

Boys are finding out what it is like to ask a girl for a date and
are terribly concerned that when they do talk to a girl they may
run out of things to say. Middle school students have long before
established very close relationships and friendships with members of the same sex, but they now begin to develop very close

relationships with members of the opposite sex. These experiences are new, and students need an environment in which they can try out new roles.

Time for Exploration

A rich part of adult life is having time to explore interests in depth. Middle school years should provide time for the student to explore an area of his choice, time to pursue interests of his own, time for some sort of depth study. The executive who delves into the stock market not only for profit but also for enjoyment, the family who thoroughly enjoys studying and growing roses, the individual who simply wants to take time out for fishing or some other type of relaxation, all enjoy pursuing their interests. The challenge that comes with being able to pursue a task in depth helps a student enjoy doing the task well. This challenging of the student to explore implies having a staff of teachers in the middle school who will encourage students to ask questions, who will accept students' ideas of topics for independent study projects, and who will consider students' suggestions and opinions without prejudging and immediately pointing out errors.

The middle school experience can be a time in which students explore their own ideas, and how the world around them reacts to them as people and to their ideas. Exploration in the middle school should not be limited to time set aside for exploration of areas of interest in subject matter only. That is, a student is free to spend an extra amount of time in art or music or some phase of industrial arts, but it is also a time in which the student can explore what kind of a person he is and examine his own values and reasons for being in school.

Right to Make Mistakes

Another requirement of humanizing education is the construction of an environment in which an individual can feel free to make a mistake or an honest error in judgment without suffering any embarrassment or ridicule from the teacher. It is not unusual to hear adults say, "I would like to ask a question, but I'm afraid of what people might think of me," or, "I would like to try something new, but I'm afraid that I might fail." Many adults are very conscious of what others might say or think about them. Many adults are also afraid that they might fail, and they would condemn themselves if they did. The middle school student has all of these fears except they are often more exaggerated than those of an adult. Humanizing education in the middle school requires that failing to achieve one's goal is not a threatening experience.

Free Expression

The middle school years are a time in which students are free of many of the adult responsibilities and yet feel very much a part of the adult world. In the adult world, one soon learns that to be socially acceptable, emotions are frequently hidden or suppressed. Students must feel free to be themselves, to laugh when something is funny, and to cry when something is sad. The students must not feel that they are always to look at the teacher to receive a clue as to what emotion they should express.

Daily Success

A middle school environment should be constructed so that learning can be fun. Daily success on the part of each student is vital. Learning can take place when students are finding it enjoyable. Students can grow, develop and become adults, even though the work may not be difficult or unpleasant. A school staff must not view learning as an unpleasant chore or a conflict between the teacher and the student. Students can be coerced into memorizing or doing certain activities if sufficient pressure is applied through grades or disapproval on the part of the teacher. Punitive measures of various sorts can change behavior. When pressures are removed, students will learn more efficiently. Students will continue to learn in a nonthreatening environment because they want to learn, not because they are forced to learn. Responsibility for learning is taken from the teacher and given to the student.

To Be Known as a Person

Humanizing education in the middle school is placing the individual above content. The subject matter material must not be remote from the learner, but must hold some present interest for him. When one cares about the individual and how the individual develops as an adult, then one will be more prone to construct a learning environment that will meet the unique needs of each learner. In this warm responsive environment the nonachiever does not exist. All children will be achieving, and the teacher will recognize varying levels of achievement. Differences will be accepted in the middle school environment.

Some students come to school from homes in which little or no value is placed on formal education. These students are provided a humanized instructional program when they are accepted and not made to conform to the same standards or exhibit the same type of overt behavior as a student who comes from a home in which formal education is highly prized. Humanizing education means accepting each student and his unique background and making him feel warm, comfortable, and appreciated in the learning environment.

Certainly high school students need this same acceptance, but the middle school student is unique in that he is becoming aware, for the first time, of many of the social taboos that can be placed upon him. At this point in the student's physical and mental development he is becoming very much aware of the world around him. He wants to become an adult who can feel confident and sure of himself. During the adolescent years when the student is neither emotionally an adult nor a child, he experiences many feelings of uncertainty. The middle school environment must not contribute in any fashion to these insecure feelings.

Humanizing education in the middle school requires that teachers recognize each individual's uniqueness. We often appreciate and cherish other adults' rare qualities. This is what makes people special. This is what makes us love someone, care for someone, and want to be around someone. Because he is unique, he is different from anyone else. The student must be able to come to school and know that the professional staff of the middle school treasures him as an individual, looks forward to having him in the learning environment, and views him with acceptance. Humanizing education may be simply stated as caring for each individual and his uniqueness and expressing confidence and trust in that individual.

Students are unsure of the roles they will play in growing up and, indeed, in the learning process. Is it the role of the individual in an educational program to try to outwit the teacher? Is the individual to accept the responsibility for his own education, or must it be a process of the teacher forcing him to learn something? Trying to identify his role in the learning process is typical of the many uncertainties and concerns students possess.

The attitudes and the way students approach the learning process in the middle school years will vastly influence how they view learning the rest of their lives. The middle school staff, at times, will need to allow the students to exercise a great deal of freedom. At other times it may be necessary for the staff to impose certain restraints upon the students. Professional judgments as to when to get out of the way of the learner and let him pursue learning on his own, and when to step in and help him, must be made. On one occasion the students appear mature and grown up, while on another they need very firm and specific directions. Teachers humanize education by knowing when to get out of the way and when to step in.

Conflicting Values

During the middle school years many values established in the home come into conflict with values established by other institutions. Suddenly the set of values belonging to the family clash with values expressed by fellow students. At this point in a student's development, it is not uncommon for the student to become disillusioned with what the adult world says and what the adult world does. Such things as honesty are taught, yet practices of dishonesty are frequently observed. Adults say one should always be honest and open, but in other instances they say that the truth must be withheld for some reason.

Many of the inconsistencies with which adults have learned to live confuse and trouble the middle school student who is trying to see the world as an adult. All of these issues will not be resolved during the middle school years, but these years are a time in which many goals are examined and issues come to the fore. It is the role of the middle school to provide a forum for the student to express and feel free to explore his feelings in order to help him learn to cope with them.

Learning to Learn

The middle school student frequently is not nearly as concerned with content and subject matter as he is with how he relates to the world. Certainly students must be able to read, to write, and to do a certain amount of mathematics. Mastering basic skills is also important in the middle school, but the emphasis should be on *how* students learn rather than on *what* they learn. There must be certain skills developed and certain amounts of general education. It is important for a student to be able to trace the development of his own nation. Many concepts are vital, but the importance of having a student memorize all of the presidents and repeat them chronologically is doubtful.

It is vital that the middle school student develop certain key concepts and that he learn how to deal and cope with problems. The student should be helped to go beyond such fundamentals as reading, writing, and arithmetic. He must become an independent learner. He will learn to identify a problem, to gather information to solve this problem — synthesize, sift, analyze, and collect data — finally, to derive some solution to the stated problem.

It is also important that the student be able to evaluate his own progress and assume the responsibilities for his own progress.

The student must be helped to recognize when he has mastered a concept or skill. When learning has a purpose and is meaningful the middle school student will develop an insatiable appetite for learning.

Testing the Limits

Middle school students are delightful, but because members of the staff are adults and subject to all the weaknesses and frustrations of all adults, teaching in a middle school can be a trying experience. Frequently a student will try to discover his limits, the limits of a given situation, and will try to push them to the utmost. These attempts must be viewed as just a process of exploring and trying out, not a process of defying the adult world. Whenever anyone, middle school student or adult, is in a new situation the limits must become clear. Adults have very sophisticated and clever ways of testing and determining limits. The middle school student has not learned or devised all the subtle means of testing limits; thus, frequently one can observe what many people classify as undesirable behavior on the part of many students.

It is not the goal of the middle school to make the student submissive to all adult wishes and demands. It is not the goal of the middle school to place all the adult taboos on the student. The student must be able to live in an environment where it is acceptable to ask questions and display an eagerness for learning. Trying out and questioning authority is not bad behavior but can be desirable. The middle school must make the methods and tools for inquiry so much a part of the students that their quest for answers will never end.

Why Innovation

Despite all the talk about innovation in the last fifteen years, changes in education remain isolated, piece-meal, and are often temporary. Innovations, ideas, and concepts have been reduced in effectiveness by teachers who do not know how to integrate

them into their daily operation. Effectiveness has also been reduced by installing only a single innovation rather than developing many innovations into an integrated system. Innovation can
result in a more appropriate learning program for students.

The professional staff of a middle school is concerned with package materials, independent study, small groups, behavioral objectives, student involvement, time allocation, facilities, aides,
continuous progress, curriculum committees, team teaching, evaluation, diversified learning activities, and differentiated staffing.
These ideas, innovations, or concepts will assist the middle school
staff to humanize and personalize the educational program for the
young adults attending the middle school.

Chapter 2

History of the Middle
School Movement

As a replacement for junior high school, the middle school offers great hope for providing a needed humaneness toward youth during a unique growth and development period. The story of the history of American education provides insight into the reasons for the birth of the present middle school.

Education in America had its early roots in the religion and mercantile occupations of the Puritans. The urgent task given to the schools was that of making it possible for a child, conceived in sin, to save himself from damnation. In order to save himself, he needed to be able to read the Holy Scriptures (165:494).*

The emphasis upon religion in education is evident in the general educational law passed in 1642 by the colonial legislature of Massachusetts. This law required that, in addition to learning a trade, knowing the major laws, and learning to read, all children had to know the catechisms. Parents were responsible for carrying out these educational goals. Town officials were authorized and required to observe whether or not parents obeyed the law and to levy fines upon those who disobeyed (66:33-48).

During the next five years, Massachuetts began to feel a need for a more concentrated and unifying effort to improve the educa-

---

*Numbers within parentheses refer to References at the end of the book.

tion for youth. This need was recognized by the legislature in 1647 when the members passed a second law requiring all towns of fifty or more families to appoint a teacher to assist in the educational process. The legislature permitted towns to pay the teacher out of public taxes provided the people voted for such taxation. Hired to teach reading and writing, the appointed teacher was probably classified as an elementary teacher. For towns of 100 or more families, a teacher of Latin Grammar, a secondary teacher, was also required (66:33-48).

The Latin Grammar school offered Latin, Greek, and rhetoric in its curriculum. These subjects were considered proper background for young men entering the ministry, law, or medicine (199:27). Although the school was supposed to meet the needs of students during that time, it failed on at least three counts. First, there was a total disregard for young men who did not plan to enter one of the three chosen professions. Second, the academic needs of women were completely neglected. Third, the organizational pattern reflected little concern for the individual needs of the young men enrolled in the school. Predetermined content, predetermined methodology, and predetermined administrative practices comprised the organizational structure of the schools.

Since the Latin Grammar school did not satisfy either the needs of the enrollees or the society it served, it declined and was replaced by the American academy in the eighteenth century. (The American academy had been founded by Benjamin Franklin in 1751.) The academy represented the "progressive point of view" of that time and constituted a rebellion against the formal and nonfunctional programs of the Latin Grammar school (199:27).

The academies were sometimes referred to as "corporate" schools since an educational charter granted businessmen and landowners the right to incorporate as a board of trustees. These trustees could then buy land, build buildings, appoint teachers, and manage a school (66:33-48).

Although free from denominational control, the incorporated academies were classified as "private" schools in American terminology. The "private" status resulted from the high tuition which made the schools available only to children of wealthy families (66:33-48). In spite of the high tuition charge, the academy grew in acceptance and stature. However, it too failed to keep pace with the changing times. As the academy took over the accepted role of the Latin Grammar school — the role of cultural preservation and college preparation — it relinquished the goals for which it had been established (199:28).

The academy served as the forerunner of the American public high school. Public high schools were born just prior to the middle of the nineteenth century. At their inception they gave promise of becoming institutions designed to truly meet the needs of American youth; however, they too often failed to meet the diverse requirement of a hodgepodge society (199:27-28). Although there were several public high schools by 1850, graduation from elementary school was considered the ultimate education for most children until after 1900.

As public high schools gained acceptance, and a growing middle class enrolled more and more children in them, elementary schools had to begin to concentrate on preparing children for high school. A compulsory curriculum became more and more inclusive so that children going on to high school would be fully prepared. Many children were required to repeat grades if they could not meet certain standards (165:494-495). All of these hastily developed practices gave little attention to individual aptitude, interest, mode of learning, or motivation. The main concern was preparation for the next group level.

Instruction in school was teacher centered rather than student centered. The teacher dispensed a body of knowledge which was supposedly learned by students and returned to the instructor in oral or written expression. Students either passed or failed according to a value judgment by the teacher. They were classified early in their school life as bright, average, or below average based upon predetermined standards established by the teaching staff of the school. Little or no allowance was given for the varying rates of student readiness. Encouragement was given to students to enter high school based on cognitive accomplishments during the elementary school years.

Around 1910 educators became disenchanted with the 8-4 organizational arrangement, and the junior high school began to gain popularity. This new organization was intended to be more than an administrative reorganization. It was designed to bridge the gap between elementary school and high school, making the transition easier. Educators anticipated that more children would remain in school because the curriculum was more interesting and useful than that of the upper elementary grades. Children were also expected to remain in school longer because, before they

reached the usual end of the compulsory attendance period at age fourteen, they had already entered a different building (125:441).

The main idea behind the junior high school was that by the age of twelve the child became clearly adolescent, individualistic, and independent, and should no longer be treated as a child. Hence, exploratory courses and guidance services were introduced. This central idea was further enhanced by the development of adolescent psychology. Through his work in child study psychology, G. Stanley Hall made a great contribution to one of the chief functions of the junior high school — that of helping the family, church, and community to guide children through the early adolescent period. (Hall published *Adolescence* in 1904, *Educational Problems* in 1911.) (125:442)*

By the middle of the twentieth century, arguments for the junior high school had begun to lose force. The legal age for children to leave school had been raised to 16 in most states and to 18 in others. The mean age of puberty had dropped approximately one year. At the same time, educators began to question whether or not sixth grade youngsters might relate better to a social atmosphere which embraces seventh and eighth graders.

The name "junior high school" is unfortunate for the term itself implies a scaled-down version of a "senior" counterpart. The major fault of the junior high school is that it has become a social copy of the senior high school with excessive emphasis on activities such as varsity athletic teams, pep rallies, marching bands, cheerleaders, class proms, and even graduation exercises. Considerable pressure is exerted on the junior high school student to excel physically. This pressure may present emotional danger for students who cannot at this age measure up to the ideal (79:108-110).

The curriculum for the junior high school also tends to parallel that of the high school. Very little core-type or interdisciplinary-type programs exist in these schools, making the opportunity for student exploration very restricted (79:108-110). The study program has generally been initiated through departmentalization with an emphasis upon the mastery of subject matter. Student interest, feelings, and emotions receive little attention at this level.

The Carnegie-unit credit in grade nine is partly responsible for the pressure senior high schools exert on the offerings of junior high schools. High schools either accept the credits of the junior high schools or control the granting of these Carnegie credits in grade nine. There has generally been more controlling than acceptance. When the ninth grade is included in the high school, the senior institution does not feel impelled to dominate the program of the junior institution (79:108-110).

Another junior high school deficiency pertains to the teachers assigned to them. Very few university teacher education programs distinguish between the preparation needed for teaching junior high students, whom the psychologists designate as unique beings, and the background required for teaching senior high school students (79:108-110). Teachers of the 10- to 14-year-old youngsters should have a differentiated training program. The special needs of students of the "in-between age" require conscious efforts by a professional staff that is aware of such needs and trained to meet them.

Because of the noted junior high school deficiencies, the middle school began to emerge in the late 1950's and early 1960's. The middle school organization provided a concentrated effort to meet the special growth and development needs of youth from 10 to 14 years old. Justification for housing students in this age group in a separate building lies in the concept of transescence:

There is a growing body of research evidence to substantiate the transescent designation. There is no major line separating the child and the adolescent but rather a gradual change involving physical, mental, and social elements.

Transescence is a period of physiological change. These changes of characteristics are peculiar to this level of development, producing a common set of social and emotional reactions which are different from those represented in children of the elementary or high school years. Biological changes taking place alter not only the physical child but also his social and emotional status.

Mental maturation, like physical development, is in transition during the middle school years. Stage level psychologists present strong arguments that during transescent years, youngsters move from a cognitive modus operandi involving concrete operations to a level characterized by their ability to interact in the abstract.

Transescence is also marked by the youngster's transition from dependence upon the family for security to a similar dependence on the peer group. Prior to transescence, the elementary child is heavily reliant on the family for interests, attitudes, and values, and after, on the peer group subculture (99:111-113).

The middle school is attempting to provide for the stage of development (transescence) which begins prior to the onset of puberty and extends through the early stage of adolescence by:

1. Developing a unique program adapted to the needs of prepuberty and early adolescent students;

2. Providing a wide range of intellectual, social, and physical experiences;

3. Providing opportunities for exploration and for development of skills involved in individual learning patterns;

4. Maintaining an atmosphere of basic respect for individual differences;

5. Creating a climate that enables students to develop abilities, to find facts, to weigh evidence, to draw conclusions, to determine values, and to keep their minds open to new facts;

6. Recognizing and understanding the students' needs, interests, backgrounds, motivations, goals, and especially their stresses, strains, frustrations and fears;

7. Providing smooth educational transition from the elementary school to the high school while recognizing the physical and emotional changes taking place;

8. Providing an environment where the child, not the program, is most important;

9. Providing an environment where the opportunity to succeed is insured for all students;

10. Offering guidance to the pupil in the development of mental processes and attitudes needed for contributing, constructive citizenship and in the development of life-long competencies and appreciations required for effective use of leisure;

11. Providing competent differentiated instructional personnel who will strive to understand the students whom they serve and who will develop professional competencies which are both unique and applicable to the transescent student; and

12. Providing facilities and a flexible use of time to allow students and teachers to achieve the goals of the program to their fullest capabilities. (168:1-2)

Education has seen many changes in America since the days of the Latin Grammar school and the American academies. The middle schools concept is one of the most recent. Because society has changed, children have changed — particularly middle school aged children. Each one progresses through school with different abilities, different backgrounds, different needs. A direct focus on these needs (in the affective and psychomotor domains as well as the cognitive domain) through the middle school concept will provide a way to humanize education and to meet the unique requirements of each student.

Part 2

The Learning
Environment

Chapter 3

Behavioral
Objectives

Although curriculum content and organizational arrangements are important in the middle school, instructional objectives must be stated clearly in behavioral terms before curriculum content and organization are determined. "You cannot concern yourself with the problem of selecting the most efficient route to your destination until you know what your distination is." (192:1) According to Robert Mager an objective is an intent communicated by a statement describing a proposed change in a learner (192:3). The statement should describe what the learner's behavior is when he has successfully completed a learning experience. A properly stated objective is a description of a pattern of behavior (performance) that the learner should be able to demonstrate.

Behavioral Objectives
in the Middle School

Most educators would undoubtedly agree that middle school students should learn to think independently and to become self-reliant. These behavioral objectives are often stated in terms so vague that it is neither possible to define specifically what needs to be learned nor to measure what has been learned. If middle school teachers want these end purposes to be achieved and be measured, it is essential that they approach the goals in a more exact manner. Teachers must have goals that enable *both teachers and students* to identify what the objectives mean if a change is going to transpire in the middle school instructional program.

Behavioral objectives should be used by every middle school teacher for the following five reasons.

First, there are many special needs of middle school students.

They have a large number of concerns other than the development of their cognitive or intellectual being during these critical three or four years of life. Student concerns may be about:

<blockquote>

a. successful peer relationships

b. how they are perceived by adults

c. the development of their own values

d. slow or rapid physical patterns they are experiencing

e. sexual maturity

f. understanding themselves

g. other areas that may be unique to each individual or may be shared by many others

</blockquote>

These concerns are very important to middle school students and certainly create pressures for them. The "guessing game" that often exists when students wonder what they are going to encounter and what is expected of them only provides additional pressures. Some pressures could be eliminated or at least reduced by behavioral objectives that are stated as precisely as possible. By reducing or eliminating the unknown aspects and providing a general "roadmap for learning," the teacher can ease additional strain. Hence, a more humanistic approach to learning is made possible.

Second, what each student needs to learn must be determined.

This forces the middle school teaching team to focus on objectives that can be accomplished. Covering a textbook from the first page to the last page is no longer an acceptable objective. Objectives must be based on what students need to learn, and students must be able to identify how the teacher expects them to demonstrate accomplishment of objectives.

Third, after objectives are determined and stated in behavioral terms, a middle school teacher must select relevant learning activities for students.

Objectives that are stated correctly make the selection of relevant activities much easier. Some activities may have been used for considerable lengths of time or may sound like enjoyable activities for students, but they have no place in the middle school curriculum if they do not assist a student in accomplishing an objective or clarifying a concept for him. Activities should be selected so that the student can actually behave in a particular way as stated in the objectives after the instructional unit is concluded.

Fourth, the clarification of instructional goals is another primary reason for stating objectives in behavioral terms.

Clarification permits more accuracy in assessing students in terms of the stated objectives. A teaching team can then make a wise decision concerning the need for altering stated objectives by adding to goals, or reducing standards that might be expected.

Fifth, behavioral objectives are a necessity in the middle school to determine if teaching has been effective after the completion of the unit.

Teacher satisfaction with student responses on a true-false examination or with interest displayed by student oral responses is not enough to determine if the teaching-learning process has been effective. Effectiveness must be based upon student behavior as a result of the instruction.

Teachers need to examine the behavior of students after instruction to determine whether the learning activities constructed by the teaching team have produced the desired results. Therefore, it is of vital importance that objectives be stated precisely so the postassessment can be accurate. Unsatisfactory performance after instruction is an indication that instruction has not been effective. The teaching team should propose changes so that later attempts at the accomplishment of objectives will provide more satisfactory progress. Decisions that are made by the professional team of middle school teachers are vitally important in determining instruction that will lead to the attainment of the behavioral objectives. A valid way for teachers to determine if the instructional sequence has been effective is through student attainment of the stated objectives.

Selecting Worthwhile Objectives

Objectives that are stated in behavioral terms are not necessarily good objectives. There is a real need for teaching teams to determine the appropriateness of the objectives. Some objectives, although stated in behavioral terms, are of little value to student or teacher. The least significant objectives can be stated very precisely while the more important objectives may evade being stated at all. Important objectives may be considerably more difficult to accomplish in behavioral terms. For example, the task of having students recite from memory ten different minerals for a science course is easier than having students identify minerals by chemical analysis. Likewise, an easier task for a middle school student might be to list the names of five authors studied in English class rather than to contrast the writing styles of five different authors that have been studied in class. Teachers should not fall into the trap of thinking that all objectives deal with only trivial forms of the learner's behavior. The appropriateness of educational objectives can only be determined after the objectives have been established. Stated objectives should be able to stand up under any criticism of the teaching team or outside observers and should not be considered satisfactory for the instructional sequence if they cannot be defended.

Determining the
Value of Objectives

Some criteria for determining the value of objectives are:

The objective should state what it is that a learner will be able to do upon the completion of the objective. A student can easily misinterpret a teacher's statement that the student should understand and gain knowledge, appreciation, or insight into a topic. These terms permit considerable latitude in student and teacher interpretation. Action words such as identify (identify object properties such as porous or nonporous), classify (assign plants or animals to groups according to family or species), describe (name all of the necessary categories of event properties), or interpret (identify objects or events in terms of their consequences) should be used in the statement of objectives rather than ambiguous abstractions.

A second criterion which can be used in determining the value of educational objectives is a taxonomy. A taxonomy is a system of classification that places educational objectives in hierarchical order of difficulty. Taxonomies have been developed for three major divisions of educational objectives called domains (cognitive domain, affective domain, psychomotor domain) and help classify human behavioral characteristics. All of the intellectual processes of the learner are included in the cognitive domain, and the majority of the objectives for an educational program would be included in this domain.

Benjamin Bloom identifies six subdivisions and various skills within the subdivisions of the first category, the cognitive domain (42:201-207). The cognitive domain, emphasizing the mental processes, begins with the concrete behavior of knowledge and continues through the more abstract processes of analysis and synthesis.

1. *Knowledge* involves the recognition and recall of facts and specifics.

2. *Comprehension* the learner interprets, translates, summarizes or paraphrases given material.

3. *Application* involves the use of material in a situation which is different from the original situation.

4. *Analysis* involves separating a complex whole into its parts until the relationship among the elements is made clear.

5. *Synthesis* involves combining elements to form a new original entity.

6. *Evaluation* involves acts of decision making, judging, or selecting based on a given set of criteria. (These criteria may be objective or subjective.)

These subdivisions are very useful in evaluating objectives since they can be used to determine which objectives require more complex responses from students. With an awareness that different levels of cognitive behavior do exist, a concentrated effort can be aimed toward higher thought processes, and an instructional program can be projected toward behavioral objectives that are more likely to result in learning as opposed to memorization.

Knowledge

The first and lowest subdivision of the cognitive domain is knowledge. This level involves basic recall of specific facts and universal principles of methods and processes, or of a pattern, or structure, or setting. To accomplish this lowest level, students need only recall certain facts that they have read, discussed in class, heard in a lecture, or experienced. This activity requires little more than bringing to mind the appropriate material and making the correct response. Some examples of knowledge are:

Knowledge of Specific Facts. The recall of specific facts is referred to as the element from which more complex forms of knowledge are constructed. Quite often students are asked to show evidence of knowledge of facts including dates, events, persons, and places. These facts may entail information that is precise such as the month, day, and year that the Japanese attacked Pearl Harbor. Teachers may also ask students to display approximate or relative information such as a minimum knowledge about the organisms studied in a biology laboratory.

Knowledge of Terminology. Students may be asked to define technical terms by stating their attributes, properties, or relations or to become familiar with many words in their common range of meanings.

Knowledge of Ways and Means of Dealing With Specifics. Knowledge of ways to organize, to study, to judge, and to criticize is more abstract than terminology or specific facts but less abstract than knowledge of universals.

Knowledge of Conventions. This area involves characteristic ways of treating and presenting ideas and phenomena. On this level students demonstrate the correct forms and usage in speech and writing as well as familiarity with the forms and conventions of the major types of work including verse, plays, and scientific papers.

Knowledge of Trends and Sequences.   Trends and sequences can be focused upon in relation to time. For example, a student may be asked to construct a chart showing cattle prices during the past twenty years. Trends can be shown by selecting the peak periods for the twenty year span.

Knowledge of Classifications and Categories.   This area requires knowledge of classes, sets, and divisions which are regarded as essential for a given subject field, purpose, argument, or problem. Demonstration of this area of knowledge may be accomplished by having students classify selected plants into species through certain distinguishable characteristics.

Knowledge of Criteria.   Criteria are used to judge or test facts, principles, opinions, and conduct. Knowledge of criteria can be established by having students list the various principles used to evaluate behavioral objectives such as the incorporation of verbs that denote overt action.

Knowledge of Methodology.   Knowledge of methodology can be demonstrated by having students list or state methods for judging criteria. Students are not asked at the knowledge level to demonstrate how to "use" the method.

Knowledge of the Universals and Abstractions.   This level of knowledge is concerned with the major schemes and patterns by which phenomena and ideas are organized. Large structures, theories, and generalizations pertaining to a subject field are involved in this level of knowledge, which represents the highest level of abstraction and complexity.

Knowledge of Principles and Generalizations.   Particular abstractions which summarize observations of phenomena are identifiable features of this area of knowledge. These abstractions aid in explaining, describing, predicting, or determining the most appropriate action to be taken. For example, students may be asked to state generalizations about particular cultures.

Knowledge of Theories and Structures.   This area of knowledge shows the interrelation and organization of many principles or generalizations. Demonstration of students' mastery can be shown, for example, by having them relate a fairly complete formulation of the theory of evaluation.

Comprehension

Comprehension is the second subdivision that Bloom identifies. It represents the lowest level of understanding. This level and the other remaining subdivisions require more intellectual ability or skill than basic recall. A student comprehends when he is able to use an idea without fully understanding all of its ramifications, or when he knows what is being communicated and can make use of the material or idea without necessarily relating it to other material or without seeing its fullest implications. Translating German into English is an example of comprehension. Another example is interpreting a graph without necessarily understanding the graph's usefulness. Three classifications of comprehension are:

Translation Comprehension can be judged according to accuracy of translation from the original communication. For example, students need accuracy in translating mathematical verbal material into symbolic statements.

Interpretation Interpretation involves the explanation or summarization of a communication. This skill is concerned with recording, rearrangement, or a new view of material. An example of this process is the ability to interpret different types of data.

Extrapolation It is desirable for students to extend trends or tendencies beyond the given data to determine implications, consequences, and effects which are in accordance with the conditions described in the original communication. Students may observe financial data at the national level, for example, and predict a continuation of trends.

Application

Application is Bloom's third subdivision of the cognitive domain. A student applying artificial resuscitation in an emergency situation after having learned the procedure in a physical education class is an example of a student being able to apply a principle. Applying a principle from a scientific journal to an everyday practical situation is another example. A middle school teacher uses application when he applies instructional principles correctly in preparing packaged materials.

Analysis

Bloom's fourth subdivision is analysis. Analysis can be observed when a middle school student thoroughly identifies and examines subideas of main ideas so the relationship among these subideas is clarified. Analysis should clarify the communication to indicate how it is organized and the way it conveys its effects.

Analysis of Elements The analysis of elements involves the identification of the elements included in a communication. For example, when a student determines which written thoughts are facts and which are opinion he is able to analyze elements.

Analysis of Relationships This area concerns connections and interactions between elements and parts of a communication. It may include comprehending the interrelationships among the ideas in a passage of literature.

Analysis of Organizational Principles Analysis, as it relates to organizational principles, deals with the systematic arrangement and structure which hold the communication together. One example of organizational analysis would be for students to develop the ability to recognize form and pattern in artistic works as a means of understanding their meaning.

Synthesis

Synthesis is Bloom's fifth level of the cognitive domain. Synthesis involves the assembly of different parts to form an original idea. Synthesis can be observed when a student in a science class forms a more complex substance through the combination of various elements. The process of reasoning must take place with this level. The science class cannot merely be following directions in a lab manual.

Development of an Original Communication A writer or speaker develops a communication to convey ideas, feelings, and/or experiences to others in this form of synthesis.

Development of a Plan or Proposed Set of Operations The development of a work plan or a plan of operations should satisfy requirements of the task which may be given to the student or which he may develop for himself.

Derivation of a Set of Abstract Relations   This area of developing a set of abstract relations is for the purpose of classifying or explaining particular data or phenomena, or for the deduction of propositions and relations from a set of basic propositions or symbolic representations. A student can demonstrate accomplishment in this area by making mathematical discoveries and generalizations.

Evaluation

Bloom's highest subdivision for the cognitive domain is that of evaluation. Evaluation describes behavior in which a decision is made concerning the value of different approaches to a particular problem. This process can take place through a student's reading of several different articles both pro and con on a certain subject and then determining which ideas are expressed in a way that he feels is proper. A student, therefore, must make a value judgment based on certain criteria. The criteria for making this value judgment may be determined not only through reading but also through communication in small group discussions.

Judgments in Terms of Internal Evidence   During the evaluation process judgment is made based on such evidence as logical accuracy, consistency, and other internal criteria. The identification of logical fallacies in arguments is one example of evaluation through internal evidence.

Judgments in Terms of External Criteria   Evaluation through external evidence results from comparing major theories, generalizations, and facts about particular cultures.

The classification of the cognitive domain into six subdivisions is very important for the middle school. All of these six subdivisions should be used at appropriate times for the instructional sequence of a middle school student. The knowledge or basic recall level will undoubtedly be used more than any of the other subdivisions unless serious effort is exerted for emphasizing higher levels. Hopefully, the stress will be on the writing of objectives so that comprehension, application, analysis, synthesis, and evaluation will be used quite regularly. If the middle school student is to be active and challenged, higher level domains must be stressed.

Sometimes it is difficult to determine if the objective should involve only one subdivision or whether the objective should contain another, higher subdivision. Therefore, middle school teachers may find it helpful to classify objectives at the cognitive level in two ways: 1) knowledge or basic recall and 2) any higher level pertaining to the remaining five subdivisions. It should not be difficult to determine which of the objectives in the cognitive domain are stated at the lowest level. Then one can try to change these objectives or identify new higher objectives.

There is nothing wrong with knowledge or basic recall of facts, but students should be able to apply these facts to the overall concepts. Certainly realistic challenges for middle school students must be stressed. This necessitates identifying not only the lowest subdivision but also subdivisions that are higher than just knowledge. A careful analysis of more complicated goals may reveal some of the lower level cognitive behaviors that need to be mastered before higher levels of learning can be accomplished.

Now that you have read about the various skills, test your knowledge of the cognitive variables. In the following exercise, try to recall the six appropriate cognitive variables or terms. On the provided space to the left of each item write the correct term for the cognitive behavior.

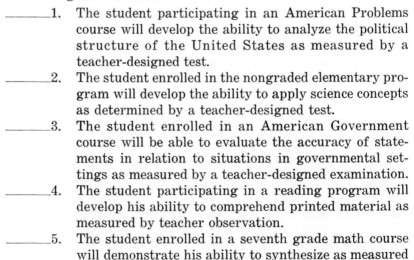

_____1. The student participating in an American Problems course will develop the ability to analyze the political structure of the United States as measured by a teacher-designed test.

_____2. The student enrolled in the nongraded elementary program will develop the ability to apply science concepts as determined by a teacher-designed test.

_____3. The student enrolled in an American Government course will be able to evaluate the accuracy of statements in relation to situations in governmental settings as measured by a teacher-designed examination.

_____4. The student participating in a reading program will develop his ability to comprehend printed material as measured by teacher observation.

_____5. The student enrolled in a seventh grade math course will demonstrate his ability to synthesize as measured by the teacher's observation of his ability to design an original numeration system.

_____6. The student enrolled in a general math course will improve his knowledge of computational skills as measured by the arithmetic computation section of Iowa Tests of Basic Skills.

Answer Key

1. Analysis
2. Application
3. Evaluation
4. Comprehension
5. Synthesis
6. Knowledge

The second descriptive category identified by David Krathwohl, Benjamin Bloom, and Bertram Masia is the affective domain (170:176-185). Attitudes, emotions, and values are reflected by interest and are included in this category. The affective domain is a much more difficult area to determine if changes in student behavior have taken place for a stated objective. However, it is also a very important area in that attitudes can affect everything a middle school student does. Attitudes can definitely affect the cognitive or intellectual domain. For example, we hope that in the intellectual domain a student will effectively analyze a scientific process and not learn to dislike science during the process.

The affective domain emphasizes the need for the middle school curriculum to focus on relevancy, which demands that the curriculum deal with current concerns of students and society. Values and positive attitudes must be considered in the teaching-learning process since popularity, individuality and conformity, self-understanding, feelings and emotions, decision-making processes, and physiology of sex are all areas of great interest for students of middle school age. During the middle school years, values are established to a great degree in these areas.

The teaching of values does not mean that facts and concepts that fall within the intellectual processes can be discarded. Facts and concepts are essential since students need them to relate to when establishing their own value systems.

Some value questions that may be appropriate for middle school youth are: "Where do you stand on man's efforts to control pol-

lution?" "Some people feel that marijuana should be legalized
and sold to those that wish to buy it, since they must live their
own lives. What is your opinion on this subject?" "Abortion is
legal in some countries. Should it be legalized in the United
States?" Developing a sound value system for one's self permits
students to become independent and self-reliant. Students do not
need to make, in fact, will not make decisions just to be "one of
the group."

Krathwohl et al., have broken the affective domain down into
receiving, responding, valuing, organization, and characterization by a value or value complex (170:176-185).

The affective behavioral variables are defined as the interest,
attitudes, values, appreciations, and adjustments of the individual. In recent years we have reached a point in the evaluation process where we are concerned not only with the knowledge gained,
but with the willingness of the student to identify himself with
a given subject. The affective domain, emphasizing the emotional
processes, begins with the simple behaviors of receiving and responding and continues through the complex process of characterization.

1. *Receiving*	the learner is aware or passively attending to certain phenomena and stimuli (i.e., listening).
2. *Responding*	the learner complies to given expectations by attending or reacting to certain stimuli or phenomena (i.e., interests).
3. *Valuing*	the learner displays behavior consistent with the single belief or attitude in situations where he is not forced to comply or obey (i.e., internal commitment consistent with external behavior).
4. *Organization*	the learner is committed to a set of values as displayed by his behavior (i.e., successful internalization of values).

5. *Characterization*   the total behavior of the
learner is consistent with
the values he has internalized (i.e., philosophy of
life — totally behaving as
you believe).

Receiving (Attending)

At the receiving level the student must be sensitized to the ex-
istence of certain phenomena and stimuli. This sensitizing process is the first step if the learner is to be properly oriented to
learn what is expected. Previous experiences cause students to
bring different views to the teaching-learning process. These
different views may enhance or obstruct the recognition of the
phenomena.

Awareness Awareness is the first and lowest of three levels of
receiving. At this stage the student is merely conscious of a situation or a state of affairs. An awareness can occur without specific discrimination or recognition of the characteristics of the
object, even though these characteristics must be presumed to
have an effect.

Willingness to receive   Students who are willing to receive stimuli have progressed past the awareness state. They are willing to tolerate a given stimulus, not to avoid it. The learner, if given the opportunity to attend in a field with relatively few competing stimuli, will not actively avoid stimulation. Hopefully, the learner will take notice of the phenomenon and give it his attention.

Controlled or selected attention   As the student moves from the willingness to receive stage, he attends to certain stimuli. The student controls his attention, so that the favored stimuli (i.e., listening) are selected and attended to despite competing and distracting stimuli (i.e., viewing).

Responding

Responding is concerned with responses which go beyond mere attending to phenomena. The learner must be sufficiently motivated to do more than just be aware. During the first stage of the *learning by doing* process the learner is committing himself to some degree to the phenomena concerned.

Many teachers find the responding category best describes their *interest* objectives. The term is often used to indicate the desire a student exhibits in a subject or activity so that he seeks it out and gains satisfaction from working on it.

Acquiescence in responding   This term describes compliance or a passiveness on the part of the learner as far as the initiation of behavior is concerned. This response suggests the element of reaction to a suggestion rather than the implication of resistance or yielding unwillingly. The learner, although making the response, has not fully accepted the necessity for doing so.

Willingness to respond   The term *willingness* implies voluntary activity. It implies that students are sufficiently committed to exhibiting certain behavior voluntarily. This level is characterized by having students proceed from their own choices while acquiescence in responding denotes an element of resistance or of yielding unwillingly.

Satisfaction in response   Students may proceed from the willingness state to behavior that is accompanied by a feeling of pleasure. Satisfaction may be displayed, for example, if students read for their personal enjoyment.

Valuing

If a student possesses this third level identified by Krathwohl, he has behavior that is sufficiently consistent and stable to be classified as a belief or as an attitude. A concern is emphasized at the value level for a set of specified values but not for the relationships among values.

Acceptance of a value   The concern at this level is one of certainty. There is more of a readiness to reevaluate one's position, although this position may be somewhat tentative. A distinguishing characteristic of students displaying this behavior is consistency of response to phenomena with which a belief or attitude is identified. The consistency is to the degree that others perceive the learner as holding the belief or value.

Preference for a value   Preference for a value implies that the learner is sufficiently committed to the value to pursue it. An example of behavior at this level would be for a student to purposely examine a variety of viewpoints on controversial issues with a view to forming opinions about them.

Commitment (conviction)   This highest identified area of valuing involves a high degree of certainty. Students possessing this behavior act in such a way as to extend the possibility of the thing valued. A deeper involvement exists with the valued item. A tension exists that needs to be satisfied and a real motivation occurs to act out the behavior.

Organization

Krathwohl's fourth identified area of the affective domain is organization. The organization of values is important after students successively internalize values and a situation is encountered for which there is more than one relevant value.

Conceptualization of a value   The conceptualization level of organization permits learners to see how the value relates to the values that he already possesses or to new values that he will gain in the future.

Organization of a value system   Objectives that can be related at this level are those which require the learner to bring together complex values and to bring these values into an ordered relationship with one another. This ordered relationship should be one which is harmonious and internally consistent, although this is not always possible.

Characterization by a value or value complex

The fifth and final area identified by Krathwohl for the affective domain reveals that values are organized into some kind of internally consistent system. The internalization of values has controlled the behavior of the learner for a sufficient time that he has adapted given disposition. Certain behavior is not aroused unless the student is threatened or challenged. A consistent behavior occurs for the learner in accordance with the values he has internalized at this level.

Generalized set   This level provides an internal consistency to the system of values and attitudes at any particular moment. For example, generalized set occurs when students respond to new evidence by changing judgments and altering behavior.

Characterization   Characterization is the highest level of the internalization process identified by Krathwohl. Objectives found here concern a value system having as its object the whole of what is known or knowable. The development of a consistent philosophy of life by a student is an example of characterization.

After just finishing reading about the affective domain, test your knowledge of the affective variables. In the following exercise, try to recall the five appropriate terms for affective variables. Write on the provided space on the left of each item the correct term for the affective behavior.

_____1.   The teacher enrolled in a philosophy of education course will develop a characterization of a social system in education which will be reflected in his continual work toward improvement of instruction in his school district as measured by instructor observation.

_____2.   Teachers using Beginning Algebra course materials will develop a positive interest toward teaching of mathematics as measured by their responses to an attitude inventory.

_____3. The student enrolled in music education will receive an awareness of different types of music as determined by his ability to rank these types of music in order of their presentation in class.

_____4. The teacher enrolled in an in-service education program on the teaching of modern math will develop an organization of a value system as measured by Edward's Personal Preference Schedule.

_____5. The teacher enrolled in a teaching methods course will develop a value for a certain teaching technique as measured by his ability to discuss, without being asked, the factors which make it a good method for him.

Answer Key

1. Characterization
2. Responding
3. Receiving
4. Organization
5. Valuing

The psychomotor domain, the third behavioral category, is concerned with skills that can be acquired in such areas as physical education, typing, and the unified arts. The psychomotor area combines physical activities with intellectual activities.

The psychomotor variables describe those behaviors which involve neuromuscular coordination. Handwriting and physical education utilize this domain to draw conclusions about special programs. The following variables are used to classify those behaviors which can be included in the psychomotor domain.

1. *Perception*	the process of becoming aware of objects, qualities, or relations by way of the sense organs.
2. *Set*	a preparatory adjustment or readiness for a particular kind of action or experience.

3. *Guided response*	the overt behavioral act of an individual under the guidance of the instructor or in response to self-evaluation where the student has a model or criteria against which he can judge his performance.
4. *Mechanism*	the learner has achieved a certain confidence and degree of proficiency in the performance of the act.
5. *Complex overt response*	the individual can perform a motor act that is considered complex.
6. *Adaptation*	the learner alters motor activities to meet new demands.
7. *Origination*	new motor acts are created.

This third domain is one about which educators and parents must be very conscious. Erratic physical growth and development for middle school youth necessitates that each student be treated individually in the skills area. Some students are growing so rapidly that their endurance will be reduced and the mile run, for example, may be an impossibility. Students will differ greatly in many other areas due to their growth pattern as well as inherited and natural ability. To expect all students to achieve the same objective is not a humane approach to the teaching-learning process.

Many of the activities in the psychomotor domain should be aimed at developing physiques as well as balance and coordination. The trampoline and skipping rope may be excellent tools to develop balance and coordination for boys who are extremely clumsy at this stage in their physical growth. Objectives that encourage each student to develop his psychomotor traits to their fullest are highly desirable.

Elizabeth Jane Simpson has identified the following taxonomy of psychomotor skills (248:110-112; 113-144).

Perception

Perception is the first step in performing a motor act. It involves becoming aware of objects, qualities, or relations through the sense organs. Through perception a student surveys the situation, interprets, and then performs motor activity.

Simpson has subdivided perception into three areas: sensory stimulation, cue selection, and translation.

Sensory stimulation   This area pertains to a stimulus upon one or more of the sense organs. Hearing, sight, touch, taste, and smell all respond to sensory stimulation. Kinesthetic cues that result in activation of receptors in muscles, tendons, and joints are also included in this area. Simpson emphasizes that the sensory cues that direct action may change from sense stimuli to kinesthetic cues as learning progresses.

Cue selection   The selection of cues pertains to deciding what stimuli a learner will respond to in order to satisfy the particular requirements of task performance. The decision may be made by grouping of cues in terms of past experience and knowledge. Relevant cues are accepted and irrelevant cues are rejected.

Translation   At this stage a student translates perception to action. It requires determining the meaning of the cues received for action. For example, a student may demonstrate perception by translating or relating music to dance form.

Set

This next step pertains to a preparatory adjustment or readiness for a particular kind of action or experience. Mental, physical, and emotional aspects of set have been identified.

Mental set   Students must prepare mentally at this level to perform a certain motor act. Prerequisites of perception and its subcategories are required. The knowledge of appropriate tools for the performance of various sewing operations in unified arts is one example of the mental set.

Physical set   Physical set requires readiness in the sense of having made the anatomical adjustments necessary for the performance of a motor act. Readiness involves both the receptor set and the postural set. The receptor set is the focusing of attention on the needed sensory organs while the postural set pertains to the positioning of the body. For example, students must achieve correct body stance in preparation for bowling.

Emotional set   An emotional readiness or a favorable attitude is needed for the motor act to take place.

Guided response

The third identified step emphasizes the abilities which are components of the more complex skill. This response is the overt behavioral act of an individual under the guidance of a teacher. Two major subcategories of guided response are imitation and trial and error.

Imitation   Students are sometimes requested to imitate the performance of a teacher. A student positioning his hands correctly upon the typewriter keys after the teacher demonstrates the correct position is an example of imitation in the psychomotor domain.

Trial and error   An opportunity should sometimes be provided for students to experience different responses and then determine an appropriate one. The appropriate response is the one that gets the job completed most effectively and efficiently.

Mechanism

At the mechanism level the student has achieved a certain confidence and degree of skill in the performance of an act. Mechanism may involve some patterning of response in carrying out the task. A student can demonstrate mechanism, for example, by correctly mixing chemicals for a science experiment.

Complex overt response

At Simpson's identified fifth level, students can perform a motor act that is considered complex because of the movement pattern required. A high degree of skill has been attained at this level.

Resolution of uncertainty   Students know the sequence required at this level and proceed without hesitation to acquire a mental picture of task sequence.

Automatic Performance   A student, at this level, can perform a finely coordinated motor skill with a great deal of ease and muscle control.

Finished with the section on psychomotor? If so, test your knowledge of the psychomotor variables. In the following exercise, try to recall the seven appropriate psychomotor variables. Write on the space provided to the left of each item the correct term for the psychomotor behavior.

_____1.   The student participating in the home economics course will demonstrate the ability to follow a recipe in preparing food.

_____2.   A unified arts student imitates the process of stay-stitching the curved neck edge of a bodice.

_____3.   Skill is demonstrated by an industrial arts student in setting up and operating a production band saw.

_____4.   The student enrolled in drama class creates a modern dance.

_____5.   Another drama student develops a modern dance composition through adapting known abilities and skills in dance.

_____6.   A first year biology student demonstrates the ability to pollinate an oat flower.

_____7.   A physical education student will demonstrate the achievement of body stance preparatory to bowling.

Answer Key

1.   Perception
2.   Guided response
3.   Complex overt response
4.   Origination
5.   Adaptation
6.   Mechanism
7.   Set

The advantage of classifying objectives according to cognitive, affective, or psychomotor domains is that middle school teachers can discern whether or not they are utilizing all three categories. If teachers find that their teaching activities lie only in the cognitive domain, they may wish to change their instructional sequence and behavioral objectives. The instructional program must not overemphasize one domain. Through a careful examination of objectives one can include the various sublevels of the three domains when appropriate.

Determining
Performance Standards

The writing of behavioral objectives must also include the determination of performance standards. One criterion for a middle school program is that the program must encourage the student to be active — to be involved. A student who performs is active. Performance standards state, prior to the instructional phase, the minimum level of student achievement. If an objective is stated properly in performance terms, a teacher should be able to determine the minimum level of student performance.

Many intellectual activities such as comprehending are actually performing. However, they are not directly observable. One cannot determine in all cases whether a student is actually comprehending. The statement of performance must specify the behavior that can be observed. The following is an example of an objective that is stated properly in performance terms:

Given twenty short stories, each story written by a different author, a student will be able to determine which author wrote which story according to an analysis of writing styles. A student will correctly identify at least eighteen of the twenty stories. This identification will include more than just the quantitative standards such as the identification of eighteen of the twenty authors as matched with the stories correctly. The analysis may require the student to identify the writing style of each author. The level of quality in this case would be higher than the lowest level of knowledge or recall in the cognitive domain. Another example of qualitative performance standards would be to determine whether paragraphs included a topic sentence with 90 percent accuracy.

Objectives stated in performance terms provide a way for the middle school teacher to look at achievement of students and a method to evaluate the instructional program.

A middle school teacher should not wait until after the instruction and evaluation sessions have taken place before determining performance standards. Otherwise, a teacher may be inclined to think that the instructional phase was needed for all of the individual students. Many kinds of rationalization can take place to determine the success or nonsuccess of a student's performance if performance standards are not stated prior to the learning activity. Excuses will become less valid in determining the success of a student in an instructional sequence if performance standards are stated prior to the instructional phase.

Middle school teachers should look closely at the capabilities of their students in establishing minimum levels of performance. Before performance levels can be established for each student, it is necessary to determine present achievement levels. A pretest can help determine the student's present achievement level. In some areas such as foreign language, there are definite concepts and skills a middle school student must master. Therefore, a minimum performance standard could be established for the mastery of the particular skill. Students must master certain basic skills before they can expect to achieve the next highest skill level. In other areas, where the mastery of a certain skill is not considered as essential prior to going to another skill, the teacher would establish a minimum level as a tentative proposal and then revise the standards when appropriate.

The establishment of minimum levels of performance in the writing of behavioral objectives is a way of using objectives as aids to the classroom teacher's effort. Specific objectives and minimum levels of performance will enable a teacher to gather information about his instructional sequence and the learning that takes place. Meaningful changes can then take place in the preparation for instruction.

Selecting Appropriate Activities
According to Stated Objectives

There are many activities that can assist learning for the middle school student. However, the question should be asked, "Which activities are appropriate for the objectives that are stated?" The middle school student should be given the opportunity to engage in activities that will help him master the objectives. Some activities will relate directly to the objective as stated; other activities may be similar to, but not identical to, the terminal behavior as stated in the objectives. For example, a student may engage in small group discussions when the activity called for indicates a writing activity. A speaking activity may be substituted for the writing activity when appropriate.

However, a middle school student should not be asked to engage in activities that are irrelevant to his needs. If the middle school teaching team provides activities that are appropriate, the student has a much better chance of mastering the stated objective.

Appropriate practices stated in performance standards and worthwhile objectives that are coupled with systematic planning and appraisal will be transmitted into benefits for the middle school student, which will, in turn, enable the middle school teacher to receive satisfaction for a job well done. Certainly, there are other factors that determine good teaching and the amount of learning that takes place, but objectives can assist the teaching team in increasing the effectiveness of the learning. Properly stated objectives with appropriate activities serve the purpose of preplanning and eliminate much of the confusion on the part of teacher and students as to what is to be accomplished.

Chapter 4

Assessment and Evaluation

Traditionally, students have been assessed for the purpose of determining their rank in class. Information was gathered to determine who was number one in the class, who was number two, who was number three, and so forth. Of course, some unfortunate student always ended up last.

The purpose of evaluation has been to determine where the student would fit into the normal distribution curve. We have been convinced that in any given number of students the majority would receive "C's," a few would receive the "A's" and "B's," and an equal number would receive "D's" and "F's."

Assessment has also been viewed as a means of judging mastery of facts. Teachers have insisted that a student has had to demonstrate he has mastered facts by proving his ability to recall memorized data. Facts memorized for a test are soon forgotten.

Traditionally, too, assessment has been viewed as a game played by both the teacher and the student, with clearly defined roles for each. The role of the teacher has been to keep secret the questions she planned to ask on a test trying to trick the student into studying all of the assignments. The role of the student has been to attempt to outguess the teacher, studying only the material which he was sure would appear on a test.

In the middle school, however, we do not view evaluation or assessment of students in a traditional manner. Tradition may be of value, but not for its own sake. In the structure of a successful middle school a traditional concept of assessment does not enhance the program.

When one applies the criterion of physical development, great differences in middle school students are easy to recognize; students in their seventh year of school have wide physical differences. Some boys are beginning to shave while others will wait several years for this experience. Some girls are attractive to older boys and are interested in dating while other girls are more comfortable climbing trees. Though harder to identify, psychological and mental differences are just as great as the physical differences in middle school students.

Therefore, rather than employing traditional concepts, assessment of students must be used as a means of individualizing the instructional program so that the differences in middle school students can be used to best advantage for the most successful education of each. By individualized instruction we do not mean that every student is expected to master the same concepts at different rates; in an individualized program, different students may be learning different things. The goal is to have every student achieving whatever he is capable of achieving. Success for each student is dependent upon having goals and objectives that are appropriate for his achievement level.

As we consider assessment, we must consider objectives because it is most difficult to evaluate or assess anything unless we first define our objectives. Evaluating is actually determining whether or not an objective has been met.

Educational objectives should be stated in terms that are measurable. For example, it would be most difficult to evaluate whether or not a student could "understand mathematics" without a further delineation of what one means by "understand." But, it would be quite possible to assess whether or not a student could add or subtract two digit numbers. In the past, teachers have found it relatively easy to evaluate students at the lowest level of the cognitive domain — that is, to ascertain what facts or knowledge the students possessed. Evaluations of this nature have been frequently determined by paper and pencil tests.

Teachers often do a very good job of assessing psychomotor skills such as typing or manipulating various devices. These techniques are easy to assess. However, it is sometimes difficult to measure items in the affective domain, which is concerned with feelings and attitudes. When teachers attempt to measure such things as a change in a student's disposition towards something, the objective must be so stated that there is something to evaluate. For example, in a health class, a teacher might try to measure a student's disposition toward brushing his teeth. In order to do this, the instructor might ask the student to keep a chart noting the number of times he brushed his teeth after breakfast, after dinner, after a snack, or before going to bed for a two-week period. From the completed chart, the teacher might infer that there had or had not been a change in the student's disposition toward brushing his teeth. In a language arts class the teacher might want to measure a student's disposition toward increased reading and his disposition toward reading a variety of literature. It could be inferred from a chart or list kept by the student over a period of time if there had been a change in inclination.

If one is unable to identify what he is trying to evaluate, then it is doubtful that he will be able to evaluate it. Educational objectives must be clearly stated in terms that are measurable.

Why Assess?

Teachers assess frequently in order to determine the present achievement level of students. In some literature this is referred to as a pretest. The pretest need not be a paper and pencil test. The teacher can check past achievement records or simply ask the student involved selected questions. Observation is also an acceptable means of pretesting.

An example of the usefulness of a pretest occurs when students are assigned a term paper or research paper. The teacher needs to determine or assess whether or not the students are able to use a card catalogue and if they possess certain other skills needed in order to complete the assignment. If it is determined that some students do not know how to use a card catalogue, those students might be grouped together to master this skill before attempting the original assignment.

For another example, let us look into a social studies classroom. Before asking students to make certain judgments about the Supreme Court's involvement in the present desegregation cases before it, the teacher must make sure the students possess the concepts dealing with the checks and balances in our government.

Teachers evaluate student learning styles in order to construct a learning environment appropriate for each student. Some students learn best through manipulative devices. They need to construct a model or work with tools, while other students work best with abstract concepts. Some students learn best by listening, others by viewing, while still others learn best by becoming involved in some action. Each learner has his particular learning style.

Have you ever been in a situation where you wished the instructor would leave you alone and let you master the concept your way rather than being forced to do it the way the instructor wanted? Perhaps you had not wanted to listen to the lecture or participate in a panel discussion, but would have preferred to go to the library to study in isolation. Or perhaps you do not like to study by yourself, but enjoy interacting with others in a small group. You have your own learning style — the way you learn best — and probably you could achieve more if instructors would permit you to use your most effective style.

Is not the same true for students? There are no hard and fast rules that will help a teacher determine when to let the student choose his or her own learning style, or when to help the student expand his experiences. This decision must be left to the professional judgment of the teaching team. Teachers must expand their professional expertise by permitting multimodes of learning.

It is recognized that students have many learning styles, not just one. The teaching team has the responsibility of identifying the various learning styles of students through joint evaluation or assessment and then constructing proper learning activities in light of the team evaluation. Frequently, teachers have stated that, "Students must learn to get along in all kinds of environments. The role of the school is to make sure that students can handle themselves in any situation." If the student is hesitant about being an active participant in a group, and resists various modes of learning, then it is the teacher's role to entice the student into the group, to encourage him to take an active part. A teacher we know — let us call her Mrs. Evans — might handle it this way. After listening thoughtfully to their comments, she delineated a task heretofore unthought of by the young people but one that she knew would be necessary to fulfill. At the same time she urged a less confident one to "give it a whirl." "You handled this type of material quite well the last time." "Good show, Tom." "Sheila, you have a talent I never suspected." Other students must see the need to acquire good listening skills. Each student must be able to take both active and passive roles for effective group dynamics.

Occasionally a student might be identified as one who needs frequent help. To make his learning meaningful, the team should construct learning activities in which frequent additional help is available for this student. At the other extreme, a student might be known to work best with little assistance from a teacher. In this case, the middle school team should construct a learning environment that allows independent study at appropriate times. Many students seem to learn some things best when they are passive members of a group. Other students need to actively participate in some project. Learning environment can be constructed to fit all these requirements.

Educators know that most students have a particular time of the day in which they learn best. Some students come to school wide awake and eager. Their best time for learning is morning, and their achievement level begins to taper off past noon. Others come to school almost asleep, and their most productive time is in the afternoon. As the day wears on, they become stronger. Teachers wish this were not true, but we must recognize these differences in students. Middle school teachers must take these differences into consideration when planning an effective learning environment.

In order to determine grouping patterns, teachers assess students. Educators frequently have pulled students together because it was assumed all students in a particular group needed help in mastering a given concept. To have an entire group listening to instruction or participating in a learning activity that some have already mastered is wasteful.

Group composition should be determined in a team meeting. The shy reserved girl, who seems to learn best when with close friends, should be placed with her friends. The team identifies certain combinations of students that are likely to produce the best learning environments. The old idea that learning has to be painful to be effective is no longer valid. This concept is difficult to remove from the schools of America. The "if it hurts, it must be good for you," is almost a part of our culture. When certain antiseptics are applied to wounds we often hear the patients remark, "It must be helping, it hurts so much." One can purchase antiseptics that do not sting and are just as effective. Neither antiseptics nor learning has to be painful. The objective is to make learning as pleasant and as attractive as possible. The middle school goal is to make learning a pleasure so the student will want to continue to learn all his life. Teachers do not want students to view learning as a painful experience.

Middle school teachers should evaluate in order to determine if the instructional program has been appropriate. If teachers find that all the students have failed to master a certain concept, then it might be that the teacher or the teaching team is at fault. Perhaps the failure was not the fault of the students. Some aspect of the learning environment might not have been constructed properly. Evaluation is for the purpose of determining the effectiveness of the learning program as well as for measuring pupil progress.

Of course, educators must also evaluate in order to report to parents. Teachers must collect certain kinds of evidence so that they will be able to report to parents precisely what their son or daughter has done in school. The parents should receive a report of not only how their child is doing in relation to the total population, but also a report of how he is doing in relation to his own competencies.

How Do We Assess?

Teachers should evaluate on an individual basis. The goal is not to compare one student with the entire class or one student to another student. Traditionally, evaluation seemed to be geared to comparing an individual to a specific group, at a specific time, against a specific standard, as best understood by a specific teacher. The goal should be to compare where a student is today in relation to where he was yesterday. Is the student making acceptable progress considering all the information we have about him — such as his ability level, his reason for being in school, his interest in the subject, and the opportunities that he has to work with media that are most appropriate for him?

Teachers have often been reluctant to state that certain judgments or evaluations are subjective in nature. Subjective judgment should not be considered unacceptable, but most acceptable and respectable. The danger occurs only when subjective judgments are recorded as objective judgments. There are educational goals that are most difficult to measure objectively. An example would be measuring the ability to apply principles already mastered to problems that will arise in the future. This can be evaluated by the team's subjective judgment; but, perhaps little objective evidence exists to support the evaluation. Generally, the teaching team's judgment is accurate, but teachers should obtain objective evidence if possible. The collective judgment of a group of professionals on a teaching team might be more valid than many paper and pencil tests.

The specific technique used for assessment is determined by what one is evaluating. If the members of the teaching team were evaluating attitude, for example, they might use one technique. If they were evaluating retention of facts, they might apply different methods altogether. The technique for evaluation must be selected only after the objectives are clear.

In evaluating student performance, it is very easy and natural to fall into the trap of evaluating behavior rather than performance. Frequently behavior is evaluated rather than actual performance. If a middle school student must choose between receiving a high mark for his performance and derision from his peers or a lower mark and acceptance by his peers, the student will often choose what is acceptable to his fellow students.

The middle school teacher must constantly recognize that pleasing a teacher is not nearly as important to the student as the respect of his peers. Teachers must be careful not to have their evaluation of student performance colored by the need of the student to be accepted by his classmates.

If one is trying to measure student attitude, a questionnaire study might be appropriate. For example, student attitude toward independent study might be measured in order to evaluate the independent study program. The student could be given a survey form to fill out and return to the teacher. From such a study, information for improving the instructional program might be obtained. Students could identify specific weaknesses, such as, "There are no teachers around during independent study time." In addition it could be determined whether all students shared the same view of the independent study programs or whether various groups of students tended to view the program differently. Such information would be helpful in improving the independent study program.

A school staff might evaluate a change in the instructional program by comparison of attendance data and/or the number of discipline problems under both the old and the new programs. The discipline problems considered might be those referred to an administrator for disposition or the number of discipline problems identified by the teaching team. This kind of information will also assist teachers in improving the instructional program.

In order to be effective, we need to evaluate as few objectives at a time as possible. If a teacher is asked to make an evaluation of the student effort, his actual accomplishments, his behavior, his motivation (as best determined by the teacher), and to assign a single mark to all of these factors, it would be virtually impossible. If teachers evaluate one objective at a time, then the method of reporting is more realistic.

In evaluation, it is helpful to have a checklist in chart form of the major concepts or objectives that most students will master. The objectives or concepts are printed on one side of the sheet and, as the student completes the objective or masters the concept, it is checked off. The team is charged with stating the objectives that the student must accomplish in performance terms. Any member of the team should be authorized to make a judgment as to when the student has reached his objective. Ideally, all students should not be held accountable for the same objectives.

As teachers attempt to humanize the middle school, they must consider how the student will perceive evaluation. The methods of evaluation are of utmost importance. The student's social development must be considered. For example, after two students had a debate in a social studies class concerning a local issue dealing with pollution, the teacher had the class vote on who should win the debate. After voting, the teacher then proceeded to ask the student who lost the debate such questions as, "Can you see why you lost the debate?" The teacher compared how one student made his points very clearly and concisely with how the other speaker was vague and nonspecific. The teacher had good intentions and felt that the review of the debate was not embarrassing to the students. After the evaluation the one student was heard to say, "She really made me look stupid." In this case, the teacher had failed to consider how the student would view the evaluation.

Assessment frequently takes place in team meetings. In teaming the group analyzes students, making professional judgments about learning styles, about present achievement levels, and about what kinds of learning experiences should be prescribed for individual students. The middle school student is viewed not only through the eyes of the team members, but by the counselor, teacher aides, and any others, that the team might like to invite to participate in the team meeting.

Accountability and performance contracts are very popular today. Teachers are wondering how performance contracting and accountability will influence their own evaluation as well as how they evaluate students. Unfortunately, many educators and citizens feel that the concept of accountability and performance contracts is concerned only with improving the cognitive or factual knowledge of a student.

Accountability

Accountability is the extent to which an individual or institution is willing and able to stand behind its work or its product and to correct a demonstrated or perceived fault. In public education, it refers to the commitment of teachers, administrators, and board members to being responsible for their performance and answerable for the results of their instructional programs (271:31).

Performance Contracting

Performance contracting is a procedure by which a school system enters into a contract with a business to carry out a specific instructional task such as teaching reading or mathematics. For a stipulated amount of money, the firm guarantees to produce specific results within a specified period of time (271:49).

Perhaps the greatest contribution of performance contracting and accountability is nothing more than helping educators to think more precisely about what really matters in education. Humanizing education and making the process more personal is the goal of the middle school staff. A personalized and humanized education is the chief concern of the school staff and has the highest priority. It is not inconceivable that gains in cognitive knowledge and an individualized program can be compatible. A more personalized learning program probably will result in cognitive growth equal to or greater than that occurring in a traditional program. The question is not, "Are accountability and performance contracting better than an individualized program?" The question should be "What goals or objectives should have the highest priority in the middle schools?" Next, educators need to decide if performance contracts will assist in meeting those goals. A personalized and humanized program at the middle school will not necessarily accept all of today's prevailing standards of success. A staff will take care that success is not evaluated just in terms of cognitive growth. It is necessary for a successful program to be evaluated in terms of what preparation the students will need for an uncertain future.

Methods of Reporting
Student Progress

Some middle schools still have traditional report cards which are sent home every six to nine weeks. The report card lists the subjects the student is studying and his progress is reported by "A," "B," "C," "D," or "F." This reporting procedure is familiar to most teachers and does not require any further elaboration. If this reporting procedure is the practice in your school, it is suggested that the staff seriously examine the procedure to see if it meets the needs of the students, parents, and teachers. The advantage of traditional reporting is convenience. Most parents feel that they understand the traditional procedure and any changes in the report method would require elaborate explanation.

However, many school staffs are replacing the traditional report cards by a parents-student-teacher conference. Each teacher is assigned a group of students, approximately twenty. Her role is to assist the student in preparing for a reporting conference. Conferences are generally scheduled at the end of six to nine weeks. Conference members include the student, the parents, and the teacher, acting as advisor. The student during the conference explains to his parents what objectives or progress he has accomplished since the last conference, what objectives he is trying to accomplish, and what goals or objectives he plans to pursue in the near future.

In assisting the student in planning the conference the advisor asks the student such questions as: "How do you want to run the conference?" "What is it that you want to tell your parents?" "How will you explain your progress or lack of progress to your parents?" Experience has shown that this reporting procedure is well received by parents. Students tend to be very critical of themselves and make many negative comments about their own behavior or seriousness of intent. The teacher-advisor offers positive reinforcement to the student and to his parents. Teachers who have participated in the advisor-student-parent conference tend to support the procedure. They report that such conferences offer several advantages. Students seem to acquire a deeper commitment to their learning programs and a better understanding of what it is they are trying to accomplish.

Another reporting procedure which can be used in the middle school is the parent conference with each subject specialist. Generally a time is set aside at the end of each six to nine weeks in which the parent has a short conference with each subject specialist. Rather than reporting a grade, the teacher comments to the parent on student accomplishment. An effort is made to note student progress rather than comparing a student with group norms or reporting failure. Emphasis is upon progress and success, not upon failure.

Community pressures, tradition, and parental concerns require that schools develop reporting procedures. But there is no reason why these procedures cannot be more personalized than today's standard report cards. The reporting system must reflect the humanistic approach.

Teacher Evaluation —
A Way To Improve Instruction

To many teachers, evaluation is a process whereby an administrator visits the class and then after class in the hallway, tells the teacher what she did right or what she did wrong. Or, perhaps, the teacher is invited to the principal's office where the principal, comfortably seated at his desk, relates his reactions. In a routine fashion the principal indicates both positive and negative observations. Positive observations frequently were such things as, "You had good rapport with your students," or "You got started on time, got the students settled, and didn't waste a lot of time at the beginning of class." Negative comments frequently took the form of, "I noticed you didn't use any audio-visual devices," or "You spent too much time taking attendance."

The above represents an outdated concept of evaluation. This stereotyped approach to evaluation adds nothing to the improvement of instruction and, in fact, probably does a great deal of damage to the teacher's self-concept, thereby, damaging the learning program.

To improve the teaching-learning process, evaluation is a necessary function. Evaluation, simply defined, is a process whereby one or more individuals observe a teaching-learning situation, analyze it, and then share their analysis with the person responsible for the learning situation. The teaching-learning process can be improved only if a teacher is able to identify practices and behaviors that facilitate the learning process and identify activities that are hindering the process.

One professional observing and evaluating another is an excellent way to assist teachers to grow professionally. Evaluation cannot be accomplished by casually walking into a classroom, observing a teacher working with one or more groups of students, and making casual comments to that teacher. Evaluation must be systematically planned and organized to be effective. The greatest advantage to all personnel is gained when both the teacher and the evaluators are members of the same teaching team. When members of a team observe another team member, that activity can be related to the team planning sessions. It is then possible to consider how the observed learning situation relates to the team's long range and intermediate plans.

Preobservation Session

Objectives Clarified   During the preobservation session, one or more teacher evaluators should examine the plans for the day with the teacher or the teaching team. The job of the evaluating personnel will be to help the teacher or the team state objectives for the learning session in performance terms. Frequently, a teacher will say, "Well, I know what I want the students to understand or to appreciate." This statement is unsatisfactory. The evaluating teacher must assist the instructor to verbalize and state in performance terms exactly what he or she hopes to accomplish during the learning session. An evaluator can judge the effectiveness of a learning situation only when he has identified what the teacher is trying to accomplish. Evaluating personnel should also determine how the objectives relate to previous and succeeding activities.

If objectives are questionable or inappropriate, the evaluator might assist the teacher in changing objectives. However, if changing objectives would be impractical because of time limitations or a teacher's sensitivity to change, then questioning objectives should be postponed until the evaluating sessions. This is a decision evaluating personnel must make.

Procedures   The evaluating team asks the teacher to outline the techniques he plans to utilize. His report should include grouping criteria. If the students are to be in a large group, what criteria were used to determine that all students needed the same learning situation? If the students are to be in small groups, what was the reason for grouping in this mode? Were the students grouped because of interests, abilities, or because they were all working on the same objective? The outline must answer all the questions. In addition, evaluating personnel will ask the teacher what materials were selected, and why.

Mechanics of Observation   The observation session should not interfere with the teaching-learning process. There should be no misunderstandings about when the evaluators will observe the teacher, where the observation will take place, how long it will last, and how free the observers will be to move about the room. The teacher should make known in advance whether it is permissible to talk with students or whether she would prefer the evaluating personnel to remain as inconspicuous as possible. Teachers may have certain problem areas to which they would like the evaluating personnel to give particular attention. Therefore, teachers should be given an opportunity to note their special needs.

If an observing team is used, a leader or chairman should be identified. A team makes possible a division of labor. For example, a teacher may ask for an analysis of her questioning technique. One member might observe and record the types of questions asked. Another would note the attention of students during a large group presentation. One member of the evaluating team could focus on such things as the amount of talking between students, the facial expression of students, or perhaps the amount of movement in the room.

The objectives, procedures, and mechanics of evaluation are all determined and precisely defined at the preobservational meeting:

> *Summary of Preobservation Session*
> 1. What are you going to do?
> 2. Why are you going to do it?
> 3. How are you going to do it?

Observation Session

The observation session should be viewed as a data gathering mission. It is not a situation in which an observer goes into the classroom to collect "good" or "bad" evidence. During the observation session the teachers must not feel pressured. Although descriptive information and general impressions are being recorded, value judgments are not. Emphasis is not on content, but on process. Information should be gleaned on teacher performance, on what the students were doing, and on how the students participated in the learning activity. General impressions are more important than isolated incidents.

The Analysis Session

Playback of Data During the analysis session the teacher is not present. The evaluating personnel examine the information collected. They concentrate on what actually took place. They compare what they observed against the information given to them by the teacher during the preobservation session.

The question must be answered in light of what the teacher said he was trying to accomplish; did the teacher accomplish the objectives? If the teacher did accomplish the objectives, did she do so in a professional, effective manner? If objectives were not accomplished, why not? What was wrong? What hindered the learner?

The evaluators must determine whether the learning activities were individualized. Did the instruction meet the needs of individuals? Indeed, the basic question is: Was the learning environment appropriate for the individual?

Plan for Helping the Teacher   If evaluating personnel are not entirely satisfied with the teaching-learning situation, they have a responsibility to suggest constructive alternates. It is not acceptable to imply that the objectives for the day, the grouping criteria used, the methodology of instruction, or the materials utilized were inadequate or substandard without proposing suggested solutions. *The purpose of evaluation is to assist the teacher to become a more professional person, not to evaluate performance.* Therefore, if the teacher is to improve, constructive alternates are necessary.

Teachers must be helped to know and to understand what happened during the learning situation. A plan should be devised that enables the teacher to reflect on what took place in the classroom.

Strategies for the Evaluating Session   Who is going to take the lead during the evaluating session? What kinds of opening comments will be made? What kinds of questions will be asked? Who will do the talking during the evaluating session and what will he say? Interaction with the teacher must not be left to chance, but carefully planned. Preparation must be made to reinforce desired teacher behavior and to identify and correct inappropriate behavior.

The Evaluating Session   The evaluating session occurs when the evaluating personnel and the teacher sit down together, preferably in an informal relaxed atmosphere, and discuss what took place during the observation session. This is not a time for the evaluating personnel to dominate. Avoid this approach — that of making positive comments to the teacher followed by, "Now, I did notice," negative comments. The teacher should be assisted in analyzing her behavior. She should not be put on the defensive, but helped to grow professionally. By asking questions, the evaluating personnel try to get the teacher to think about what took place. Evaluating personnel must be careful not to exercise value judgments or make value statements, but should preface statements with remarks such as "I observed this" or " I felt that," asking the teacher if this really did occur. One must offer perceptions as perceptions, not facts. An attitude of helping the teacher to grow professionally must prevail. The atmosphere must reduce any threat to the teacher.

If the teacher is unable to focus on the learning situation observed, the following questions might be asked:

1. Considering your objectives for any given day, what are your ideas about how to construct a number of learning situations so that students can learn in different ways at different times?
2. Is it necessary that all students in any course master the same concepts and skills, or might some objectives be different for different students?
3. Do you feel students have any need to read the textbook if teachers always cover or lecture on the assignment?
4. Does a teacher always need to lead the discussion?
5. How could what happened in your classroom today be made more relevant to today's world?

Role playing is a technique that may be employed most effectively in the evaluating session. If the evaluators assign the teacher one role and themselves another, then it may be possible to talk about areas that are quite sensitive to the teacher. By utilizing role playing techniques, it is possible for the teacher to verbalize her feelings without being defensive.

Postevaluation Session

During the postevaluating session, the evaluating personnel examine their performance. They might ask themselves the following questions: What agreements did we reach? Did we help the teacher? If so, how? And, if not, why not? Always try to collect evidence during the evaluating session as to its effectiveness. For example, it might be noted whether the teacher was defensive or receptive. Evidence might be gathered by observing facial expressions, tone of voice, or the degree of defensiveness.

Not only should the evaluating personnel examine their effectiveness, but the teacher's opinion should be considered also. For example, the teacher might be asked, "What were the evaluators saying?" Another question would be, "What could the evaluating personnel have said or done to be more helpful?" The evaluating session was designed to help the teacher grow professionally. Therefore, her opinion as to the usefulness of the session is most important.

Summary

The greatest value of evaluation will be to the teacher since the result of the session will be more effective instruction. In the analysis session the learning situation should be completely dissected; a lively exchange of comments encouraged. Objectives are examined, procedures identified, and constructive alternatives proposed.

The job of evaluating classroom teachers has been the job of a supervisor or principal for too long. Evaluation must move from a judgment process to a process whereby one professional helps another to improve teaching-learning situations. This is what evaluation is all about. The purpose of evaluation is not to praise or condemn, but to improve the instructional program.

Chapter 5

Team Teaching

There are many definitions of team teaching. Some educators would call "You take the class today, and I'll take it tomorrow," team teaching. Most educators would reject this definition.

It is suggested that in team teaching all of the following elements be present:

1. Teachers control the organization. No rigid class schedules determine the duration or frequency of instruction. Teachers make decisions regarding the appropriate length, number, and composition of instructional sessions.

2. Teachers may have joint responsibility for objectives.

3. There is role specialization. Teachers specialize in those aspects of teaching that they do best.

4. Student evaluation is a team responsibility.

5. The team meets and works together in regularly scheduled planning sessions.

6. Several teachers are assigned a number of students whom they meet regularly.

7. Teachers will work together with the assigned students in diagnosing difficulties, prescribing appropriate activities, aiding students in becoming self-directive individuals, and in making experiences in schools humanistic.

Role Specialization

Teachers who "do their own thing" in traditional classrooms, with very little consultation or helpful criticism from their professional colleagues, tend to become satisfied with one particular approach to learning. In the self-contained classroom, we are asking teachers to be experts in all phases of learning. This is an unreasonable demand.

We often talk a lot about individualizing instruction for students, but very seldom do we consider the needs of individual teachers. Each teacher certainly has some areas where she feels more confident, and, if she were to remain in a self-contained classroom, she would usually spend more time in these areas of competence. In teaming with other teachers, these strengths are used to best advantage while possible weaknesses are compensated for by the proficiencies of other team members. Team teaching not only takes into account the individual needs of teachers, but also has the potential to individualize instruction. The middle school must acknowledge the uniqueness of students. Team teaching is one approach or organizational pattern that permits teachers to provide for this uniqueness. In addition, teaming tends to provide for a much stronger curriculum for students.

Joint Responsibility for Objectives

Decision making is an essential part of team teaching. What kinds of decisions do team members need to make? Stating instructional objectives, identifying learning experiences, determining time allocations, identifying the different tasks that teachers are to perform, and evaluating progress represent some of the tasks that must receive top priority in team planning. A team needs time set aside during the day and a place where the members can meet to think and plan constructively without interruption.

A middle school team must design a curriculum for the individual student. The total needs of one child are likely to be quite different from that of another. Variations of these needs can be taken into account when curriculum decisions are made. Therefore, the essence of the team teaching concept is the provision of learning experiences for students by joint efforts of teachers. These plans include the use of teacher aides working as a part of the team.

The combined skills, talents, and interests of two or more teachers in a discipline offer a stronger instructional program to the student than one teacher can possibly offer alone. Students can also benefit from the enriched educational experiences provided by various organizational plans coupled with team teaching — such as assembly group instruction, inquiry or small group instruction, and individualized instruction, planned and executed by the team members. The teaching team can adjust the size of a particular group of students depending upon the activity that is to take place and upon the needs of the students involved at that time.

The middle school team has a joint responsibility for fostering interests, developing abilities, and establishing value systems for each learner. Meeting individual needs can be best accomplished by having students meet with teachers in large assembly groups at times, in small inquiry or discussion groups at other times, or on a one-to-one basis on occasion. It is not implied, however, that the middle school student needs to be involved with teachers or other students at all times. Certainly there is a need to give the student the opportunity to work alone. Teachers should guide, diagnose, and direct learning to stimulate the student's interest.

Middle school students must be active. Teachers in a team can perform the companion process of determining what the students need and proposing varied activities for the self-development of each student. The middle school must also be a place where the teachers in a team are free to observe and work with students, to talk with their fellow team members about a psychology and philosophy of learning, to jointly evaluate a student's progress, and to exchange ideas about teaching methodology. Students should also have the opportunity to observe many teachers and to identify with several teachers rather than just one.

Types of Team Organization

The phrase "team teaching" has many different connotations. One team teaching arrangement could be classified as a hierarchical arrangement. This is one where one teacher is designated as being the leader of the team by an administrator. That person is responsible for the management of the team, ordering supplies, and sometimes evaluating other team members.

In another team teaching arrangement the team members select one of the members for the leadership role. This is a more democratic approach than that of an authoritatively designated leader. The team selection procedure fulfills the need of staff involvement. The administrative role of the principal is thus integrated by permitting teachers to assume a participatory role.

A third type of team teaching organization plan has a team leader neither assigned by the administration nor selected by the members of the team. The leadership role is passed from team member to team member depending on the circumstances involved and the strengths required. This approach could be classified as the involvement organizational plan where the leadership evolves as the need arises.

Team teaching can also be classified in terms of the functions team members perform. Team members may specialize in a single discipline such as mathematics or science. A single discipline team may have one teacher who, because of her expertise, assumes the responsibility for content. Other team members support the instruction by their knowledge of the learning process. An example might be a science teacher motivating and exciting the students by presenting some introductory ideas and posing questions in a large group lecture. After the initial lecture, the other members could lead inquiry groups though they do not have in-depth knowledge of the content.

Another pattern calls for several teams to identify objectives and to have the subject matter specialist from each discipline determine activities within the respective discipline as it relates to the objective. An example might be identifying factors contributing to pollution, to the quantity of waste causing pollution, to the effort or lack of effort by local, state, and federal government to control pollution, and, finally, making recommendations for possible solutions to these problems. Teachers in each discipline would concern themselves with assisting the students to master specific objectives as they relate to respective disciplines.

Still another pattern might be an arrangement where specialists from each discipline combine their instruction to perform interdisciplinary teaching. Broad general concepts are identified and it is the student mastery of concepts that is of prime importance. One example of a major concept is "dependency." A subconcept of dependency might be that "man is dependent upon others."

Although the success of an interdisciplinary approach is contingent upon the cooperation of all teams, it is suggested that the single discipline teams first identify the important concepts. Representatives from each discipline, including unified arts, can then get together for a special team meeting to discuss appropriate concepts and ways to "join forces" for the instructional sequence. Middle school teachers may decide to combine learning activity packages or relate disciplines through an assembly group. Certainly, the amount of specialization in a content field or a particular arrangement depends on many things, not excluding the teachers themselves, and will vary from school to school, even from team to team within a school.

While there are many different functions the team members can perform and many different organizational arrangements for team teaching, there must be one approach that is preferred over the others. It has been our experience with team teaching at the middle school level that teams function more effectively if the leadership evolves from unit to unit, from concept to concept, or function to function. We feel that all team members are more receptive and willing to share in the decision-making process with this kind of arrangement.

To provide a smooth transition from the fifth year into the middle school, we suggest that teams operate with a sixth year social studies and language arts team and a mathematics and science team. The number of teachers on these teams may then be divided into separate teams in each of the four major disciplines — i.e. language arts, social studies, mathematics, science — and a related arts team. The related arts team should include teachers of foreign language, physical education, music, and typing. A unified arts team would consist of industrial arts, art, and home economics teachers. As teachers gain proficiency in teaming there are distinct advantages for interdisciplinary teaming. Advantages also exist of combining various age groups for a continuous program.

Representatives from all teams should meet weekly to discuss what they are doing, the concepts they will cover, and how instruction can best be related in a different content area. This is one approach of interdisciplinary teaming to remove the fragmentation that can easily occur in specialization teaming. The

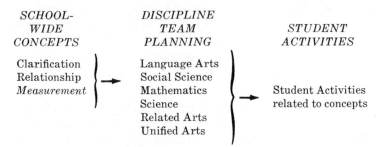

Measurement is shown as one of the concepts that may be appropriate for middle school youth. The following activities would be considered appropriate for the various disciplines:

a) Language Arts   —   Time relationship

b) Social Science   —   Map skills

c) Mathematics   —   Ratio problem

d) Science   —   Measurement with a micrometer

e) Related Arts
    1. Physical Education   — Distance or heighth
    2. Typing   — Margins
    3. Music   — Note measurement
    4. Foreign Language   — Map skills using kilometers

f) Unified Arts
    1. Industrial Arts   — Board feet
    2. Home Economics   — Measurement of ingredients
    3. Art   — Perspective

objective is to couple discipline areas so that the student no longer sees language arts as isolated from mathematics or other areas. We feel that this arrangement combines the best features of discipline teams and at the same time builds on the merits of interdisciplinary teaming. While teachers integrate the curriculum, they share information about the instructional requirements of their students.

Types of Planning Sessions

Some educators feel that in a team teaching situation where teachers plan together, think together, and evaluate together, the teacher's individuality is forgotten. Nothing could be further from the truth. The individual approaches taken by various teachers are considered good psychologically and theoretically. Moreover, the uniqueness and creativity of the individual teacher are never forgotten in the team planning phase. A spark of creativity by one teacher may serve as a catalyst for other teachers. Hence, one good idea may become a better idea as a result of team interaction.

Every middle school teacher and principal should be aware that there are different types of planning sessions for teaching teams. None of the following types can be omitted.

> I. Organizational Meeting
> This is one of the first meetings of the teaching team. The principal discusses with the team any decisions that have already been made. Such decisions might include:
> 1. Time school starts and ends.
> 2. Lunchtime.
> 3. Space assigned to the team.
> 4. Specialists available (counselor, nurse).
> 5. Additional human resources available (student, teachers, teacher aides, parent volunteers).
> 6. Policy on field trips.
> 7. Budget policy.

Teacher responsibilities:
1. To determine team organization. Team members will be selected for a single discipline or interdisciplinary approach.
2. To tentatively determine major units to be taught during the year.
3. To review pupil assessment for initial assignment.

II. Long-range Planning
The team will meet from one to four hours at the beginning of each major unit. (A major unit might be from two to eight weeks.)

Team responsibilities:
1. To determine and/or to reestablish major objectives or outcomes for a unit.
2. To determine role specialization or division of labor for the teams.
3. To determine and assign writing of learning activity packages.
4. To establish tentative grouping patterns.
5. To establish a rationale for time utilization.
6. To determine and plan how the objectives can be translated into an operational program.

Individual teacher responsibilities:
1. To inform other team members of special strengths, skills, or interests in the unit under consideration.
2. To identify appropriate material based on past knowledge of individual learners.

III. Intermediate Planning
The team should meet a minimum of two hours per week for intermediate planning.

Team responsibility:
1. To evaluate the teaching-learning process that has taken place.
2. To review plans for future learning experiences.
3. To consider and plan for:
    a. Grouping patterns by assessment of the students' needs and abilities.
    b. Staff assignments, including teacher aides.

    c. Equipment needs.

    d. Arrangement of physical environment and space.

    e. Assessment of students during the learning process.

    f. Community and home involvement.

Individual teacher responsibility:

1. To make operational decisions about daily confrontations between the teacher, the student, the curriculum, and the total environment.
2. To structure daily activities considering how each student differs in ability and aptitude, in social and economic background, in motivation, in study habits and skills, and in interest and needs.
3. To vary teaching techniques, materials, human resources, and time so that each student has the opportunity to learn at his own pace, in his own style, and within a framework of what is significant to him.
4. To allow each student to progress as rapidly as he is able or as slowly as he must.

IV. Short Range Planning

The team will generally meet informally a total of fifteen to twenty minutes a day in addition to other team meetings. This need not be a single time span — for example, this might be a thirty-second conference in the midst of learning activities.

Team responsibility:

1. To make daily adjustments in the instructional program.
2. To move students from one group to another.

Individual teacher responsibility:

1. To identify problems that require a team decision.
2. To determine when additional teacher input would enhance a student's learning effectiveness.
3. To adjust material, space, equipment, or individual student objectives as the situation mandates.

V. Special Team Meetings
    Pupil assessment:
    Once or twice during a unit the team should
    meet and discuss only pupil assessment. Each
    teacher assumes the responsibility for the as-
    sessment of a specific number of students.
    This is to serve as a check to insure the con-
    tinuous assessment, and each team member's
    judgment and observation is considered.

    Extending horizons:
    Individual team members meet with other
    teachers in the school who are not members
    of their team. One example of this would be
    a meeting of all social studies teachers.

    Subteam:
    Two teachers may jointly assume responsibil-
    ity for a part of the team plans.

    Special teachers:
    The team meets with special teachers to coor-
    dinate activities. (Special teachers might be
    art, music, home economics, industrial arts,
    and physical education instructors.)

    Team evaluation:
    The team needs to review its effectiveness as
    a unit at least three times a year.

    Curriculum council:
    Representatives from each team meet to dis-
    cuss matters of interest to all teams; i.e.
    scheduling, curriculum, facilities, equipment,
    assessment procedures, and community in-
    volvement.

Process in Moving from
Traditional to Team Teaching

Before teachers venture into team teaching, they need to visit
other school systems that use teaming; they should read and discuss materials with one another, attend local workshops, and experiment with actual teaming procedures. During the first year
especially, additional consultant help should be available as teach-

ers feel the need for it. Growth in team teaching should be a constant, ongoing process.

Teachers should be involved in planning for team teaching from the very beginning. Some principals make the mistake of outlining the teaming arrangement, selecting the teachers, stating expectations, and then stepping out of the picture. Although the principal must take a positive leadership role in encouraging teachers to team, he must involve the teachers in staff selection, in the development of the teaming philosophy, and in the identification of operational procedures. The principal should act as a guide, an encourager, and a resource person.

Often it is easy to find two teachers who get along well together and who desire to team teach. From this point, they need only to be encouraged to become involved in selecting other staff members. They should be instructed to select teachers for a team on the basis of interpersonal compatibility, similar educational philosophies, balanced intellectual strengths, and balanced skills. Skill strengths may be in such areas as writing, assembly group presentations, or inquiry group leadership. The initial team of two would select teachers who could complement their strengths and offset their weaknesses.

To secure proper teammates, it might be necessary to transfer and promote within the school system. A teacher with certain personality traits may work out perfectly with one team within the school district while she is undesirable for another team within the same building. It may also be to a team's advantage if the team consists of both experienced and inexperienced personnel. A team needs members who can provide fresh ideas and a lot of energy. On the other hand, teachers that have had some experience are vital in providing stability within the team.

Once teachers decide to team, they must be committed to continued teaming. This commitment is necessary to improve instruction and to meet truly the needs of each middle school student. Teams should begin forming with the realization that difficulties will undoubtedly be encountered in the initial stages. An understanding and supportive principal will enable these difficulties to be met and conquered much more easily.

Students should be helped to understand the philosophy behind team teaching. An orientation program for all new middle school students should establish the role of the student in team teaching.

Students should have an opportunity to discuss this role with the professional staff. The advantages of team teaching must be readily apparent to the student body.

When moving from a self-contained approach to team teaching, it is essential that the community be thoroughly informed. Community support is especially necessary today when school systems are constantly seeking increased tax levies and bond issues. The solid support of team teaching and other innovations will be reflected by financial responsibility.

Parent-teacher organizations, newspapers, surveys, monthly or quarterly reports, radio interviews, and other media offer excellent opportunities to inform the public about team practices. The extensive use of volunteer mothers and other community resources are ingenious ways to assure not only acceptance but assistance as well.

Administrators must convey to the community the reasons for team teaching and the advantages teaming offers to the students and to the community. This communication should exist prior to the initiation of team teaching and continue throughout the ongoing phase of teaming. It would be deplorable to have a team teaching program fail because parents felt that their students had less contact with teachers, or that students were not receiving the attention that they should. A two-way communication program that explains the concept to the community and permits free discussion is vitally important to the success of the program.

The building principal has the additional responsibility of providing adequate time and space for the team to plan and evaluate instruction. The principal may have to be the spokesman to obtain additional multimedia materials or the money necessary to change the facilities to meet the requirements of innovative types of instruction.

Certainly, these responsibilities are not all–inclusive.

Developing Team
Member Compatibility

Successful team teaching is much easier if those directly involved realize that compromise may be necessary at times. Many hours can be wasted and team effectiveness reduced when agreements cannot be reached. "My" instructional program now becomes "our" instructional program; "my" students become "our" students.

Teams should be permitted to resolve internal conflict themselves. If they can solve their problems effectively, a smoother organizational arrangement is assured. Whenever a principal or an arbitrator steps in, the team's chances of resolving future controversies is lessened.

A principal should encourage discussion and exchange of ideas between team members and between teams. Such exchanges inspire creativity and, hence, become the source of many new ideas. An atmosphere of openness and receptivity will result in a more stimulating educational program for middle school students. As teachers gain the firm belief that teaming is the best approach, their doubts about teaming advantages will disappear.

Disadvantages of Teaming and How to Overcome the Disadvantages

There may be some disadvantages of team teaching; middle school teachers and administrators should be cognizant of these disadvantages prior to the initiation of a team teaching organizational plan.

In any program of change when something new and different is about to occur, teachers need to be involved in the decision-making process. Teachers can be encouraged to team teach, but they must be fully committed before they venture into the new organizational arrangement. If the idea to team is initiated and supported by the teachers, teaming will quite likely succeed. If the teaching staff has not made this decision, team teaching may experience many difficulties simply because the idea was forced upon them before they were fully committed to the teaming approach.

The second area of difficulty may be due to the inability of some people to get along in a close team teaching effort. Inability to cooperate may be due to immaturity or personality clashes.

Some teachers just do not work comfortably with other teachers. This does not mean that the teachers are not doing a good job of teaching, but simply that they are more effective when working by themselves. When possible, the present team members should interview prospective new members and participate in the selection process. Candidates for the new position might also view their possible future colleagues with an eye toward probable compatibility.

There will be a need to resolve differences from time to time in the team functions. There may be disagreement concerning the selection of concepts, the structuring of different size groups for instructional purposes, or the selection of evaluation procedures. Team teaching implies sharing and mandates a mutual understanding by all concerned. The success of teaming is dependent upon cooperation. Without sharing, mutual understanding, and effort, a team cannot function effectively.

A third area of difficulty may be inadequate planning time. To assume that teachers can meet and plan together prior to school, after school, or in the evening is erroneous. Teams need regularly scheduled planning times during school to achieve maximum effectiveness.

Although it would be nice to have facilities that provide flexibility, aesthetic value, and comfort, the lack of such facilities should not be used as an excuse for poor teaming or no teaming at all. Open-space buildings designed for flexibility, that are acoustically treated, attractive, and comfortable, are highly desirable. But an older, more traditional building should not discourage a group of teachers from starting to team.

Although one must be aware of possible problems in teaming, the advantages of the team teaching arrangement far outweigh the disadvantages. Let us now consider the advantages that team teaching offers to a school, to students within a school, and to the educational program.

Advantages of Teaming

Team teaching offers teachers the opportunity to become true professionals. Through teaming, they can become more effective in individualizing instruction by being free to diagnose, prescribe, and guide learning activities. Individualizing instruction can be more than just lip service to something that looks good on paper. Team teaching makes this approach a reality.

Flexibility can be provided by teams working together to organize the instructional practices, the curriculum concepts, and the content. Not all teachers do all things equally well. This approach not only permits, but demands that teachers specialize in what they do best. Not only does this provide more satisfaction to teachers themselves but, more importantly, it is beneficial to the students because greater quality in instruction exists.

Middle school students need the exposure to teachers with different and varied backgrounds and areas of specialization. Students become more stimulated and more excited about learning due to a break in the monotony of having one teacher and only one teacher. Because of the planning that takes place in a teaming situation, students are much less likely to encounter the lecturing and telling situations that often prevail in self-contained classrooms.

Because team teachers preassess the needs of the students, they are able to organize their instructional patterns to meet the specific requirements of each student. The evaluation phase is benefited by having several different people view the process. Planning and evaluating jointly make for more efficient use of teacher time and free teachers to work directly with students.

Team members are charged with the responsibility of evaluating each other, of determining instructional materials to be used, and of selecting the instructional techniques that will be used by their professional colleagues. It is difficult for one to effectively evaluate his own instructional techniques and methods. Praise and, at times, helpful criticism from colleagues can make instruction more meaningful to students.

Team teaching permits the possibility of greater student participation since team teaching permits inquiry group instruction in a one-to-one situation. A student should have the opportunity to express himself and the teacher must be available to listen. When the teacher becomes a listener at times and the student becomes the active participant, learning takes place. There should be a setting in which the customary teacher-student roles can be reversed.

Paraprofessionals and clerical aides can perform many routine tasks as well as a professional. Although teaching teams do not always include clerical aides and paraprofessionals, the professional role of the teacher is certainly enhanced by the acquisition of such people.

Summary

Middle school students have varying levels of maturity and, hence, have different needs. Team teaching can reach the student regardless of his maturation point, and challenge diverse intellectual, emotional, and interest levels. Student needs are met more effectively through increased flexibility, role specialization, and a sharing of ideas about individuals and their unique learning styles.

Teachers can learn from one another about how to teach. Most teachers possess sufficient subject matter knowledge, but this is not enough. Knowing how to identify the individual needs of students and knowing how to meet these needs most effectively is much more important. The sharing process between team members on how to teach is vitally important. By sharing knowledge of how to best meet the needs of students through improved teaching techniques and through better student evaluation, a more humanizing experience for middle school students will prevail.

Chapter 6

Inquiry Grouping

Middle school students will enjoy school more if they encounter *success*. Different grouping arrangements can contribute much to the students' chances of success. Indeed, inquiry grouping makes success and individualized instruction possible.

Participation in inquiry group discussions permits the students to become actively involved in learning. In a class of twenty to thirty students all cannot possibly be involved in discussion. But an inquiry group of seven to ten allows each member to participate freely.

Learning is best facilitated when middle school students meet together in appropriate groupings. In interaction with other students, learning is mutually reinforced. Inquiry groups permit a deeper level of communication than is usually found in a traditional classroom. The free exchange of ideas encourages students to be open and honest with one another. When a student has the opportunity to express himself and to actively participate in a quest for knowledge, his commitment to learning is greatly increased.

Learning in the middle school should certainly be more than just the accumulation of facts and barren information. The middle school student should master the process of inquiry. If middle school students are to become individuals who can think for themselves, they must experience the satisfaction of conversing in inquiry with their peers. Students need to communicate with their peers in a way that will satisfy their own needs and, at the same time, contribute to their learning. In small groups, where the number of students is limited, such communication is possible. Purposeful interaction among students demonstrates the importance of the social aspects of learning.

The small inquiry group is one innovation or organizational arrangement that must not be obscured in the middle school. The inquiry group arrangement permits and encourages students to explore ideas gained from the assembly groups, from reading of and doing exercises in learning activity packages, from the reading of supplementary materials, or from their own experiences. Students must have the opportunity to discuss, question, appraise, and criticize ideas that have been presented by teachers or other students.

Many times, we as adults have clarified our ideas and been stimulated to inquire further as a result of a conversation. We use every opportunity to persuade others to accept our thoughts and beliefs. Life would be incomplete and dull without the daily small group discussions that adults typically enjoy. This process of inquiry is just as important for middle school youth as it is for adults.

A sound middle school program must not be perceived as simply "telling" the learner. Instead, emphasis must be placed upon identifying the ways that each student learns best. The middle school staff needs to concentrate on stimulating and motivating youth to become active thinkers and inquirers. There are certain questions the teacher can ask that will produce a degree of tension. Some tension is needed to encourage initial investigation and to promote discussion afterward. It is quite a challenge for teachers to create the conditions that will encourage learning and inquiry.

The Teacher's Responsibility
for Inquiry Grouping

When the inquiry group is planned and conducted successfully, a student cannot become lost as a passive listener. Successful inquiry demands that the teacher possess a knowledge of group dynamics. Middle school teachers must thoroughly understand inquiry group concepts. They must then provide opportunities for students to grasp dynamic skills. Once teachers understand the rationale of small groups, it is unlikely they will lecture to students. Teachers may examine the rationale of small groups through an inservice training program.

As mentioned above, one of the first responsibilities of the middle school teacher is to help students to understand group dynamics and the inquiry group process. An initial meeting to explain the students' role in inquiry could occur in an assembly group. This assembly or large group might be formed by bringing together all the students who need greater knowledge of group dynamics. The number of students might range from five to two hundred. This first orientation could be accomplished by lecture, films, video and audio tape, or demonstration. Eventually, students will have to actually participate in inquiry themselves to fully understand the process.

The assembly group can be used to identify the purposes and responsibilities of student leaders, recorders, and observers. Students need to examine and understand the various roles. Each middle school student should have the opportunity to be a student leader, recorder, or observer. As the students begin to function in these roles the teacher must constantly observe to determine if the designated leader is truly the leader or if joint leadership has occurred, to evaluate the effectiveness of the group leader as he is perceived by his peers, and to ascertain the total involvement and enthusiasm within the group. If a student leader is experiencing difficulty, the teacher must make a special effort to assist the student in mastering leadership techniques.

The teacher must insure that the middle school student can identify the specific objective of each group in which he participates in addition to stating the rationale of the inquiry group. To bring students together on a particular day and say to them, "This is the day that we are to discuss osmosis in an inquiry group," is not adequate. Objectives must be established for each group.

Through the small group, students learn to discuss controversial subjects and can easily communicate with their peer group. The small group provides an opportunity for students to listen and to learn from other students with different backgrounds and viewpoints.

The teacher should help students realize that all members of a group must be free to express their ideas on any topic. Each member of the group should be encouraged to participate and his ideas should be considered important by all, regardless of agreement or disagreement by others. If a teacher effectively communicates this point to students, individual members will feel free to participate and the effectiveness of the inquiry group will be enhanced.

Another responsibility of the middle school teacher is that of observing small groups in action to determine whether common needs exist that could be more effectively met in a larger group. If there is a common lack in certain basic skills or information, it might be more expedient to present the necessary background material in an assembly group.

Participation in small groups provides students with the opportunity to investigate concepts in depth. The small group may stimulate a student to further investigation during his independent study time. Small groups are concerned not only with content but with the process of the interaction as well. *Process* refers to the way that the inquiry group handles communication problems and decision making. Teachers should not worry if the group is not covering a predetermined amount of content. Successful small groups depend upon students' free exchange of ideas and their active involvement in the decision making and the processes of the group.

Teachers must change the composition of the small inquiry group frequently. One reason to change group membership is student personalities. For example, as the teacher observes a small group in action, he may notice that some students are overly concerned about their own participation and are trying to decide what they are going to say next rather than listening to what others are saying. It is necessary for students to listen to all ideas expressed and to observe attitudes from their peers' point of view. By removing a student who is thinking about what he is going to say rather than listening, the group effectiveness might be appreciably improved. The student who has been removed from one group may require tutoring before assignment to another group.

Grouping demands that the teacher know many things about students: their special interests, the friendships that may exist between students, vocational or educational goals, and many other considerations. To know a great deal about a great number of students is a lot to ask of one teacher. Therefore, it is important that a teacher communicate with other teachers in a team and with anyone else who may have knowledge about certain students — people such as counselors, principals, and teacher aides. A continual information flow between professional people is necessary to maintain and improve effectiveness.

To be an effective member of a small group, the student requires certain background information during his independent study. Teachers must see that proper resources are available to the students. Some students may need assistance in locating basic material. Teachers might identify articles and other materials and make them available to learners.

Students may be encouraged to use as many different research materials as possible. They should be encouraged to read conflicting sources of information, clarifying the conflict in the inquiry group. Examining conflict is an excellent way for students to realize that frequently there are different ways to perceive information. Students must learn to weigh all evidence and arrive at their own conclusions.

The involvement of students is very important to individualizing learning. The middle school student must be active in the learning process. Passive listening must be minimized by encouraging students to become active participants — by reading, writing, discussing, discovering, interpreting, and evaluating. To accomplish these tasks, the traditional role of the teacher — that of doing most of the talking and asking specific questions — must be eliminated. A teacher should be a consultant to the small group. Being a consultant to the small group requires the teacher to let students assume a greater responsibility for learning. Students may look to the teacher for suggestions and advice at times or may actively seek her knowledge and experience concerning a certain topic. But students must see the teacher's role as that of a consultant and only very rarely that of active participant.

One exception to this role would be if the teacher were to identify a gross error that may influence the group in the wrong way. She may then relinquish her role as observer to clarify a misconception. It is important, though, for the teacher to be certain that the incorrect statement or error would cause irreversible damage. Perhaps, in some cases, it would be better for the students to eventually realize that an error had been made than for the teacher to identify the error immediately.

A teacher may also have the task of helping students to identify problems than can be actively undertaken in the small group. The purpose of the inquiry approach is to assist the middle school students to increase their confidence as learners. Confidence is a natural result of students becoming more independent. The role of the teacher should rarely be to tell the student what she thinks the problem is or what the small group needs to accomplish. It is true that at times the teacher may assist the students in identifying the problem, but it is hoped that often the students will be able to diagnose the problem themselves. Teachers and students together determine when the students are prepared to participate in small group activities. Each small group has a specific objective. The objective may be very general, such as the free exchange group where students get together to discuss concerns of their own (122). Generally, however, a specific objective is identified and considerable planning is done prior to the inquiry session.

Student Responsibilities and
Roles in the Inquiry Group

A very important role in the small group is that of student leader (122). The student leader must help the group to determine the issues they wish to discuss, to clarify the issues, and to practice the discussion process. The leader and all members of the group must realize that the success of the inquiry group is the responsibility of the entire membership of the group. Although the leadership role is extremely important in determining the effectiveness of the group, this responsibility does not reside entirely with the group leader, it is shared by all members.

The group leader should make a valiant effort to involve everyone in the discussion. He should try to identify concerns, interests, and abilities, and then he must build on this knowledge by asking different members specific questions that he feels they can answer. He should try not to make members uncomfortable by

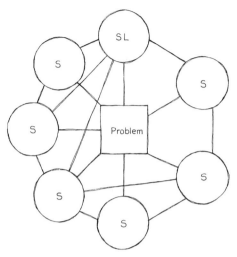

SL – Student Leader
S – Student
T – Teacher

asking them questions he knows they cannot answer. One must remember that many questions may not be considered as either correct or incorrect. This is true if questions are asked that provide directions to living. There are value related concerns resulting from alternatives as an outgrowth of inquiry discussion. A leader should try to establish a climate where personal feelings and attitudes are accepted and students are willing to relate their thoughts to the group.

Another student responsibility is that of recorder (122). The recorder must keep a record of the discussion. He records areas of agreement and of disagreement. He is not concerned with recording who made what statement. The recorder has information available upon request from the leader or other members of the group so that issues can be clarified during the process of group discussion. Normally, the recorder will summarize the discussion and report back to the total group.

The observer plays still another role in the small group. He does not necessarily enter into the discussion (122). He observes and keeps track of who participates in the discussion. The object is to make sure that everyone contributes to a meaningful discussion.

The observer also attempts to analyze why a group is successful or unsuccessful. After analyzing the group in action, the observer may be called upon by the group leader to evaluate the group progress. It is important that he make suggestions in a positive vein so that students are "turned on" rather than "turned off" after the critique. An observer helps a small group to grow in quality and quantity of discussion.

The teacher should make certain that all members of a discussion group have a clear understanding of what an ideal group would be before an observer is appointed or selected. Until the group has this understanding, it may be better to have the teacher serve as an observer. The observer's role should be rotated among all students so that all will have the opportunity to study the interaction that takes place in a group.

Another technique that may help the group to understand the communication process is to divide the group into two separate groups. One group would then sit back and observe the other group to determine who talks, how long and often they talk, whom they look at when they talk, and what style of communication they use.

The style of communication involves the tones of voice, gestures used, and the questions and assertions that take place. The observing group then can determine what communication barriers, if any, exist.

Students might also benefit by having several groups evaluate their discussion and by sharing suggestions for growth within their respective groups. A group can be divided into three or four subgroups that could meet with other subgroups. These subgroups could discuss problems and the solutions to problems. After talking over these problems, they can then go back to their main group and share the information that they have gathered. This process may lead to the identification of new solutions to problems, thus enhancing the effectiveness of the small group.

After an inquiry group session has ended, the teachers need to determine the success of the overall discussion. This evaluation phase is related to observable behavioral changes in learners. These behavioral changes may concern: the number of valid ques-

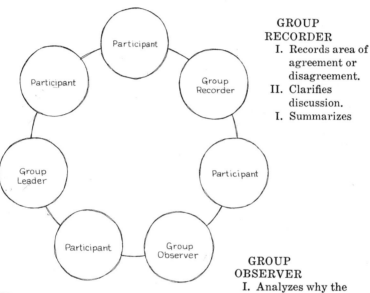

TEACHER
I. Insures all members participate.
II. Available as a resource.
III. When necessary:
— explains group process
— assist group in determining objectives
— gives group specific
assistance when
appropriate.

GROUP
RECORDER
I. Records area of
agreement or
disagreement.
II. Clarifies
discussion.
I. Summarizes

GROUP
OBSERVER
I. Analyzes why the
group is successful
or unsuccessful.
II. Makes positive
suggestion to improve
the group.

GROUP
LEADER
I. Encourages participation.
II. Ask questions.
III. Keep discussion moving and
centered on objective.

tions asked by students; the degree of pursuit of understanding by learners themselves; the degree of self-initiated and self-motivated questions and reactions by students; the students' ability to apply universality to unique conditions; and the increased humaneness of students as evidenced by the tolerance demonstrated for variant comments.

Meaningful learning takes place through effective interaction. Without this interaction, the effectiveness of the learning situation is greatly reduced. For this reason, the small group is of primary importance; the assembly group is used much less. Students need the opportunity for pupil-pupil interaction and pupil-teacher interaction. Such exchanges cannot take place in the assembly group.

Summary

Middle school teachers should try to concentrate upon the processes by which students learn. A student learns when he is involved in the learning process, when he is successful, and when he has a positive self-concept. A small group is designed to achieve student involvement. By proper grouping patterns, a student can be successful and make positive contributions to the group. Successful involvement builds a positive self-concept.

Opportunity must be available for middle school students to make choices about what they will investigate, study, collect data on, and eventually discuss in small groups. They should be encouraged to have ideas and then to communicate these ideas to their peers in the form in which the ideas were created. Both peers and professionals must use humane approaches in reacting to the ideas presented. In a nonthreatening atmosphere, students will research, debate, and finally determine if an idea or statement should be accepted, modified, or rejected without feelings of defensiveness, defeat, and/or despair. Indeed, students should emerge from an inquiry group with a feeling of exhilaration, challenged to investigate further on their own.

The middle school can offer fresh and improved ways of teaching and learning. Teachers need to use new approaches and new ideas in these times of expanded knowledge and rapid change. The development of the middle school can provide the full potential for utilizing the advantages of small groups.

Chapter 7

Independent
Study and
Open Laboratories

It has become professionally fashionable to institute some form of independent study. Who can be against either independence or study? Combined, *independence* and *study* makes an appealing label. However, *independent study* means different things to different people.

Independent study has become an umbrella sheltering a variety of practices. Actually, it is little more than homework if not integrated into a systematic organization for instruction which calls for learners to spend a significant portion of their time working alone.

The approach encompasses all three learning domains: the cognitive, or intellectual; the affective, or attitudinal; and the psychomotor. All are important in the middle school, but none, perhaps, is more important than the affective domain due to the opportunity to develop positive attitudes in students. James Espich and Bill Williams refer to the affective domain by saying,

> Among the many teaching tasks within the affective domain are such items as promoting enthusiasm, self-confidence, responsibility, and trustworthiness, and developing team spirit, curiosity, and the will to learn (106:5).

If properly implemented, independent study can accomplish all
of these very worthy goals. It is so important to effective learning
that unstructured time be made available for each student. The
approach is as appropriate for slow learners as for rapid learners,
as valuable in the sciences as in the arts, and as applicable in the
middle school as it is in the twelfth year of school or college.

Independent study activities can be classified as either teacher-
suggested or student-assumed projects. Teacher-suggested independent study activities are prescribed by the teacher with the
student's interests, abilities, and learning styles in mind. Ideally,
the student and teacher work together to construct or design the
independent study project.

Student-assumed independent study activities are formulated
by the student. The teacher may give the student appropriate advice as needed, and the student is free to consult with the teacher
or teachers during the process of the inquiry.

Broadly defined, *independent study* consists of all learning activities that take place when the teacher stops talking. Most often,
students work alone during independent study. However, the term
may be used to describe research projects carried out by a student
in cooperation with one or more other students.

In *Independent Study: Bold New Venture* we find:

> While the use of independent study often calls for an interdiscipli-
> nary use of ideas and knowledge, it has a broader invitation. It
> opens the opportunity for the student to pursue his interests, an-
> swer his questions, and deal with his concerns (35:196).

The extensive opportunity for a student to work independently
at his own pace is the sign of a truly individualized instructional
program.

Independent study helps the student to develop the ability to
plan and work toward a goal. It can bring about creativity and
a sense of inquiry. Independence is what education is all about.
The goal is to bring the student to the point where he is able to
recognize there is a problem, can identify the problem, can plan
its solution, and is capable of evaluating the results of his efforts to verify that the solution is satisfactory to him.

Some teachers falsely proclaim "independent study" when they
allow students to miss class one day a week to work in the library.
This view falls far short of our goal of independent study. Perhaps it is time to stop and answer the question "Who is learning

what from whom: how and why?" "Who" pertains to all students. The sum of human worth is not related to an intelligence index. "What" refers to individual programs in all disciplines. Individual programs are concerned with personalization and attention to unique needs. "From whom" indicates that the total middle school staff needs to free the learner from the need for constant teacher direction. Sufficient material and equipment for all ability levels should be available to facilitate rapid retrieval of information in a learning environment. "How" requires specialized teachers coupled with flexibility in scheduling. Student commitment and a sense of responsibility are developed for the learning process through decreasing faculty supervision. It is hoped that the last ingredient, the "why" of independent study, is clarified in this book and through involvement in the actual process. Developing the independent learner, who works at his own rate in his own style, can be a gratifying experience.

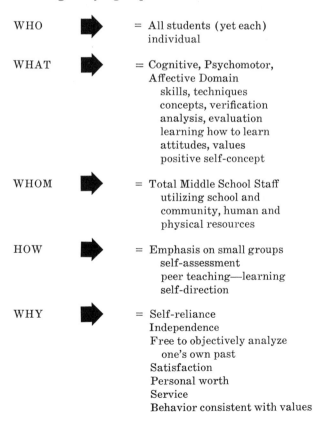

WHO   ➡️   = All students (yet each) individual

WHAT   ➡️   = Cognitive, Psychomotor, Affective Domain
      skills, techniques
      concepts, verification
      analysis, evaluation
      learning how to learn
      attitudes, values
      positive self-concept

WHOM   ➡️   = Total Middle School Staff
      utilizing school and
      community, human and
      physical resources

HOW   ➡️   = Emphasis on small groups
      self-assessment
      peer teaching—learning
      self-direction

WHY   ➡️   = Self-reliance
      Independence
      Free to objectively analyze
        one's own past
      Satisfaction
      Personal worth
      Service
      Behavior consistent with values

Independent study is supported enthusiastically and advanced verbally, but it must receive more than lip service. This concept, if put into practice, could be another force to lessen the gap between theory and practice, intent and action, abstract proposal and concrete accomplishment in individualizing instruction.

Independent Study
for All Students

Independent study is workable for all students, although students with limited skills, interests, and creativity will need more detailed direction. It is difficult to believe that a student would not be excited or, at least, very pleased to know that a learning program was developed just for him. If the learner is provided with opportunities to be successful, independent study activities are willingly assumed and zestfully carried out to completion. The job of the middle school teacher is to gear independent study to the student's level of operation and to focus on his interests.

Students should know that subject matter information and current knowledge rapidly become obsolete. The information explosion makes impossible the idea that we can teach or feed a person all the things he will need to know for the next twenty years. The rapid expansion of knowledge certainly indicates the need for self-directed learners. Educators can help each student select the activities that will fulfill his potentialities.

Modern education should provide incentive for the learner to seek retraining and give him the ability to retrain himself. The learner's hope for the future is his knowledge of how to learn. The teacher's most enthusiastic mission is to provide the student with such satisfaction in learning that he develops an insatiable appetite for it. Independent study practices help students become individual inquirers.

It is most difficult to encourage an insatiable appetite for learning without independent study. Independent study necessitates that the student become active in the learning process.

In some traditionally organized schools, students can tend to develop a passive attitude toward learning. Their day may consist of class after class, and independent study might not be expected of them. Learning can be fragmented into many small unrelated classroom subjects and much time wasted in going from place to place, from subject to subject, and in the frequent adjustment periods required in the process.

Flexibility in scheduling is also required to develop learners responsible for their own learning. It is nonsense to think of independent study without thinking of schedules that provide freedom from rigid time structures. If independent study is to be consistently and universally enjoyed by students, free time must be provided, and teachers must be available to give assistance and counsel. Independent study practices, to be useful, require flexible forms of school organization.

The Student's Responsibility

Maturing students must face the fact that teachers will not always be there to make them study, to tell them where to find the answers, to explain minute details, and to plainly tell them

whether or not they have learned something. Fundamental characteristics of an educated person include the capacity to solve problems, the desire to learn, and self-evaluation. The amount of time students spend in study and the nature of the projects in which they engage will vary with the maturity and needs of the individual, but the sooner the learners engage in a program of independence, the better.

Students like to do the things they do well. And, conversely, they do well the things they like to do. The role of the teacher is to diagnose a student's content and skill interests and suggest task oriented activities that remedy deficiencies.

The Staff's Responsibility

A school of 1,200 students may have 1,200 individual programs. Each individual student should be given the opportunity to develop his unique talents and interests. Each individual program will be developed by the student, the teacher, the counselor, and the administrator. A student's test scores, past records, learning styles, motivation, and readiness are carefully considered in developing his learning program. The teacher, student, and other interested persons can identify what is expected of the student because objectives are stated in performance terms and evaluation procedures are clearly defined.

Other individuals must be brought into the planning: the librarian, the multi-media expert with his training in the psychology of communication, and perhaps other specialists.

Specific instructions are discussed such as:

> —Where is the student to study?
>
> —What resources are at his disposal?
>
> —Does the student have the necessary background tools? For example, does he know how to use the card catalogue?
>
> —What records are to be maintained so that teachers, students, and parents know what individuals are doing?

The above list is far from complete, but it is a starting point. It suggests the cooperative nature of the planning demanded of all the school's human resources.

The most salient issue will be the attitude of the staff toward independent study. Students are quick to pick up clues. If independent study is valued by the staff, students will respond. Staff attitude soon reflects in student behavior. If discipline becomes a serious problem, then perhaps it is the staff that needs the "castor oil."

If students are not involved in purposeful study, it is the professional staff's responsibility to find out "why not." The humanizing aspect of middle school education then continues with positive reinforcement to bring about desired changes of behavior in students. Rather than resorting to punishment when a student abuses independent study privileges, positive reinforcement is encouraged. An example might be to say (to a young man who is having difficulty finding anything productive to do), "Have you selected any media in working on your project?" Upon the reply, "No, but I have considered some filmstrips," the teacher could give positive reinforcement by stating, "Good, let me give you some assistance. I think filmstrips are fine."

Inservice Requirements

To install an independent study program is to alter the role of the teacher. Independent study programs require teachers to be more than subject specialists. They require that teachers become masters at diagnosing individual learning problems and at motivating students. Inservice programs are a prerequisite for any school that adopts independent study. Teachers must have opportunities to discuss and to internalize techniques for working with individuals. In addition, teachers must share responsibility for policy determination in regard to school schedules. Some teachers within a school may never meet with formal class groups. Instead, they are available throughout the day to work with individuals and with small groups. The inservice program permits these teachers to take charge of the school's schedule and to agree on appropriate teaching assignments or roles.

A SOCIAL SCIENCE TEACHER SCHEDULE

8:00 — 8:50	Meet with other discipline teachers in a steering committee. The agenda for this meeting may include: a) "What concepts will all teachers be working on for next week and how can we relate these to various disciplines?" or b) "How can we individualize instruction now so students can explore quest areas in greater depth?"
9:00 — 9:20	Assist seven students in identifying appropriate activities for quest projects.
9:20 — 10:00	Moderate inquiry discussion group on the topic of the pros and cons of legalizing the use of marijuana.
10:00 — 10:15	Work with a student who has chosen to construct a series of flip charts to show the increased degree of mechanization during the past 100 years.
10:15 — 10:45	Work with five students who have been diagnosed as having similar problems in time-space relationships.
10:45 — 11:00	Assist three students who are experiencing difficulty in locating materials for a research project.
11:00 — 12:00	Team planning session.
12:00 — 12:30	Lunch
12:30 — 1:00	Moderate a student group discussion on the topic of "What can *we* do to help reduce the pollution problem?"
1:00 — 2:00	Work with several students to help them state their objectives in behavioral terms as part of a signed contract.
2:00 — 2:20	Assist another teacher in conducting a large group session for forty students. The session, hopefully, serves the purpose of motivating students to research a timely topic.
2:20 — 3:00	Participate in a discussion with ten students on a value clarifying issue.

3:00 — 3:30   Work with several students in transcribing a video tape on a student mock trial and appeal procedure for a higher court.

3:30 — 4:00   Meet with team teachers for discussing how several identified students can be assisted in becoming more self-directed.

Guidelines

The following guidelines are suggested for a successful independent study program.

1. The school schedule and facility arrangements should make independent study a part of the regular school day.

2. Objectives of an independent project should be agreed upon by both the student and teacher. After agreement by both parties, the objectives should be written in behavioral terms. Stated objectives will not stifle creativity but will instead serve as a means of organization for the student.

3. Inquiry-group instruction and assembly-group instruction aim to stimulate and facilitate a variety of independent learning activities by students. Independent study should be the outgrowth of inquiry-group and assembly-group experiences.

4. Programmed instructional aids, audio and video devices, printed materials, machines and tools, and personal assistance are essential ingredients in student work areas.

5. Divergent interests and talents among students must be recognized in planning and evaluating independent study efforts.

6. The staff must place high value on the quality and quantity of independent study in appraising and reporting individual pupil progress and in judging the general excellence of the educational program.

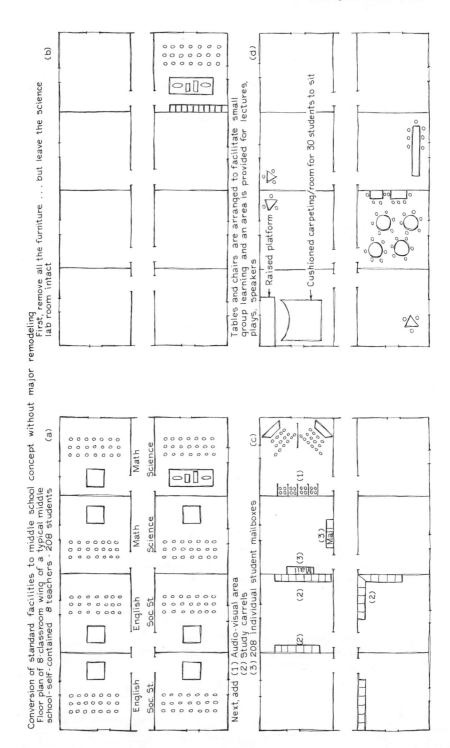

Conversion of standard facilities to middle school concept without major remodeling

Floor plan of 8-classroom wing of a typical middle school-self-contained 8 teachers · 208 students

(a)

English Math

English Math Science

Soc. St.

Soc. St. Science

(b)

First, remove all the furniture ... but leave the science lab room intact

Tables and chairs are arranged to facilitate small group learning and an area is provided for lectures, plays, speakers

(c)

Next, add (1) Audio-visual area
         (2) Study carrels
         (3) 208 individual student mailboxes

Mail (3)

Mail (3)

(2)

(2)

(2)

(1)

(d)

Raised platform

Cushioned carpeting/room for 30 students to sit

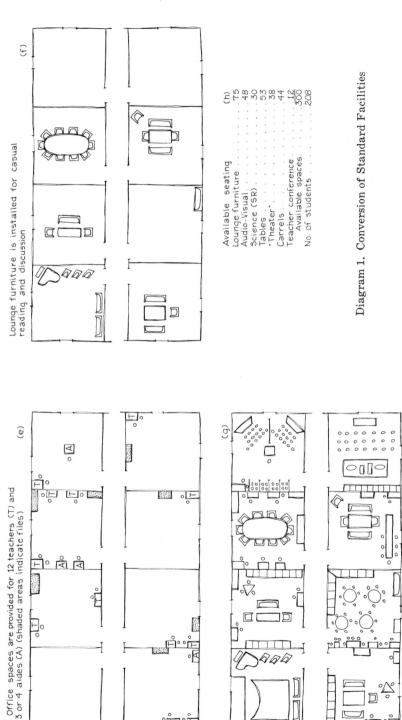

Diagram 1. Conversion of Standard Facilities

Open Laboratories

In accordance with the first guideline above, facilities must be available if independent study is to be successful. One of the most common mistakes made in independent study is the lack of a suitable place for study and investigation. The open laboratory concept should be initiated in every middle school.

Open laboratories are areas where a student can go at any time to create, to become involved, to experiment, to research, to work by himself on a topic of concern to him. It is important that such laboratories be available at all times. Otherwise, students will encounter difficulty in finding an area free at a time when it is appropriate to them. The unavailability of an area will hinder the entire open laboratory concept.

Open laboratories, including the instructional materials center, should not be mere reading rooms or places to study quietly. Rather, they should be areas that permit students to become actively involved in the learning process. When various materials or laboratories are made easily accessible to students, the effectiveness of the educational process is greatly enhanced.

Examples of laboratories designed for independent study would be a science laboratory, a mathematics area, a combined area for language arts and social science, an instructional materials center with audio-visual materials available, a home economics area with stoves, utensils, etc., an art studio, and a gymnasium. All of these areas should have a professional teacher, a student teacher, or a paraprofessional available to give students any assistance that they might require.

In regard to the materials that should be available to students in open laboratories, M. Delbert Lobb states:

> A challenge to teachers exists in the idea that one can reach proposed educational goals by varying procedures and activities. In fact, although there has long been much discussion about individualizing instruction, in far too many instances the only individuality has been the teacher's personality. Learning is natural and probably self propelling if the student relates himself to the need for it. He is more apt to do this when he has access to materials which interest him. Therefore, an enriched environment has great potential for accommodating the uniqueness of each pupil. Just as their interest and needs vary, so should the materials (183:45).

To accomplish this integral part of the learning situation, materials that will promote student interest should be available and readily accessible in the open laboratories. Examples of possible materials would be games or simulation kits for mathematics and social science, models in science, teacher-prepared audio tapes for foreign language classes, filmstrips for the unified arts classes, loop films for physical education, movie films, and video tapes. Visual materials require that equipment such as overhead projectors, film projectors, and headsets also be available to students.

Middle school students can not always direct their own independent study projects. Even after an independent study contract has been formed, the students may need help in identifying appropriate materials and in operating various machines. A teacher or teacher's aide can provide this assistance and, on the basis of individual differences, can permit a highly motivative learning experience to take place.

Lee Smith has identified certain criteria for the selection of materials (251:130-131). Although these criteria were identified for use in the library, they are equally useful for identifying materials for use in various open laboratories. They are:

1. Materials should be accurate and interesting in content.
2. The concepts treated must be within the understanding of students who will use the materials.
3. The content must be significant.
4. Materials should enrich the life of the individual by widening boundaries of thought, presenting an honest picture of live, developing and understanding of people, and fostering positive values.
5. Reference, social studies, and science materials must be kept up to date.
6. The treatment of social studies materials must emphasize desirable social attitudes, ideals, and loyalty to the principles of American democracy.
   a. Source materials must be available when needed in the learning situation.
   b. Both the accomplishments and failures of democracy should be examined.

    c. Both sides of issues should be presented.

    d. Materials should help pupils develop their own methods of propaganda analysis.

    e. The individual's obligations as well as his rights should be stressed.

    f. Materials must promote evaluation and critical discrimination rather than unthinking acceptance.

7. The reading level of books, including vocabulary, sentence structure, and paragraph structure, must be suitable for pupils who will use the materials.

8. Books must be written in a style that is appealing, readable, clear, and dynamic.

9. Factual books should have an appropriate number and variety of illustrative materials—including pictures, maps, charts, graphs, and diagrams — which contribute to the understanding of basic relationships and which clarify and enrich content.

10. Factual books should include appropriate tables of content, indexes, and appendices.

11. The authors of books should have had training and experience in the fields about which they write.

12. The format of books should be of high standard. Type should be clear, legible, and large enough to read without eyestrain; paper of durable weight; illustrations clear and well spaced. The books should be appropriately bound.

13. Reputable, unbiased, professionally prepared selection tools should be used.

14. Gifts must conform to the criteria for materials selection if they are to be accepted.

Independent Study Program Criteria

The criteria for assessing a school's independent study program are few, but vital. They are:

1. Students must be free to work, independent of formal class activities, from 30 percent to 70 percent of the school day. The trend is clearly toward more time for independent study.
2. Students must be able to meet with teachers individually or in small groups as needed.
3. Students must be free to use necessary materials, equipment, and facilities on an "ad hoc" basis.
4. Students must be evaluated individually, not according to group norms, by the teachers with whom they work.
5. Students must be able to identify the performance objectives of the various subjects they study.

Outcomes of Independent Study

Independent study practices have definite outcomes implied. First, such programs are intended to free the learner from the need for constant contact with a teacher. Education is intended to make the student independent, not dependent. Education is intended to make the student secure by developing his strengths, not insecure by focusing on his weaknesses. Education is intended to consider the student unique in terms of his own development, not like others in terms of his knowledge and skills.

Organizing an independent study program can be beneficial to students and rewarding to teachers. Students will benefit from the enriched educational experiences of middle school. All who have implemented successful independent study programs know the feeling of professional satisfaction that comes from seeing students develop independence.

Chapter 8

Continuous Progress

Many teachers now realize that a lock-step type of school organization is unrealistic. Middle school teachers are wondering what really should be taught. They ask the question, "What is it that all students must learn?" However questionable it might be, let us say that we can identify a body of knowledge that all students must master. This done, the next step is to diagnose the skills and concepts that each student needs to learn. We cannot presume that all students will need to master the same skills and concepts, in the same way, in the same place, and at the same time.

We must recognize that children enter school with different ability levels. These levels may range from quite low to quite high. Some kindergarten children are unable to identify any letters of the alphabet while others are able to read. Obviously, children at the kindergarten level should not be learning the same things, at the same time, and in the same way. By the sixth year of school, these same varying abilities exist, have probably increased in scope, and certainly should be provided for in the instructional program. In light of what we know about individual differences and about how people learn, the necessity of covering a given amount of subject matter in a specified length of time, in the same place and in the same way, does not make sense.

On the other hand, a continuous progress philosophy recognizes that each student differs not only in learning potential, but differs in interests, emotional concerns, personality, home environment, and all the other factors that affect learning as well. These differences make it imperative that the middle school provide a wide variety of instructional materials and techniques to reach all of the students at their individual levels. A variety of instructional materials must be available for the entire curriculum.

The middle school is organized to allow students to be more different than alike. Its organizational structure helps the teacher make education more appropriate for each learner. And continuous progress is an integral part of this structure.

What Is a Continuous Progress Middle School?

A *continuous progress* middle school (or synonymous terms such as *nongraded school, individualized instruction,* or *continuous learning*) is a new form of organization and has a different attitude toward curriculum. This new organizational form permits true individualized instruction, a goal advocated by many schools and claimed by some for years. The organization fosters opportunities for each learner to learn in his own style and at his own rate.

A continuous progress middle school is not divided into grades. In the process of instruction and learning, learners are not limited to information, ideas, concepts, skills, and attitudes designated for some relatively artificial grade level. A student is not a sixth grader or an eighth grader, he is a student in his sixth year or his eighth year of school. At the beginning of each school year, he starts wherever he left off and continues his own program at his own rate.

There is no such thing as a uniform program of instruction followed by all who are in a given classroom during a period of time. In a continuous progress program learners progress at their own speed, each learning as much as he can of a curriculum appropriate for him.

There is no one best way to learn. Therefore, a wide range of diversified learning activities is available. Some students need to write while others need to talk. Seeing a film might be very productive for one learner while listening to a tape may be more appropriate for another. The teacher is responsible for providing a number of varied activities so that each student can select the activities most appropriate for him.

The school's atmosphere impels the student to progress as rapidly as he can but as slowly as he must. Middle school teachers make it possible for each learner to fulfill his own needs. In the continuous progress school there is a great deal of difference in what individual students learn and how they are involved in learning.

Comparison of Continuous Progress and Graded School Concepts

The curriculum offered to students in the graded school is organized (into subject matter), designed to be learned in the two semesters of the school year. A longer period of time, often three or more years, is allotted for studies in the continuous progress school. Planning a program over a period of three or four years permits considerable sequencing. It is a natural and simple matter to begin where the student is and to manage his development in appropriate stages.

In the graded school, students are usually expected to advance at a standard rate in all areas of study. A sixth-grade student is expected to be at an achievement level arbitrarily assigned to all sixth grades in all subject areas. His progress is ordinarily measured in terms of his ability to cover a predetermined amount of content. The measurement consists primarily of how well the student can recall the information that he has been given. Frustration, boredom, and discouragement are easily generated. Discouragement often exists in slow learners, but the same sense of discouragement can exist in students who are capable of achieving more than the artificial grade level permits.

Meaningful learning experiences in which students can experience success must be provided. Students with high academic ability and interest in learning are not satisfied simply to achieve at a higher level than students their own age. These students might want to be achieving on a level which we traditionally have felt were within the domain of the high school. The continuous progress organization encourages students to learn at their own speed and to develop their own patterns of scope and depth. Self-respect and confidence is enhanced by the continuous progress concept.

Grade Assignment

In the graded school we assign grades on the basis of how well one student does in comparison to the group. We attempt to legitimatize our grades by applying statistical terms like *mean, median, mode,* and something called *standard deviation.* Seldom is the student's growth compared to his own past achievements. His progress is usually measured by an estimate of how much subject matter he can recall compared to how much others can recall within the same limits.

In continuous progress programs and actually in any kind of learning system, the pace of achievement for any student is more reasonably measured by considering how well each develops according to his own abilities. Thus, the student is not evaluated against artificial standards. Instead, we evaluate the point of achievement as compared to the starting point in learning. Any evaluation is related to the student's apparent abilities and interest.

In the graded school we expect all students in a class to progress at approximately the same speed. As a result the slow ones get low grades, the fast learners get the high grades, and the middle group gets mostly "C's" with some "B's" and "D's."

Awarding high grades to those students who easily excel and dispensing low grades to those who cannot compete is an inhumane practice and is unnecessary in the continuous progress plan. It is completely rational that all students can receive high grades in the continuous progress school. All students can experience success; the only difference is the degree of individual accomplishment. When the student makes progress, his report shows where he is compared to the point from which he began. Even if he does not progress as well as it appears that he might, opportunities exist to help him where and how he needs help, as often as necessary. It is progress that is predetermined, not subject matter. He is competing against himself, not others over whom he has no control.

The question is frequently asked, "What happens to the student who makes good progress in the scope of a subject?" Is this a problem? What happens if a fast learner learns concepts which are traditionally taught by another teacher later? This question suggests that teachers often establish subject matter domains. Over the years a kind of security is developed and some teachers find it uncomfortable to leave the "domain." Perhaps this is why we imagine that students must stay at "grade level" and teachers specialize in teaching specific areas of content. In some cases we work hard to keep our students within closely defined limits. In a continuous progress middle school environment teachers guide students into whatever level or area of subject matter best fits the ability and needs of the student.

There is always, in some degree, a tendency to be domain prone. There is little need for such a superstructure in a continuous progress school in that attention will naturally gravitate toward more important things.

Team Teaching and
Continuous Progress

In the graded school the ratio of one teacher to one room, with one text to one path of progress, creates the conditions where one teacher evaluates the student at the end of the year. It is one teacher who determines, essentially, the kind of learning environment within which the learner functions.

In the continuous progress middle school it is practical, effective, and perhaps required that a team of teachers guide students. A team decides how best to apply their various skills to the multitude of learner patterns. It is quite appropriate to exercise specialties in this way. The object is to provide an optional learning environment. The student, learning at his own rate, can move to new levels or ranges whenever he has mastered the last one attempted. The rationale for the continuous progress middle school makes provisions to apply actually the psychological principles and the philosophies of teaching and learning that many educators support but have never been able to activate to any effective extent.

Martha Dawson, in speaking about the relationship between team teaching and continuous progress, states that team teaching is the way teachers and pupils are placed together for instruction at any given period. Where continuous progress directs initial attention to the vertical movement of pupils, team teaching is primarily concerned with the organization of teachers and the grouping and subgrouping of pupils within a vertical structure. Teachers break out of their self-contained or departmentalized classrooms. Team teaching provides the vehicle for a teacher to share his knowledge and ability and to cooperate with others (86:1).

Dawson also states that joint planning and evaluation is essential to team teaching. These two ingredients make the teacher more aware of instructional alternatives and the need for providing a program to accommodate individual differences. Team teaching often serves as an excellent forerunner for continuous progress (86:1).

Advantages of
Continuous Progress

Educators are constantly discovering more and more about how people learn. The continuous progress plan attracts the application of the more effective practices. It frees the professional to use the best means of accomplishing a clearly defined and specifically stated objective. In essence, the teaching-learning process in the continuous progress middle school is an opportunity for true individualized instruction.

In a continuous progress environment, promoting students from one grade to the next becomes irrelevant. In the graded school most students are promoted at the end of the year to a new learning environment. They must rupture their pattern of progress and spend part of each year restructuring new patterns. It is a loss of continuity that might never be recovered.

Educators have long espoused the concept that we must "meet the needs of all the children." If we accept this concept, every learner should be involved in the learning process in whatever way is best for him. He must be in competition with himself. Grades must be abolished and replaced by achievement levels tailored to the individual and attained through individual patterns at individual rates. If a student is learning according to his ability, if he is making progress appropriate for himself, then the teacher has achieved his goal and so has the student. This achievement is what continuous progress expects of all learners.

The student is not profiled on the basis of chronological age or any predetermined grade standard. He is always making relative progress toward his optimum goals based on the combination of diagnosis, prescription, and implementation of his educational program. Promotion and failure no longer exist, only evaluation of progress and development is relevant. A wider variety of more sophisticated instructional materials is used. All sorts of media are available as resources for the student to use as he develops a desire for learning more things in more ways.

Learning Packages as an Aid to Continuous Progress

A learning package is one way to provide individualized instruction. Learning packages, varying in design and format but with certain common elements, are in use in school systems throughout the country.

Basically the package is teacher prepared. The material is self-contained so that the student can take a learning package and, without further assistance from the teacher, can work independently or with others in mastery of a concept.

A learning package is generally designed around one single concept. The teacher either assigns the student a learning package or the student chooses one. Educators must remember that learning packages are not for every student, and all students do not work with all packages. Learning packages are assigned to individuals to meet individual needs. The level of responsible independence of each student must be considered when writing and assigning learning packages. Students vary greatly in the amount of guidance and direction needed.

Phillip G. Kapfer made four basic assumptions regarding individualized learning (161 :260-263).

First, he states that it is the student's responsibility to learn and the teacher's responsibility to establish the learning environment by making that which is to be learned available to the student.

This assumption places the teaching-learning process in proper perspective. Too often teachers feel they must tell a student everything that he is to learn. The middle school student is able to, and should be permitted to, learn on his own initiative. Learning packages provide a means for the student to learn on his own.

The second assumption for individualizing learning deals with the individuality of the student himself.

This assumption indicates that the pace of instruction must vary with each individual student if the subject matter is going to be appropriate for that student. Learning packages provide for an individual pace. We know that all students cannot learn at the same rate. Neither can they all read at the same level, comprehend at the same level, or for that matter do anything at the identical level of other students within a particular discipline. For these reasons, the levels of sophistication that a student encounters should differ. Students also have varying interests, learning styles, and perceptions. All learning packages are not appropriate for all students. What is perceived as being relevant for one student may be very unrealistic to another. Therefore, the individuality of the student must be considered if true individualized learning is to occur.

His third assumption relates to the composition of a group.

The size and composition of any group of students should be appropriate to the purposes of the group. The small or inquiry group instruction, large group instruction, and learning laboratories have been subjects of previous chapters in this book.

Kapfer's fourth assumption for individualizing learning concerns the need for learning packages to provide self-paced rather than group-paced instruction.

It is this last assumption that we deal with directly in this chapter. It is our intent to discover what a learning package consists of, why it needs to be developed for middle school students, what the necessary ingredients of the learning package are, and how a learning package can most effectively be used in the middle schools.

Learning packages are self-contained sets of teaching-learning materials designed to teach a single concept. They are structured for individuals and quite often for independent use in a continuous progress school program. The materials place the emphasis on the individual and his learning patterns and depart from the materials designed for group-paced instruction.

Student learning packages are sets of teacher prepared, teaching-learning materials. Although not all learning packages need be constructed by teachers, the majority of them are and should be developed by the people who have primary responsibility for establishing the learning environment for middle school students. Who should know better what the individual interests, abilities, and attitudes of middle school students are than the teachers who work with them every day? Teachers can provide needed relevance by their deep understanding of the students within their own school.

Individualized instruction is a term that has become quite popular, especially in the past decade. While the challenge to individualize instruction is clear, recommended methods and actual practices are quite vague. If individualized instruction is ever to become a reality, students must be permitted to move at their own pace. By receiving a learning package of appropriate learning tasks and by assuming the responsibility for accomplishing these tasks, a student gains a unique plan for learning.

Learning packages are generally prepared by the teachers within the middle school. Local preparation of learning packages may have a distinct advantage over purchasing commercially developed packages. When teachers have been involved in the construction of a learning packet they tend to be more enthusiastic about the packet. This enthusiasm will likely carry over to the students during the use of such material. Some educators feel that teachers do not have the time to write learning packages and, of course, not all teachers have the writing ability to produce such packages. If teachers do not have the time or talents to write learning packages then commerically produced packages should be secured.

Essential Ingredients
of Learning Packages

Not all learning packages look alike. However, there are certain essential elements that should appear within each package. Middle school teachers need to be aware of these essentials and should make certain that each packet does contain these ingredients:

Concept   First, the teaching team must decide on the major concept that is to be studied. The concept can be considered as the main thought or "big idea" that a student is expected to absorb during his use of a particular packet. This concept is not only identified by the teaching team but is stated within the packet as well, so that students can readily see the purpose or intent of the material.

Teachers may have a difficult time identifying a single concept. Although difficult, it is vital that one concept be sorted out of the many important ideas presented to middle school students. In fact, quite often concepts are divided into subconcepts to clarify the issue for both teacher and student. If this identification procedure is followed, the process of focusing or "zeroing in" on the important topic becomes much easier. Each package can be related to a previous package and become an essential ingredient for the packages that follow it. Each package can build upon the previous packet to form a series of packages. A rigid predetermined sequence, however, is not necessary. The amount of sequence is a matter of teacher judgment.

Objectives The second essential element of the learning package is that objectives be stated in behavioral terms. Successful teachers must communicate to youngsters. An objective is the communicative vehicle of a learning situation. Objectives permit the student to understand what is expected of him. They eliminate the confusion and guesswork about what is to be accomplished. Students will be able to identify what they must do to demonstrate that knowledge has been attained, that understanding has taken place, that skill development or attitude formation has occurred. By reading the objectives of the learning package a student can identify what he must accomplish.

Not only must behavioral objectives relate directly to the concepts of the learning package, effort should be exerted by the teaching teams constructing the packet to identify various levels of cognitive learning. Frequently objectives are stated only at the lowest level of cognitive learning — that of knowledge or basic recall. Objectives can and should be stated for higher levels of cognitive learning — those of application, analysis, synthesis, and evaluation.

Preevaluation The preassessment test that is contained within the packet must be carefully developed by the teaching team. This test should be given to determine how much knowledge a student already possesses prior to studying a particular concept. A pretest indicates where students are in relation to the specific objectives listed within the learning package. It can point out certain weaknesses that may require a young person to do some background work prior to the packet. It may also show that a middle schooler has already mastered some or all of the objectives required. If this is the case, a student may go on to the next package or begin self-initiated activities.

Self-assessment is also a part of the learning package. Self-assessment is necessary to enable the learner to measure his progress toward achievement of the stated objectives. The process assures the person learning that he is achieving his goals. In fact, the self-assessment stage should occur several times throughout the packet. Checkpoints, strategically placed throughout the packet, permit both the learner and the teacher to make realistic decisions concerning the progress made and changes that might need to take place in the learning program.

Suggested Activities   Another essential part of the learning package is diversified learning activities. Various ways of active participation must be available to the student. All students do not have the same learning style. Therefore, a package should contain many suggestions for mastering a given objective. Diversified methodology includes activities such as small group or inquiry group sessions and assemblies to hear a resource speaker. To view a demonstration may be in order for the activity package. A student should be able to select the activity that will best help him achieve his objective. Generally, he should be free to determine his own learning activities if those suggested in the package hold little or no interest for him. There must be greater freedom of choice than in the past.

Suggested Materials   Frequently students need assistance in identifying materials that are available. Some students lose interest when resources are not readily available and when the materials are difficult to locate. Some learning packages will identify specific pages and textbooks or other resource materials. Transparencies, tapes, filmstrips, physical models, films, loop films, and other media can be used to provide diversity. It is well known that we can all learn more easily and retain longer that which we are permitted to see, feel, smell, taste, and hear. Granted, it is difficult to involve all the senses in each learning package, but teachers should try to provide every opportunity possible.

When developing diversified learning materials, teachers must not think only of commercially developed resources. Slides, filmstrips, single concept loop films, transparencies, and other resources can be developed through the audio-visual department. Many can be made by teacher aides and by volunteer people in the community. For example, listening center tapes are quite commonly recorded by volunteer mothers with pleasing voices.

Postevaluation The postevaluation stage is an assessment of the progress that has been made by the student. This evaluation can take place in a small group seminar or in a pupil-teacher conference. Most frequently it is accomplished by a test administered by the teacher. Relative gain from the pretest can be measured by observing results from the posttest. Hopefully, the posttest will clearly illustrate a student's ability to achieve stated objectives. Paper and pencil tests are probably easier to construct and take less teacher time than performance tests or conferences.

Student Initiative Activities In-depth and quest activities are always included in the learning package. This permits the interested student to pursue a subject further. Suggested activities are not necessary to the development of the concept, but do add greater meaning to it. In-depth activities are usually suggested by the teacher, while quest activities are thought of as being student oriented work. Quest activities banish the notion that everybody learns only what exists in the established curriculum. They provide opportunities for students to deeply probe areas that are of particular interest to them.

Probably the most important factor in determining success of learning packages in the middle school is the attitude of the teachers. Unless teachers are convinced that learning packages have value and unless they are enthusiastic about their use, learning packages cannot improve the instructional program.

Learning packages are one way to move from group paced instruction to individualized continuous progress. But let us reiterate — individualized instruction is far more than having all students do the same things only at different rates. Therefore, not all packages are for all students. Some learning packages are appropriate only for some students.

Continuous Progress —
An Emphasis on
Humanizing Conditions

It is possible for a middle school staff to be sold an organizational pattern without an in-depth understanding of the concept. It is also possible to focus on "How do we nongrade?" rather than "How do we meet the unique needs of middle school youth through a continuous progress program?" Full knowledge of the continuous progress concept, coupled with a direct focus on organization to meet the unique needs of middle school youth, results in an extremely effective approach to teaching and, consequently, results in humanizing experiences for the students. In the following paragraphs, Lester Abbenhouse describes continuous progress as an approach designed for children.

Continuous progress has been represented as a response to cultural conditions, a philosophical position, and an attitude of mind. The representative program may appear to be a position overbalanced in favor of effect. However, continuous progress is actually an organizational position that permits youth to maintain a balance of human attributes in the cognitive, affective, and psychomotor domains. There are conditioning features that are built into the social structure, the student behavior management techniques, the instructional style, and the attitudes of teachers that assure more of a good effect. The intellectual domain can then be approached with the assurance that the affective side of being and becoming is emphasized.

The continuous progress program is disassociated with the traditional homogeneous grouping practice that segregated children on the basis of intellectual skills only. Nonsegregated approaches with continuous progress programs assist teachers in their attempts to unify middle school youth behind common purposes. The mixing of middle school youth with ages of 11, 12, and 13 results in higher interest levels for youth. The mixing of various ages also increases differences and tends to develop habits of cooperation and mutual aid.

Continuous progress middle schools offer a constructive alternative to the adult tendency to underestimate youth's ability to act responsibly. We must expect all youth, within reason, to be responsible and effective in individual and group action. The middle school staff establishes the classroom atmosphere in which cooperative relationships are carried out. An organized setting provides assurance that a democratic and an enjoyable atmosphere prevails for all.

Many people today are accusing youth of being rebellious and defying authority. One of the reasons that defiance is shown in youth may be the fact that teachers have been accustomed to forcing children to learn what was being taught. Forcing children to study can cause rebellion against authority thus undermine the enthusiasm, confidence, and self-regard of middle school teachers. A well-organized continuous progress program can minimize rebellion and defiance since children are considered in terms of what they are rather than in terms of what we feel they should be.

Teachers can enhance the effectiveness of a continuous progress program by providing an atmosphere of mutual respect and trust. If a teacher admits mistakes, he conveys the idea that he is secure enough to accept another person as he is. Kindness or firmness by itself leads to unstable relationships. Mutual respect allows the teacher to use firmness accompanied by kindness. It then becomes possible for teachers to work with students rather than against them.

The middle school principal also plays an important part in creating humanizing conditions with a continuous progress program. He establishes the atmosphere in which teachers work and youth learn. The way a principal wields the power of his position helps determine the way teachers wield their power with students. Clarity, consistency, and integrity of the principal elicits the same features from teachers and, in turn, influences the student's role as a learner in a middle school.

The middle school principal must have a high regard for others. This high regard for others is projected to teachers through understanding of them and support for them in their difficult assignments of working with youth who are different in age as well as different in all domains. The principal expresses his regard through regular discussions of real issues with the entire staff, groups of teachers, or individual teachers.

A continuous progress program provides for various differences in youth by eliminating failure in favor of continuous growth, by eliminating unrealistic accomplishments through artificial grade levels, and by facilitating self-pacing. However, the students, the teachers, and the principal must create the proper atmosphere after the organizational framework has been provided. Positive attitudes by all, a high regard for others, and a cooperative and supporting relationship are all necessary to develop a humane approach to middle school youth (1:1-4).

We can summarize this discussion on continuous progress by printing two letters. The first letter was written by a first year teacher to a well-known educator; the second is his reply.

Dear Sir:
  My principal told me I am in charge of developing a continuous progress program in our school.
I think I am sold on the concept of continuous
progress, but what do I do? Help!
                Sincerely,

                Jane Price

Dear Miss Price:
  The willingness to try something new is probably the most important prerequisite for a continuous progress program. Obviously, this will
take more than the commitment of one individual
teacher. Support will be required of the administration of the school, as well as from the public
which it serves. Lack of such support probably
ranks high among the forces that tend to weaken
the continuous progress concept. (Also, we tend
to measure the work of a continuous progress
school in terms of criteria more applicable to
the graded program.)
  Communicating with parents in the community
represents one of the most crucial tasks you

face. Nothing can beat face-to-face communication with your parents. We can exchange a lot of paper without exchanging ideas.

Teachers in a continuous progress school will sense a need for a greater variety of books, materials, and equipment. Most significant is the need to reallocate resources. Simply stated, this means that rather than buying every youngster in the sixth grade a sixth grade text, a whole series of books ranging above and below what is normally termed "sixth grade level" ought to be available. Textbooks are but one source of material. There are many others.

Some teachers have purchased or developed materials wherein skills and concepts are sequenced. A continuum is outlined and diversified learning activities designed to assist the student in mastering skills and concepts. The fact that certain skills and concepts have been predetermined or identified does not mean that every student must master every one of them. Nor is a rigid learning sequence implied.

Other teachers have developed learning activity packages. Each package focuses on one concept and includes a pretest, posttest, and various suggestions for learning activities.

Many commercial programmed materials are available. There are also a large number of reading, mathematics, science, and social study "laboratories."

The curriculum is the heart of continuous progress. In a continuous progress school the individual pupil determines the curriculum. Teachers are not concerned about a predetermined amount of content for all students in a specific sequence. Teachers are concerned with diagnosing individual needs and planning an appropriate learning program for each individual.

Curriculum and curriculum materials will, I believe, be the most difficult task for you. Developing curriculum requires a great deal of

time. I would strongly suggest you consider many
of the materials available from commercial pub-
lishers. You might also consider securing
materials from schools that have already
developed continuous progress programs. I am
always amazed at the generosity of educators.

Needless to say, the physical structure in
which teachers must operate does have an impact
on how they teach. The flexibility of an open
school makes it easier to adopt the continuous
progress approach. There are many examples of
continuous progress programs operating in traditional school buildings, however: the type of
building should never be the determining factor.

In closing, I'd like to stress one final
thought . . . Continuous progress schools must
emphasize process.

I hope these thoughts are helpful. You have
my best wishes.

                         Sincerely,

                         Charles L. Willis

                         Program Officer*

---

*Letter used by permission of Charles L. Willis, Program Officer of
/I/D/E/A/, Dayton, Ohio.

Chapter 9

School-Wide Curriculum Committee

We are living in an era of rapid technological and social change. These changes must be recognized and used to improve educational opportunities for middle school youth. All change is not progress, but most people will concur that today's society provides more opportunities and more challenge than ever before.

There is little doubt that society will continue to make demands of schools which will bring about practices that are radically different from those that exist today. Change and modification are constantly needed in middle schools to meet the demands of a forceful society. There is widespread demand that our middle schools make more provisions for individual differences. Although administrators are faced with increasing enrollments, inadequate funds, and a constant need for improved facilities, experimentation must be made with various curricular, technological, and organizational modifications. Experimentation must be done if middle schools are ever to achieve maximum educational effectiveness.

M. G. Abbott and J. T. Lowell state that if schools are to remain dynamic and viable forces in American society, ways must be found to increase the rate of adaptation to a social order in which they exist (2:40-52). They also indicate that educators must increase their ability to recognize and assess the social changes which are occurring so that the schools may not only adjust to changing conditions, but may also aid in providing directions for those conditions.

The middle school curriculum committee can provide a framework to constantly evaluate the educational program. Members of the committee can also become the activators of change and innovation by keeping current on the new approaches that are occurring throughout the country. The more important part of their role, though, is to "brainstorm" in an attempt to define directions in education that will provide new ideas to stimulate and enhance the efforts of others.

The school-wide curriculum committee is based on the assumption that change occurs more easily and is more lasting if teachers are directly involved in developing the program. If teachers are given support and guidance through the curriculum committee, they will look at their jobs more creatively and will be more receptive to new ways to do their work effectively.

Some educators might question the use of middle school teachers for a curriculum council. They might argue that too much of the teachers' time will be taken up in weekly council meetings with not enough time devoted to team planning, to becoming creative within a single discipline, or to working with individual students. One argument might be to let the principal assume the task of sorting through and suggesting innovative ideas. It is true that the principal's role should be one of causing innovative activity to occur, but it is questionable whether he can bring about innovation by being the sole initiator of ideas. Rather than becoming the lone innovator, he should be more concerned with building a structure that will support innovative activities.

Others might contend that rather than having teachers get together at least once a week to evaluate, to be creative, or to bring about change, the school board should hire someone to do this for teachers. Some educators might suggest employing a "change agent" because change occurs by methods such as research, development, diffusion, and adoption. This person could then provide all the information that the teachers need to put innovations into action. Although the employment of a change agent might seem desirable, one might also question whether one person should ever become the sole innovator.

R. L. Foster states that when change occurs by the agent method, the change agent is directing the change process and is manipulating for the desired change (111:288-291). He feels that, due to the unusual amount of direction provided in order to arrive at the expected change, little additional change comes from the self-actualization or inventiveness of the teacher. The responsibility for the change rests with the inducer of the change; and consequently, there must be continued reinforcement by the outside agent to insure movement toward the desired goals. Foster would encourage, instead, an open system where change is induced through experiences which develop new understanding, new perceptions, and new skills. Such an open system might consist of a school-wide curriculum committee.

Mark Chesler and Robert Fox would be prone to encourage the open system, too (75:25-26). They state that, in order to establish a healthy climate for innovation and change, we must first develop ways for individual teachers to share new ideas with other teachers and to gain support for worthy change. They feel that there is a need to make teachers feel that they have had some influence in developing changes by adopting new administrative styles which decentralize decision making.

Functions of the Curriculum Committee

One of the first functions of the middle school curriculum committee is to determine what the different disciplines are doing now. The teachers must analyze not only what learning experiences are provided but must also evaluate student outcomes. Some practices are fairly easy to evaluate, such as academic achievement as determined by standardized achievement tests. Achievement results can be compared with national norms to determine how students do in a particular area according to the results of a standardized test. Consultants can also give a middle school staff some insight into what has been accomplished.

Certain aspects of the educational program, however, are more difficult to evaluate. For example, it is difficult to evaluate a student's self-concept and his growth toward independence. Standardized tests do not provide answers to such questions. Although independence and one's self-concept are difficult to evaluate in many respects, they are more important than academic achievement. The "humanizing effect" of the educational program must be given top priority.

Therefore, the first function of the curriculum committee is to evaluate the ongoing program.

A followup study of students who have gone on to high school is essential. Followup studies can reveal strengths as well as weaknesses in the middle school instructional program. Telephone surveys, parent-teacher organization meetings, and teacher and counselor contacts with parents are all ways of determining whether the present program is meeting the needs of the students. Again, the priorities should be in the areas of humanizing education. Parents should be asked such questions as, "Is your child happy in school?" "Is your child eager to come to school in the morning?" "Does your child get along well with his peers?" These are questions that give some insight into the human aspects of the educational program.

Many times the discipline committees that are established for K-12 can provide insight for the curriculum committee. For example, the language arts committee that is studying conceptual schemes from kindergarten through grade twelve, and applying values to these concepts, can provide the middle school curriculum committees with information about the ways in which the language arts program is individualizing instruction. It is of the utmost importance that true communication exist between the members of the curriculum and discipline committees and each teacher.

It is also important that members of the curriculum committee fully understand their roles and, if certain limitations exist, be aware of their limitations. The job of helping teachers to identify the purposes of the committee and of giving specific instructions or assistance belongs to the principal and central office staff. Assistance for the teachers should also be provided in the form of literature on pertinent research and prevailing trends. Such information enables teachers to be much more effective in their committee work.

The teachers on the curriculum committee should be teachers who are eager to spend extra time in furthering the educational program of the middle school. Hopefully, they will come to the meetings with an open mind, willing to listen, observe, and present sound ideas for investigation and/or action. Teachers should admit that they do not "have all the answers" but must be willing to research, investigate, and communicate their findings to their fellow teachers.

After evaluating the present program, the curriculum committee must determine what teachers want to do that is different from what they have been doing.

This second function is a natural flow in that the curriculum committee must first identify a problem before it can encourage change to take place. If after evaluation teachers feel there are no existing problems, recommendations cannot be expected for change. But after problems have been identified, the curriculum committee needs to thoroughly investigate the causes of the problems to provide suggestions for solutions. Committee members may decide, at a certain point, that it is necessary to involve other teachers, to acquire more possible solutions through research, or to consult with experts from other school systems or from universities.

The third function of the curriculum committee is to establish a priority rating of changes they wish to initiate.

This committee, for example, may identify two problems that seem more important than others. One of these problems might be that students have a poor self-concept. The other problem may be that students appear to have difficulty in establishing value systems. The committee may experience difficulty in establishing priorities and might consider both problems to be top priority. They must then try to identify ways of meeting both of these important needs. Questions that are asked and the way that they are asked may be contributing to this problem. Perhaps inquiry group discussions with students may be beneficial. Organizing the conceptual scheme to help students tune in on a value system may be another solution. There are, of course, many other possible solutions.

After identifying possible courses of action, the fourth function of the committee is to determine what teacher and student preparation must take place for changes to occur.

Certainly everyone must see the problem as a real problem before positive changes can occur. One solution might be that both teachers and students need to emphasize small group discussions with the focus on values. After this plan has been identified to reduce or eliminate certain problems, it is very important that teachers be given in-service assistance so that they can work to solve these problems in a professional manner. Teachers may need to acquire new skills so they can implement small group discussions with proper techniques. They may need some assistance in small group dynamics so that all students are encouraged to participate and are free to express themselves without fear of ridicule. If teachers are given assistance, they will confidently attack their problem and the results will be encouraging. Proper preparation of teachers and students will result in a stronger, more dynamic, and certainly, a more humanizing program for middle school students.

After new ideas and/or adapted research have been implemented, the fifth function of the curriculum committee is to evaluate what effect the changes have had.

The committee must, with the help of the entire faculty, test out the plans of action and assess the impact of this action. The evaluation procedure should determine to what degree objectives have been accomplished.

During the evaluation phase one must consider that certain objectives may have been unrealistic for all students. An objective, for example, may have been for all students to assume full responsibility for identifying their own needs and their own learning experiences. The evaluation phase may reveal that very few students can fully identify their own needs and learning experiences. Rather than to conclude that this objective still needs to be met as stated, it may be determined during the evaluation phase that the objective is unrealistic. Although one must always give students every chance to mature, perhaps they were not ready for this much responsibility. Teachers should determine if some of the action advocated is too demanding for some students. If this is the case, the objective must be restated to meet the needs and concerns of these students.

The curriculum committee can and will, if properly employed, encourage a middle school program to be active and to truly meet the needs of students. The committee can produce a program that will assist teachers to develop new understandings, new perceptions, and new skills for both teachers and students. They can help the middle school identify forces that need to be reduced or eliminated if certain practices are to change in a positive way. They can help the staff project for the future and to identify a sequence for changes to take place.

In addition, the committee can help teachers to identify present and future needs. They can create a middle school that is vitally alive and creatively challenging for teachers and, consequently, for students.

Finally, a curriculum committee can help teachers realize that ideas are generated not only by principals or by central office personnel. Consequently, the morale will be high, communication lines will be open to all, and all will experience the professional satisfaction of trying out their own ideas. This satisfaction will definitely carry over to the teaching-learning situation. The committee's efforts will result in a better instructional program with a greater humanizing effect on middle school youth.

Chapter 10

Diversified
Learning Activities

"Teaching is more than talking and learning is more than listening." This statement implies that in teaching the lecture method alone is not adequate. Frequently the lecture fails to reach students; teachers themselves are the first to admit this.

Why do teachers report that the old tried and true lecture method is no longer adequate? It could be that reliance on the lecture method in the past was never quite satisfactory and that evidence of this fact was not realized until we became serious about individualizing instruction. Today the professional journals are filled with reports of student unrest and dissatisfaction with the instruction programs in our middle schools, high schools, and colleges. We must strive for the most up-to-date, effective, and humane practices possible.

Our response to student criticism is an attempt to individualize the instructional program. Individualizing instruction requires that a program be designed and conducted for and with each student — a program specifically tailor-made to fit his learning needs and characteristics. This means that there must be a number of diversified learning activities available for mastering each objective. From the activities suggested each student will be able to select those most appropriate for him. The middle school teacher must remember that it is not enough to have a variety of learning opportunities available; the student must be free to select the activities he feels he needs. No learning activity should be imposed by the teacher; there must be a choice on the part of the student as to how he will master each objective.

Today's middle school teachers have rejected the concept of limited learning activities. In the continuous progress middle school the curriculum is student-paced. Therefore, teachers know that students must be presented with a variety of ways to master a concept or to achieve an objective. Lesson plans that offer a number of diversified learning situations replace the textbook and lecture as the sole means of instruction. Once a student has identified a concept to be mastered, he is free to choose from a wide range of opportunities the activities that appeal to him. He will constantly use the self-evaluation instruments provided in the lesson to determine his own progress. Teachers realize that learning programs that effectively individualize instruction include all sorts of learning activities, media, and materials. They have to provide efficient learning experiences for each student.

Checklist to
Assay Lesson Plans

1. Do the learning activities ask that each student take an active part in the learning process? (If an activity merely obligates the student to listen and to do seat work I must examine the activity with care. When a student is active rather than passive he will have a greater commitment to learning.)

2. From the number of learning activities available, is each student free to choose the learning activity he feels is most appropriate for him? Further, is he able to determine the number of activities he must do to reach his objective? (The learner should be able to check his progress as he moves through activities by using the self-evaluation devices I've built into the program.)

3. Do I as a middle school teacher accept the fact that my position in the classroom has changed with increased activities available for students?

Am I willing to disengage myself as a doer to become an observer, a diagnostician, a prescriber, and an evaluator of learning activities? Have I more time for the students because I am spending less time doing things for the students that they should have been doing for themselves? Am I willing to allow the students to be active, busy, and productive; recognizing that in the process the classroom may not look orderly in the traditional sense? Am I willing to accept that an orderly and passive group is not necessarily a learning group, nor is a noisy and active classroom necessarily an unproductive one?

4. Am I secure enough as a professional to realize that individual progress sometimes produces noise that to a visitor or a supervisor may indicate disorder? As a professional, do I recognize that noise is a constructive part of the learning environment?

5. Am I willing to accept learning activities suggested to me by students? Can I recognize that many times the most effective learning is learner devised? Do I believe that the lesson plans developed and the learning experiences innovated may be adequate today but inadequate tomorrow? Do I accept that to keep the learning experiences viable, flexible, and appropriate for the learners, they must be ever changing?

6. Are the learning activities conceptually oriented? Am I striving to identify the main ideas or concepts that are considered essential in the disciplines? Am I identifying subconcepts or subideas within generalizations that are important for students?

7. Are value systems for middle school youth a natural outgrowth of conceptual schemes? Are students exposed to various views and not just my opinions? Are my students encouraged to read and discuss various viewpoints of authors with an eye toward values for themselves? Do my students respect the rights and opinions of others in their search for a value system for themselves?

Our major goal in education is to develop the independent learner. Hopefully the student will create an insatiable appetite for learning that will impel him to continue to learn throughout his life. As a middle school student moves on into high school, into college, or into the world of work, he needs to be able to continue learning on his own. As he begins to mature, the protective arm of the teacher cannot always be around him, and the student will need to assume greater responsibility for his education. Eventually, the middle school student will need to answer the questions, "What is it that I need to know?" "How can I construct a learning situation that will allow me to learn the things I need to learn?" And, finally, "Have I learned enough?" Independent learners are not developed overnight; it is a long process. The middle school is an ideal place to develop the independent learner.

Instructional Materials

Instructional materials and methods used in the middle school must decrease dependent learning and increase independent learning. The middle school student must be exposed to variety. He must be able to read, to listen, to question, and to view critically and thoughtfully. He must be equally able to use human resources and material resources. He must be able to use adequately a number of learning devices, not *a* learning device. The ability to utilize multimedia is a great asset as the student continues to learn throughout life. The goal is self-direction and self-instruction.

Somehow a student must acquire the wisdom to select the instructional materials that will best help him meet his objective, whatever the objective might be. To gain this wisdom, the middle school student must have the opportunity to interact with a number of learning materials and to become comfortable in various learning situations. Diversified learning activities provide this opportunity.

One of the most frequently voiced objectives of teachers is to provide for individual differences. If learning materials are carefully selected and skillfully used, this goal may become much closer to reality than is otherwise possible. After objectives or goals have been selected and the means of reaching them chosen, the most appropriate media for each group of students should be selected. Different students require different materials and methods if they are to learn efficiently. Thus, a wide variety of learning materials must be available to meet the individual needs of pupils (30:117).

Filmstrips

Filmstrips are of considerable value if used properly. Superior results are obtained when filmstrips are incorporated with other media. They are particularly effective when used to teach specific skills, such as stages of preparation for a particular laboratory experiment, steps in solving a mathematical equation, or the proper placement of the hands on the typewriter keyboard. The learning experience should determine when filmstrips should be used and how they should be correlated with other instructional materials.

James W. Brown, Richard B. Lewis, and Fred F. Harcleroad have identified 11 special uses of filmstrips (61:145-146).

1. To provide bases for understanding symbols. Some filmstrips can be used to aid in the understanding of work symbols and to help build vocabulary. Math symbols or symbols used in mathematics may be made more meaningful through filmstrip presentation by providing visual impressions of the realities behind the symbols.

2. To help teach skills. Filmstrips can be projected at various speeds, and students can repeat certain pictures in whole or in part, thus making the filmstrip an excellent media for helping to teach skills.

3. To provide information. Actual information can be presented via the use of the filmstrip to aid in concept building.

4. To take the place of or to reduce wear on other materials. Some materials are too expensive or too difficult to obtain. Therefore, a filmstrip can be used in place of the actual materials. (However, viewing a filmstrip is not as meaningful as active participation.)

5. To stimulate esthetic appreciation. Filmstrips that are in color can effectively build esthetic appreciation of beauty, rhythm, and works of art or nature.

6. To develop interest in further pursuit of topics. When filmstrips are used to present introductory stages of information, students may be encouraged to continue with further activities on their own.

7. To consolidate and "review" learning. Filmstrips can be used to help the student to look back over what he has studied and to view it in the light of original learning goals. Students can be asked in inquiry groups to explain or comment on a filmstrip, basing remarks on what has been learned before.

8. To focus group attention. Although students may benefit more by using a filmstrip on their own, groups of individuals could be asked to fix their attention upon a screening of the darkened room. Whether this is an advantage or disadvantage would depend upon the purpose.

9. To supplement and reinforce learning from other experiences. After taking a trip, students could benefit by seeing a filmstrip or viewing a 16mm film.

10. To provide opportunities for students to practice basic skills. The filmstrips can be used to help provide unusual opportunities to help students learn to verbalize about what they see. This activity would attempt to clarify and strengthen learning.

11. To provide opportunities for individual study. Filmstrip viewers used in carrels can permit individuals to view and analyze filmstrips as they would read or study books or other printed materials. This may be one of the most important advantages in the use of filmstrips.

Whether a middle school teacher uses filmstrips for an entire class, or whether one student uses them on his own during indepent study time, depends upon the particular purpose in mind. Regardless of whether they are alone or in a group, students should be prepared before viewing a filmstrip. If no preparation is provided, little learning will take place. Suggestions for proper preparation are:

1. Prepare a list of questions about the concept or skill covered in the filmstrip. Questions could be contained in a learning activity package or, more appropriately perhaps, included with the filmstrip. The questions would depend on the purpose of the filmstrip.
2. Prepare a brief overview of a filmstrip. This would assist students to focus in on the major idea or ideas presented.
3. Encourage students to take notes, to go back and review any material in question, and to discuss their observations in small groups.

When properly used, filmstrips can be an excellent aid to learning. They should definitely be considered in planning for the overall instructional program for the middle school.

Slides and 16mm Films

Slides and films are examples of media conducive to individualized learning opportunities and self-paced learning.

Motion picture films are used to accomplish many objectives. They might be appropriate for any of the following: to clarify a complex idea, to motivate, to trigger discussion, to enlarge, to present subjects or events that the average person cannot hope to see or experience. There is a vast number of excellent films available dealing with nearly every subject. For example, films can be used: to make history come alive, to demonstrate scientific phenomena, to introduce social problems.

Frequently films are not utilized because teachers are not aware of the quality and quantity of films available. Purchasing films is expensive, but some rental procedures permit films to remain in the school system for the entire year at a fraction of the purchase price. Many films can be borrowed for short periods at no charge and many more are available at nominal rates. Rental often makes more sense since the capital outlay for films is reduced considerably and the school system is not stuck with unused, outdated films. (See pages 165-166 for sources of films.)

Slides are considerably more economical and are ideal for displaying a single concept. It is easy for students to select those slides that are of value to them. They offer considerable flexibility and may be used by a single student, a small group, or a large group. They are equally effective as a preview or a review. With the assistance of an audio visual media specialist, teachers can create their own slides. Middle school students could also make slides as a learning activity. Also, a relatively new idea in projecting includes the use of multiple screen projectors which makes a visual impact with the use of slides.

8mm Films

The value of 8mm films as a teaching tool is now being successfully demonstrated in many schools. Single concept 8mm films are brief motion pictures showing aspects of a single subject, a demonstration, or an experiment. They are silent and/or sound so that teachers can introduce them into learning situations in any way that is appropriate. They are highly flexible.

Since each film deals with only one concept, they are usually short in length — often two to four minutes. Also, since they are used in the form of continuous loops and reels, each film may be immediately reshown, without delay, as often as required. Cartridge loading is so simple that students can make sufficient use of films.

A major key to the successful use of 8mm films in the classroom is the attitude of the teacher. A teacher may predetermine effective outcomes of 8mm films simply by evidencing enthusiasm, knowledge, and a sensitivity to the job at hand. They are not designed to replace the classroom teacher or to serve as a substitute for activities involving vital teacher-student or student-student interaction.

The teacher must understand the purpose of 8mm films and their use and be prepared to exploit their contribution to the teaching-learning process to the fullest advantage. The use of

8mm films provides another diversified learning activity for the student.

Advantages of 8mm single concept film loops are numerous:

1. They motivate learning. The visual impact of the 8mm presentation serves as a springboard for involving the learner.
2. They magnify illustrative material. The camera can enlarge small objects to full screen size for intimate inspection.
3. They provide special instruction in all areas of the curriculum, at all levels, depending upon the needs of the participating students.
4. They exhilarate the professional teachers by making it possible for them to observe the teaching of others.
5. They provide a way to improve the curriculum and to enrich the educational program more easily than ever before. They accomplish all this by providing means of introducing new material and by bringing into the classrooms special services such as costly experiments and demonstrations.
6. They make it possible to keep all content material completely up to date. (8mm film loops are relatively inexpensive to produce.)
7. They permit outstanding teachers to reach more students and give teachers more time for planning, study, and guidance.
8. They offer greater equality of opportunity for all pupils. In culturally deprived areas and in the most affluent school districts students participate and view the same film loops. They have the same variety of courses and the same studio teachers. With 8mm films the small middle school can offer courses which otherwise might not be available.
9. They help the student to assume more responsibility for learning by providing resources with which he can work independently.
10. They are very accessible. They are easy to produce, instantly available, can be used whenever and wherever the teacher desires.

To present the other side of the coin, disadvantages of 8mm single concept film loops do exist:

1. There is predetermined pacing of material. The film can be stopped and it can be instantly reviewed; but some teachers feel the pace is predetermined and, therefore, not adequate for many students.
2. They provide little opportunity for verbal interaction.
3. They afford the studio teacher no way of seeing the reaction of pupils at the time the lesson or concept is presented.
4. 8mm films, the equipment to produce the films, and the cartridge projectors represent a high initial cost.

The middle school teacher would be well advised to review the various types of equipment available. Regular 8mm film cartridges will not work in super 8mm film projectors. At this time there is no standardization in the industry as to regular 8mm versus the super 8mm film.

There is a vast quantity of projectors on the market today. Projectors that are designed for use by an entire class or large group are available as well as projectors designed for individual use. The middle school teacher has but to choose what it is she wants to do and then select the equipment that will do the job.

A word of caution: the 8mm film is never intended to be a complete learning experience in itself. It can be meaningful only when it is followed by or integrated with some type of learning activity which makes the lesson an integral part of a total learning process.

Programmed Learning

Programmed learning can greatly increase instructional effectiveness. Since programmed materials generally are used by one student at a time, they epitomize what is meant by individualized instruction. We recommend that teachers seriously consider the use of programmed material in the middle school.

Advantages of programmed learning include:

1. Ideas are organized into an effective sequence.
2. Complex ideas are broken down and presented one small part at a time. Instruction moves from simple to complex.
3. Each student is free to progress at his own pace.
4. Students receive instant feedback.
5. Objectives are well defined.
6. Programmed instruction uniquely matches the learning style of some students.
7. Students remain active.

There are, of course, some disadvantages:

1. Programmed materials are not for everybody; they are misused when all students are indiscriminately required to use them.
2. If used extensively over a long period of time, programmed materials may become very boring for the student.
3. The student objective may not match the programmed objective.

The disadvantages listed are the result of misuse and bad judgment by the teacher.

Games and Simulation

Very few games or simulations were commercially available before 1965. Today a vast number of them are appropriate for middle school students. Basically, the objective of simulated games is to provide a learning strategy which will motivate the student to full commitment. The games are designed to take a small segment of our complex society or the world of reality and to reduce it to manageable proportions. The student, interacting with the game, finds it necessary to cope with this segment of his environment.

It is not enough simply to assign a simulation game; the educational objective must be considered. The learning experiences and the rules of the game should be so structured that the student is constantly working toward an educational objective. This objective would be to learn about a particular segment of society or some small part of the real world.

Most educational games require that students exhibit some cooperation. They are so designed that it is of mutual benefit for the players to work together. Players soon learn that little is gained by acting on their own without first considering the other players. By cooperating, by bargaining, and by reaching a consensus everyone enhances his position.

Often, as students participate in games, they are forced to step into the shoes of others thereby experiencing some of the feelings, attitudes, and emotions of others. Players tend to identify with their role and to develop a sensitivity toward the person whose part they are enacting. For example, a middle school student assuming the role of a parent frequently gains empathy for the position of parents. A middle school student who voices the English point of view during the Revolutionary conflict can gain new insight into how the English must have viewed the colonists in early America.

If, indeed, we are interested in student mastery of concepts, games have much to offer. The middle school student, rather than listening to a lecture on the duties of a senator, can actually assume the role of a senator and can come to understand the pressures on that individual. When the student, playing the part of a senator, begins to interact with the president and the Supreme Court, he *feels* the concept of separation of powers, of balance of powers. The abstract lecture is replaced by a concrete, viable experience.

After simulation games, students actually feel that they can cope with their environment, whereas before many may have expressed a feeling of complete helplessness. Through the games students become aware that they can be a real force — that they can shape the goals of an organization or make an impact on society.

Middle school students frequently report that, by being allowed to make a mistake, a point is forcefully brought home. For example, in one game when a middle school student assumed a position of leadership he failed to consult with his "advisors" and made decisions that plunged his nation into a serious depression. Later this student reported that he felt he now had a grasp of certain economic concepts that in the past were only words.

Students who are not achieving well academically are often attracted to educational games. Playing allows them a solid situation with which they can manipulate and interact. Many teachers report that this is an excellent way to involve students who are usually passive learners. Many such students find they do indeed have much to contribute. They are delighted to find that in certain situations they can compete quite well with the academically talented.

On the other hand, students who are academically talented report that they, too, profit a great deal from participation in simulation games. They are able to conceptualize the purpose of the game and to analyze how the decisions they make during the game relate to the concept that they are striving to master. Further, the more able students frequently bring greater knowledge and greater understanding to the simulated environment, to the benefit of all students.

Gaming requires that the teacher not be the focal point of instruction. The simulated environment and the students' interaction with their environment requires that students become more active in the learning process. They learn as they experience the consequences of their actions. The teacher's role is that of an advisor — a resource person who can provide assistance when her students request it. She is not the dominant person who is always giving or telling the answer.

Some educators, however, have serious objections to educational games. They feel it is impossible to boil highly abstract situations down into simple simulations where students can interact. They argue that decisions made by students have nothing to do with reality. Bad decisions are not really punished, and the student suffers no ill effects from a bad decision. For example, a student can decide to wage war on Russia and bomb Moscow with no real consequence for his action. Therefore, all games do is create unreal situations.

Some educators have stated that games offer a very simplistic view of reality. Since it is impossible to have a highly complex model, models remain very simple in design. Therefore, the games seem very simple and often mislead students into thinking that they understand concepts in the complexities of a subject when, in reality, they have a very simple-minded view.

Another disadvantage frequently mentioned is that middle school students do not take games seriously; they view simulation as child's play. They do not feel they actually learn anything, nor do they try. The games are not significant to them. They merely join in these fun activities to please the teacher.

We strongly recommend that middle school teachers at least investigate the use of games as another diverse learning strategy for their students. Games are very reasonably priced, and before they are rejected, they certainly should be examined and tried out in the classroom.

Other Media

Media such as transparencies, audio and video tapes, kits of artifacts and models, maps and countless other items can be used to good advantage in the middle schools. Various textbooks and paperbacks should also be included in multimedia programs for middle schools. As long as the concepts have been identified, different texts can be used to present a variety of viewpoints. Middle school students should be exposed to different writing styles and different reading levels; it is unusual to find one book that has all parts equally well written and illustrated.

Students who have the opportunity to use many different materials use many different senses. They learn more easily and completely when they not only see but touch, smell, hear, and speak as well. Middle school teachers face a most challenging task in the proper selection of multimedia. They must prescribe the proper blend of media for each student, the blend that will best meet his needs as a learner. Achieving this blend requires a perceptive knowledge of individual students and diagnostic skill. But when the blend is right, the media relevant and conceptually oriented, the results are spectacular.

The Community as a
Learning Laboratory

One of the most valuable resources is the community. Transportation, liability factors, time limitations, and sensitivity to "disrupting" other teachers' programs all could create problems; yet in spite of the difficulties, the exciting and unlimited opportunities available make any extra effort worthwhile.

The Community into the School

As middle school youth begin to explore such topics as pollution, urban problems, women's liberation, welfare, taxation, and the war in Vietnam, they need to meet with individuals with expertise in these areas. Usually such individuals are not teachers. Within a one hour period, via the telephone, one four-member team was able to schedule the following people to interact with their students:

1. A rehabilitation counselor was secured to explain how tax funds are utilized, what services are available, and how individuals are helped to move from the welfare rolls into productive, useful citizens.
2. A director of a council concerned with pollution was delighted by the chance to talk with students. His primary responsibility was combating industrial pollution of air and water. He volunteered a second person who was responsible for alerting the public to the role the consumer plays in pollution.

3. An individual connected with the women's liberation movement was scheduled to discuss the
   history of women's rights in America and current efforts to eliminate discrimination against
   women.
4. Several returning Vietnam veterans were not
   only willing but pleased to be asked to talk with
   students about their experiences.
5. A local realtor who was playing a neutral role
   in a very emotional "apartment-versus-single-
   family-dwelling" conflict agreed to work with a
   group of students who were studying propa-
   ganda.
6. Various county officials indicated a willingness
   to alert the middle school youth to problems that
   are not geographic in nature but require the
   cooperation of the many small village, township,
   and city governmental bodies. This briefing was
   planned to help the students realize the complexity of problem solving.

These six activities are only a small sample of the rich and varied human resources available. High school students who elect,
as a service project, to work with middle school youngsters can
be utilized in numerous ways. They can work with students in
their special areas of interest, such as art, music, science, math, or
home economics. Two high school students who assisted in the
area of gymnastics and modern dance gained quite a following in
one middle school. Two senior students even assumed the responsibility of training and assisting a group to produce a middle
school newspaper. Orientation for high school can become a continuous program through a series of weekly or monthly "rap sessions" conducted by high school students about various aspects
of high school.

A creative middle school staff will suggest many additional
possibilities for using *people* resources.

School into the Community

The advantage of actually seeing, walking around, and visiting
in various parts of the community over hearing or reading about

them is obvious. It is difficult to "walk in the shoes of another" from a distance. True understanding of situations often requires the emotional impact of a site visit.

Factories, museums, parks, community agencies, airports, churches, and businesses are all available for school use. For example, a visit to a large stock brokerage firm resulted in a "paper investment club" and was the catalyst of a large number of independent study projects in one middle school. Small groups of students could observe people at work in various occupations to become more familiar with the "real world" and to help establish long-term goals for themselves.

What other journeys into the community would enhance the learning program in your school?

SOURCE OF FILMS
(Partial Listing)

Rentals

Audio Visual Services
Kent State University
Kent, Ohio 44240

Audiovisual Instruction
Coliseum 131
Corvallis, Oregon 97331

Boston University
Abraham Krasker Film Library
765 Commonwealth Avenue
Boston, Massachusetts 02215

College Film Center
332 South Michigan Avenue
Chicago, Illinois 60604

Florida State University
Educational Media Center
Tallahassee, Florida 32306

Hank Newenhouse
1825 Willow Road
Northfield, Illinois 60093

Indiana University
Audio-Visual Center
Bloomington, Indiana 47401

International Film Bureau
332 South Michigan Avenue
Chicago, Illinois 60604

Southwestern State College
Instructional Materials Center
Weatherford, Oklahoma 73096

Syracuse University
Educational Film Library
1455 East Colvin Street
Syracuse, New York 13210

University of Arizona
Bureau of Audiovisual Services
Tucson, Arizona 85721

University of California
Extension Media Center
2223 Fulton Street
Berkeley, California 94720

SOURCE OF FILMS
(Partial Listing)

Rentals

University of Illinois
Visual Aids Service
704 South Sixth Street
Champaign, Illinois 61820

University of Michigan
Audio-Visual Education Center
720 East Huron Street
Ann Arbor, Michigan 48104

University of Minnesota
Audio Visual Extension Service

2037 University Avenue, SE
Minneapolis, Minnesota 55455

University of Utah
Educational Media Center
Milton Bennion Hall 207
Salt Lake City, Utah 84112

University of Wisconsin
Bureau of Audio Visual Instruction
1312 West Johnson Street
Madison, Wisconsin 53706

Free Loan
City and County School Systems

Ford Film Library
Ford Motor Company
American Road
Dearborn, Michigan 48120

Modern Talking Picture Service, Inc.
2323 New Hyde Park Road
New Hyde Park, New York 11040

Public Libraries
(Free loan or minimal
    service charge)

Serina Press
70 Kennedy Street
Alexandria, Virginia 22305
(Free loan of
    government films)

State Departments of Education

U. S. Atomic Energy Commission
Washington, D. C. 20545

Professional Films   Available from /I/D/E/A/ is a series of rental films dealing with critical issues in American education. In addition to films of community interest, a library of inservice training films is being produced by /I/D/E/A/. These training aids are designed to assist individuals and organizations interested in educational change. For a list of films write to:

Institute for Development of Educational
Activities, Inc.
/I/D/E/A/, Mail Orders,
Post Office Box 628
Far Hills Branch
Dayton, Ohio 45419

Many films and filmstrips are available from the National Education Association. The NEA catalog of publications and audiovisual materials is published yearly. To keep up to date during the years on new materials, consult the "New NEA Publications and Audiovisual Materials" page appearing monthly in *Today's Education: NEA Journal*.

The local college or university is a source for films. A school district can often establish a relationship with the local university so that films can be borrowed at little or no cost.

Chapter 11

Time Allocation

Scheduling is simply a way of budgeting the time of students and teachers in response to their individual and everchanging needs. A variable schedule cannot be seriously considered unless it is used in conjunction with other closely related innovations. The schedule serves the instructional program of the school; to alter an instructional program to fit a schedule defeats the purpose. Changes in the instructional program must precede and determine changes in scheduling.

Time allotments, teaching techniques, student groupings, and teacher and pupil activities should be determined by teachers and counselors, not administrators. In any schedule the principal should allow teachers to control the use of time, the grouping procedures, and the learning strategies. Teachers are capable of making decisions about the way instructional time should be used. They are closer to the needs of students and are in a better position to evaluate how time can best be used to meet those needs.

Frequently middle school teachers will construct a student's schedule simply by asking the student how much time he needs for various activities. The amount of structure needed will vary greatly. Many students can exercise a great deal of independence in the use of their time.

169

Whenever time is reallocated, teachers, parents, and students must all be involved in making the change. The teaching staff must internalize the rationale behind independent study, small group work, and large group lecture. If the large group lecture is used to cover the textbook, then independent study, laboratory experiences, and the small group process will not function well. For example, if during a large group lecture the teacher explains or tells all the facts, relationships, principles, conclusions, or generalizations then students will have little reason to pursue inquiry in small groups or independent study. The large group mode must not be used to do things for students they can do for themselves. Grouping procedures must be thoroughly investigated and understood by the teaching staff, and explained to the students and their parents.

To allocate time to take advantage of differences in the way students learn, in their abilities and interests, mandates that the teaching staff know the students. Teachers will want to become highly sophisticated in analyzing and diagnosing the strengths and weaknesses of individual students.

Flexible use of time generally allows students to work independently. Therefore, materials and facilities must be made available to the learner. Without a learning center where a variety of media is available, it is most difficult for the student to pursue subject areas in depth.

When the teaching staff is no longer restricted by time and can create a flexible schedule for each student, the principal will come to realize that he cannot know where every student is every minute of the day. Accounting for students will naturally be decentralized. Teachers will assume more responsibility for where each student spends his time.

There are many ways to allocate time; probably there is no one best way. Time allocation is simply a way to utilize the human and physical resources of a school effectively and efficiently. The flexible schedule gives the teacher freedom to construct a learning environment that she feels is appropriate for each student. Parents generally will accept a flexible use of time if they are made aware of the fact that this flexibility will provide more individual attention and help for their son or daughter. The school should communicate to parents that if the variable schedule is used, the student will no longer be locked into one schedule for an entire year. In addition, pupils will profit from a variable schedule in that they can easily switch from group to group without the traumatic experience some students feel when shifted to a different section or class in a traditional school. Pupils will gain the advantage of relating to a number of teachers and many students rather than the few teachers and students who happen to be in a particular homeroom or section.

Many middle school principals ask, "Should a different use of time or a variable schedule be imposed on my staff overnight or should it evolve slowly over a period of time?" The answer depends on the school involved. If a school has been constructed for team teaching, has the latest innovations built into the building, and is opening for the first time, it is rather difficult to see why one would not move immediately into innovative use of time. Teachers would determine how the time should be allocated, and, certainly, a creative staff would probably make each day of the week different.

On the other hand, in an older school where the staff has been working with a traditional schedule for many years, in a community that has had no experience with flexible scheduling, it might take several years to move from the conventional schedule to a block schedule. The principal might start the first year with only part of his staff varying time modules. Perhaps as few as 30 percent will use time creatively the first year. It would become the role of the administrator to encourage and to praise those who develop flexibility.

Before anyone can accept flexibility of time, he must first accept certain assumptions: assumptions about students, how they learn, and their learning program.

1. Students will have a greater commitment to learning if they help make important decisions about their learning.

2. Students should be given greater choice in what they learn and the way they will learn.

3. All students do not need to learn the same things. Each individual should have a unique learning program.

4. The task of the teacher is to free students by assisting them to become self-selecting, and independent individuals.

5. Basically students want to learn, grow, and improve. The role of the teacher is to encourage, assist, help, trust, believe in, and have faith in students. Teachers do not view their role in the learning process as a commander, controller, or dominator.

6. The learning program must be flexible enough to use alternatives when needed.

7. A student's learning program is never final, but always subject to revision and change.

8. Learning can take place without a teacher being physically present.

9. Students have the ability to assume responsibility for their own learning.

10. All classes, in all subjects, do not need to meet the same number of periods per week for the same amount of time each week. All classes do not need to meet every day.

11. The instructional program in a school can be improved, and the teaching staff has an obligation to invent and experiment with creative use of time so that it might improve the instructional program.

12. The staff must exhibit a willingness to use time creatively. If a teaching staff goes along with a change in schedule merely to please central administration or the principal, innovative use of time will not take place. The teaching staff must be convinced that there is a better way to structure time than has been done in the past; that a teacher should not have twenty-five to thirty students five days a week, fifty-five minutes each day; and that time requirements must be determined by what it is that the student is trying to accomplish rather than by some arbitrary time limits.

Following are several schedules that are operational in middle schools. Figure 1 will help you understand the block schedule.

Block Schedule (Figure 1)

You are a member of the English-Social Studies team. The team modules denote periods of time. Instead of a traditional six-period day, Figure 1 illustrates a schedule with 16 modules of time for your team through the day:

1. *Modules 1 — 4:* The team works with students assigned to Group A.
2. *Modules 5 — 7:* The team meets for planning.
3. *Modules 8 — 10:* Lunch and student activities are scheduled. (An example of a student activity might be a meeting of the Science Club.)
4. *Modules 11, 12:* The team assists the Related Arts Team. (Interdisciplinary teaming emerges from this contact.)
5. *Modules 13 — 16:* The team works with students assigned to Group B.

Next, we follow a student in Group A through the day:

1. *Modules 1 — 4:* Students meet with the English-Social Studies Team I.
2. *Modules 5 — 7:* Students meet with the Related Arts Team.
3. *Modules 8 — 10:* Lunch and student activities are scheduled.
4. *Modules 11, 12:* Students rejoin the Related Arts Team.
5. *Modules 13 — 16:* Students meet with the Math-Science Team II.

Independent study time has not been scheduled for the students and teachers. Within all team areas there is time allotted for independent study, laboratory experience, and small group work.

Viewing the English-Social Studies Team I, we find that the team has four modules allotted for both subjects. The time may or may not be divided equally. The team decides how time should be used. In practice, a different schedule evolves daily. Team I may elect to use Modules 5, 6, and 7, or Modules 11 and 12 for individual conferences with students or parents, or perhaps for helping students in remedial work. The use of this time is limited only by the team's creativity. All students do not do the same things at the same time; they can be grouped and regrouped daily within a section or even shifted from Group A to Group B or vice versa. The block schedule provides one example of how teachers can control time, the size of the group, and the composition of the group. Teachers determine the way the instructional time is used.

Team I English Social Studies	Team II Mathematics Science	Team III English Social Studies	Team IV Mathematics Science	Team V Related Arts
1 2 3 4 Student Group A	Student Group B	Team Planning	Team Planning	Student Groups C & D
				Team Planning
5 6 7 Team Planning	Team Planning	Student Group C	Student Group D	Student Groups A & B
8 9 10 Lunch and Student Activities				
11 12 Assist Related Arts Team	Assist Related Arts Team	Student Group D	Student Group C	Student Groups A & B
				Team Planning
13 14 15 16 Student Group B	Student Group A	Assist Related Arts Team	Assist Related Arts Team	Student Groups C & D

School organized into five teaching teams:

    (1) Two English, Social Studies teams
    (2) Two Mathematics, Science teams
    (3) One Related Arts team (Music, Typing, Physical Ed.,
          Home Ec., Art, Industrial Arts, Etc.)

Fig. 1. Middle School Block Schedule encompassing students
in the 6th, 7th, and 8th year of school

Block Schedule, Unified
Studies Teams (Figure 2)

This schedule encourages and promotes an interdisciplinary approach. Each team decides on the amount of time to be spent in the various content areas and on grouping procedures. Decisions are made only after preassessment of the students' abilities, interests, and needs. Not all students spend the same amount of time in each content area. For example, if one student needs a great deal of work in the language arts area, the team makes enough time available. On the other hand, if a student has already met most of the objectives in one area, his time in that area is minimal. While one team's students are involved in activities in the related arts area, that Unified Studies Team can spend its time planning.

Let us trace the activities of a teacher in Team II through the day:

1. *Modules 1 — 8:* She is involved in learning activities with students in their eighth year of school.

2. *Module 9:* Lunch is scheduled.

3. *Modules 10 — 13:* She is involved in learning activities with students in their eighth year of school.

4. *Modules 14 — 18:* She joins other members of the team for a planning session.

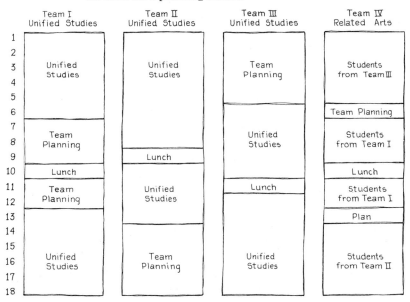

School organized into four teams:
(1) Three Unified Studies teams (English, Social Studies, Mathematics, Science)
(2) One Related Arts team (Music, Art, Industrial Arts, Home Ec., Physical Ed., Etc.)

Fig. 2. Middle School Block Schedule, Unified Studies Teams

Now to trace a student in Team III through the day:

1. *Modules 1 — 5:* He is involved in the Related Arts area.
2. *Modules 6 — 10:* He is involved in the Unified Studies area.
3. *Module 11:* Lunch is scheduled.
4. *Modules 12 — 18:* He is again involved in the Unified Studies area.

Flexible Modular Scheduling
(Figure 3 and Figure 3a)

A flexible modular schedule is actually a process of scheduling by the week rather than by the day. In a traditional school each day is the same. In a flexible modular schedule, as illustrated in Figure 3, there is a different schedule every day; therefore, teachers and students have five different schedules, each in effect once a week.

A flexible modular schedule implies that the teachers have predetermined the frequency and duration of the learning groups. It is difficult to construct and very complicated to administer. Most schools rely upon a computer program to build the master schedule. The obvious disadvantage of this type of schedule is that the school is locked into a given schedule for at least a semester and usually a year — unless, of course, the school completely reschedules at an earlier date.

The flexible schedule assumes that classes do not necessarily meet daily, and when they do convene they meet for varying lengths of time. The school day is divided into small segments of time (modules) so that teachers can request the number of modules that seem most appropriate for the planned learning activities and for the characteristics of the students involved. The length of time allotted for various groups can vary from one module to as many modules as the teacher deems necessary. The size of the group frequently varies from six students to as many as 300 to 400 students.

The four teaching-learning modes most generally used are large group instruction, small group learning experiences, laboratory experiences, and independent study. Independent study or unscheduled time comprises from 30 to 70 percent of the student's day. The amount of unscheduled time is determined by the teaching team, and varies from student to student. The trend is to

	Monday	Tuesday	Wednesday	Thursday	Friday
1	Team Planning	U.S. History S.G. Section 5 Room 218			U.S. History L.G. Sections 1-12 Lecture
2					
3					
4				Team Planning	
5					
6	U.S. History S.G. Section 6 Room 218				Humanities
7		Humanities	U.S. History S.G. Section 4 Room 219	U.S. History S.G. Section 3 Room 219	
8					
9	Lunch	Team Planning	Lunch	Lunch	Lunch
10					
11		Lunch			
12	U.S. History S.G. Section 5 Room 218				
13			U.S. History S.G. Section 4 Room 219		
14		U.S. History S.G. Section 3 Room 219			Team Planning
15					
16				Humanities	
17		U.S. History S.G. Section 6 Room 218			
18					

Key:
  L.G.= Large Group
  S.G.= Small Group
(During unscheduled time the teacher is free for student-teacher conferences.)

Fig. 3. Modular-Flexible Schedule, Teacher Copy

allow more unscheduled, independent study time than ever thought possible or desirable in the past. Students use this time to meet with their counselor, to confer with teachers, to practice skills, to work in open labs or in the learning resource center, or just to relax and enjoy a bottle of soft drink in the student lounge. This is the time when students are free to complete their assigned

	Monday	Tuesday	Wednesday	Thursday	Friday
1	Home Ec. S. G. or Lab. Room 204	U.S. History S. G. Room 218	I. S.	Biology L. G. Lecture	U.S. History L. G. Lecture
2					
3				I. S.	
4	I. S.	Art Room 16	Biology S. G. or Lab. Room 237	G. Math S. G. Room 109	I. S.
5					G. Math S.G. - Room 109
6	G. Math L.G. Lecture	I. S.			English S.G. Room 104
7		G. Math S. G. Room 109	I. S.	I. S.	
8	I. S.		G. Math L. G. Room 109		Lunch
9	Spanish I Room 314	Lunch		Lunch	I. S.
10			Lunch	Language Lab.	
11	Lunch	Biology S. G. or Lab. Room 237	Spanish I Room 314		Spanish I Room 314
12	U. S. History S. G. Room 218			I. S.	
13					
14		I. S.	I. S.	English S. G. Room 104	I. S.
15					
16	I. S.	English L. G. Lecture	Home Ec. S. G. or Lab. Room 204	Art Room	Home Ec. S. G. or Lab. Room 204
17					
18		I. S.			

Key:

L.G. = Large Group
S.G. = Small Group
I.S. = Independent Study
Lab. = Laboratory

(Options available include such areas as open laboratories, instructiona materials center, quiet study area, and talk study areas.)

Fig. 3a. Modular-Flexible Schedule, Student Copy

work as well as to pursue independent interests. Independent study time is structured to a degree in that students have learning contracts to fulfill; assignments to prepare; and must, in general, prepare themselves to accomplish objectives that they have either set for themselves or assumed under the guidance of a teacher.

The authors feel the Flexible Modular Scheduling movement is "an idea whose time has passed." Some educators feel this movement has not passed its zenith; therefore, this discussion is included.

Block Schedule,
Open Laboratory (Figure 4)

Figure 4 illustrates a block schedule in which each team meets with all grades at different times of the day. The use of time during any instructional block is left up to the teaching team.

This schedule differs from the preceding ones in that it has a block of time labeled "independent study" or "related arts" scheduled at the end of the day. This opens several possibilities for the student. He might want to explore other areas of the related arts that he was unable to schedule during his day, for example, a foreign language or typing. Another possibility is that the student might want to pursue an independent study project, and this would be time set aside during the day for this purpose. Basically, this type schedule is ideal for an exploratory program. The student has

	English Social Studies	Mathematics Science	Related Arts or Independent Study
1 2 3	Group I	Group III	Group II
4 5 6	Group III	Group II	Group I
7	Lunch		
8 9 10	Group II	Group I	Group III
11 12	Independent Study - Related Arts, Band, Choir		

Fig. 4. Middle School Block Schedule, Open Laboratory

a block of time in which to explore many areas. If necessary, the students could even be dismissed early the last two modules of the day to permit teachers to participate in teacher-parent conferences or in-service activities.

Rotating Variable
Time Schedule (Figure 5)

In the rotating variable time schedule the periods are of different lengths. This allows the teacher to choose the block of time most appropriate for a given teaching-learning situation. A ninety minute block of time, for example, would be useful for laboratory experiences; a forty-five minute block of time might be more suited for a large group presentation. By developing staff consensus, the amount of time required for each learning experience can be secured within the schedule.

Rotating Four-Day
Schedule (Figure 6)

In the rotating four-day schedule each period is of the same length, but classes meet only four days a week. Blocks of time are provided so that other activities can be scheduled — activities

Number of Minutes	Monday	Tuesday	Wednesday	Thursday	Friday
90	1	6	5	4	3
60	2	1	6	5	4
60	3	2	1	6	5
45	4	3	2	1	6
45	5	4	3	2	1

Fig. 5. Middle School Rotating Variable Time Schedule — Four-Day Schedule

such as assembly programs, basketball or football pep rallies, or band concerts. One example of how the time might be used is to devise a guidance program in which each student meets in a small group with a teacher-counselor. By having two open periods at the end of the day, students could be dismissed early to permit parent-teacher conferences, in-service activities for the teaching staff, or team meetings.

Period	Monday	Tuesday	Wednesday	Thursday	Friday
I	1	Open or Activities	6	5	4
II	2	Open or Activities	Open or Activities	6	5
III	3	2	1	1	6
IV	4	3	2	3	Open or Activities
V	5	4	3	Open or Activities	1
VI	6	5	4	Open or Activities	2

Fig. 6. Middle School Rotating Four-Day Schedule —50-Minute Periods

Rotating
Conventional Schedule (Figure 7)

Some teachers have complained that meeting with students the same time each day, every day, becomes boring. A frequent complaint is that the sixth period class, or the last class of the day, is always tired, restless, and over eager to go home. Another oft heard comment is that the period immediately following lunch finds students tired or sleepy.

The rotating conventional schedule still maintains a six-period day, but it does rearrange the periods during the day. For example, if a student has English the first period on Monday, on Tuesday his English class would meet during the second period, on Wednesday during the fifth period, on Thursday during the fourth period, and on Friday during the sixth period. The rotating conventional schedule offers little improvement over a traditional schedule other than breaking the monotony of a daily routine.

Period	Monday	Tuesday	Wednesday	Thursday	Friday
I	1	6	3	4	2
II	2	1	4	5	3
III	3	2	5	6	4
IV	4	3	6	1	5
V	5	4	1	2	6
VI	6	5	2	3	1

Fig. 7. Middle School Rotating Conventional Schedule — 50-Minute Periods

Back-To-Back
Schedule (Figure 8)

Even within the framework of a traditional schedule, a staff can gain some flexibility in the way time is used. The back-to-back schedule offers several possibilities of how an English and Social Studies teacher can, if not team teach, at least do cooperative teaching. The illustrations show how it is possible to vary student experiences during a weekly schedule. Student schedules need not remain constant for the entire semester.

The arrangement of time must be left to the judgment of the classroom teacher. The back-to-back schedule could be a first step as one breaks out of a conventional schedule. The periods do remain the same, and the schedule does restrict the professional teachers as they try to make effective and efficient use of time. Nevertheless, the back-to-back schedule does encourage cooperative planning and does provide an opportunity for teachers to work together. The back-to-back schedule may be viewed as a first step, but not a final step, toward the most effective use of time. It is an easy first step to make, and one which many teachers who are a bit hesitant to try new ideas can accept. Therefore, it might be a wise first choice for some schools. We would hope, though, that the staff involved would soon be able to advance to one of the more flexible schedules.

Figure I

Minutes	Period				
50	I	Teacher A Social Studies I 20 Students	Teacher B Social Studies I 20 Students	Teacher C English I 20 Students	Teacher D English I 20 Students
50	II	Teacher A Social Studies I 20 Students	Teacher B Social Studies I 20 Students	Teacher C English I 20 Students	Teacher D English I 20 Students

Figure II

Minutes	Period		
50	I	Teacher A,B Social Studies I 50 Students	Teacher C,D English I 60 Students
50	II	Teacher A,B Social Studies I 50 Students	Teacher C,D 50 Students

Fig. 8. Middle School Conventional Schedule Back-To-Back

Period 1

Monday	Teacher A L. G. 50 Students	Teacher B L. G. 50 Students
Tuesday	10 Students S.G. 8 Students S.G. 8 Students S.G.	8 Students S.G. 8 Students S.G. 8 Students S.G.
Wednesday	Teacher A I. S. 45 Students	Teacher B 5 Students Tutorial Assistance
Thursday	8 Students S.G. 8 Students S.G. 8 Students S.G.	8 Students S.G. 8 Students S.G. 10 Students S.G.
Friday	Teacher A 20 Students Tutorial Assistance	Teacher B 20 Students Tutorial Assistance

Key:

L. G. - Large Group
S. G. - Small Group
I. S. - Independent Study

Part 3

Staff Allocations

Chapter 12

Differentiated
Teaching Staff

Most middle school teachers would agree that the task of the teacher is no longer that of a dispenser of information in a self-contained classroom. The concept of a single teacher in a self-contained classroom, managing all phases of instruction, is outdated. Many are the tasks of teachers in today's middle schools. They realize that they must plan instructional units, diagnose student learning and student learning difficulties, and prescribe appropriate learning activities. They know that the prescribed activities must relate to the learner's experience, his interests, and needs. As a unique learning program is planned for each learner, it must be coordinated into a total learning program. Teachers must constantly make value judgments, such as when to prescribe an objective for a student and when to let the student select his own objectives. In addition to providing appropriate learning activities, pupil progress must be evaluated to find out if the learning program has been adequate and to determine student levels of performance.

Such tasks are very difficult for any middle school teacher to perform and for any teaching team to manage. The task of providing a proper learning environment is made more difficult when we ask teachers to do a vast amount of paper work: recording pupil records; marking papers; typing their own materials; running duplicating machines; and supervising ball games, lunch rooms, wash rooms, and corridors. Differentiated staffing is one way to make the job of teaching more manageable. It is an organizational design that delineates the levels of teaching responsibility.

J. Lloyd Trump and Dorsey Baynham, in their 1961 book *Guide to Better Schools*, propose a differentiated staff consisting of 1) instructional assistants, 2) clerks, and 3) general aides for supervision (268:33-34). These assistants would provide support for teachers in the teaching-learning process. In the early 1960's Myron Lieberman (*The Future of Public Education*) shocked and aroused many educators by his suggestion that teachers should not be on the same level and that some sort of differentiated staffing should be considered (181:77). Dwight Allen and Robert Bush, in a publication in the mid-sixties, *A New Design for High School Education*, also suggested a model for differentiated staffing (9:41-45). Dwight Allen's model identified approximately four levels of teacher responsibility. The most responsible level would be the curriculum associate or professor. Next would be the senior teacher followed by a staff teacher and an associate teacher. A corps of teacher aides would assist the professional staff. M. John Rand and Fenwick English proposed a differentiated staff model for the Unified School District, Temple City, California (233:265-268). Their model is under constant revision; but, basically, it separates the staff into levels: a teaching research associate, a teaching curriculum associate, a senior teacher or a teaching staff, and academic assistants.

There is a vast amount of material in professional journals devoted to differentiated staffing. In almost all models proposed, the professional staff has been divided into levels as well as the various teacher aides.

America's public school administrators have not been forgotten. Trump proposed a model for differentiating the administrative staff (266:1-4). In fact, he proposed several administrative models with delineated levels depending upon the size of the school. Just as the task of the teacher in the self-contained classroom is unmanageable, so is the role of the principal. If the principal is the sole administrative person in the school trying to do all things for all people, his job is unmanageable. If the role of the principal includes being the instructional leader in the school, then he will need assistants to perform some of the administrative chores.

Differentiated staffing can also be described as an organizational design that defines and delineates the total continuum of teaching and learning responsibilities. The continuum begins with those activities which can be performed by a teacher aide and proceeds to those highly complex activities which can be performed by only the most competent educator. This network of responsibilities can easily encompass all of our present job classifications, including teacher aides, interns, student teachers, teachers, and administrators.

There have been a number of concepts that have restrained diversified staffing. The advent of the self-contained classroom, coupled with the judgment that the average teacher could handle thirty children, has provided American education with a strong deterrent to any form of differentiation. Any differentiation that did exist took the form of a person being an *elementary* teacher as opposed to a *high school* teacher, or a *science* teacher as opposed to a *language arts* teacher.

In addition, the single-salary schedule has emphasized efforts to treat teachers as equals. The merit pay philosophy attempts to allow for the variation in the complexity of the teaching-learning act, but it has been directed toward the total skills of the teacher, rather than the degree of sophistication involved in the teaching act. The use of the subjective judgment to determine which teachers would receive different pay for doing the same task seemed to doom the use of merit pay.

In addition to individualizing instruction for the student, differentiated staffing also involves the teacher—in decision making, in curriculum planning, in method determination, and in time utilization decisions. For years teachers have been saying that they want to be involved in the decision-making process, and this type of staffing provides such opportunities. Differentiated staffing matches the various combinations of talent possessed by teachers to the specific needs of children. It creates an organizational incentive program that makes teaching a more professional career. As teachers become able to assume more responsibility, and want to assume more responsibility, they are paid accordingly. Staffing so divided into levels allows classroom teachers to assume responsibility and exercises initiative commensurate with their interests, talents, and abilities.

A diversified staffing program possesses certain elements which distinguish it from the present method of teacher utilization. While any program of this sort might take any one of a multitude of directions, there are certain elements common to all forms. Some variation of those common elements are usually found in differentiated staffing:

1. Instructional tasks are identified and defined so that educational personnel can fit their particular aptitudes or abilities to the task which they can best perform.

2. Teaching remains the primary function of all staff members within the differentiations—only the intensity of effort is changed. A differentiated staffing pattern is not designed to make some teachers primarily administrators. Generally, all teachers maintain contact with the students. Some teachers, however, work in curriculum design creating activity packages; others work with students in independent study, or plan individual learning programs, or work with students in correcting papers, or assist students in seeking resources.

3. Educational personnel are given more latitude and become professional partners with administrators in the decision-making process.

4. When the organization of staff is changed in a differentiated manner, the organization of pupils must also change. If tasks are differentiated to allow educational personnel to do what they do best, the self-contained classroom cannot be retained as an organizational technique.

Possible Degrees of Differentiation

Serious attempts to define the degrees of differentiation have usually resulted in several levels of sophistication within the teacher aide range of responsibility. These would include clerical aides, supervisory aides, material aides, and instructional aides. Also, the roles of the student teacher (intern) have been included in some patterns. The emphasis given to the use of aides testifies that while decision-making should be left to the professional teacher, there are many instructional tasks that teacher aides can perform. The important and significant factor is that educators are able to differentiate the sophistication of the teaching-learning process.

The majority of teachers are believed to possess talents consistent with the most basic level of the continuum. Tenure of position is usually granted only at the basic levels. Only those certified personnel who possess highly sophisticated levels of teaching performance are given responsibilities of a more far-reaching nature. It is at the sophisticated levels that an instructor may directly affect the largest number of pupils. At the highest level the educator would make decisions about the total school curriculum, about the kinds of materials that would be available in the school, and about matters that influence the entire teaching-learning process.

Possible Models to Differentiate a Teaching Staff

Several models were suggested earlier in the chapter. One would be advised to look further at the works of Allen, Trump, English, and others for specific models. It is also advised that each school first determine what it is they want to do as a result of differentiating their staff before devising their own model.

Schools wishing to inaugurate a program of differentiated staffing should consider the following:

1. Any study of this subject should involve these people who will ultimately assume responsibilities within the school — that is, the administration, the local teachers' organization, and the community.
2. Because the teaching roles are so diverse, it appears that any attempts to differentiate the

responsibilities of teaching must include the delineation of many teaching specialties. For example, it is rather easy to see the difference between a clerk-typist and a coordinator of instruction; but as the roles are further delineated, such as a teaching research associate as opposed to a senior teacher, the differences in responsibility are not as obvious.

3. A staff must constantly remember that the primary objective is to define differences in responsibility, not to assign additional administrative assignments to teachers.

4. Design several models defining the various roles a teacher might assume.

5. Select the model that best fits your middle school situation.

6. Give specific attention to the task of studying the responsibilities for each role, the selection of each role, and the salary which will be assigned to that position.

7. Initially neither teacher nor administrator will be able to operate effectively within the framework required for differentiated staffing. Therefore, in the beginning, define how additional study and in-service education can best be obtained. Before a program can be successful, both teachers and administrators will need in-service training.

8. In any plan include specific recommendations for ways to evaluate the program.

Implications for the Future

In the future the questions will not be, "What is the student-teacher ratio?" but, "What is the ratio between students and adults?" Without significantly altering the financial structure of the school today, by differentiated staffing, it is possible to change the student-teacher ratio from one to twenty or twenty-five to one adult to twelve or fifteen students. The question is no longer, "Are there enough teachers available?" but, "Are there enough adults available to meet the needs of all the learners?" Adults with specialties in curriculum development and writing learning activity packages, communication experts, library aides, custodians to maintain facilities, and a host of other specialists will be needed.

If the teacher's role were merely that of a dispenser of information, today's technology would make her obsolete. Computer assisted instruction, programmed material, audio tapes, individualized learning packages, and a great deal of hardware have been and are being developed. For example, we know that machines can assist students in mastering facts. Machines do rather well in communicating cognitive information. More complex teaching tasks, however, require both a teacher and a machine, each having something to contribute to the learner. Through a differentiated staff a teacher at one level might be able to conceive and design programs for both teachers and machines in an instructional system. Other teachers would actually test and use the program. Another staff person at still another level would possess the skills to make it technically possible for the system to operate. Machines can effectively prescribe learning situations for students — provided the machine is programmed with the right information.

It is quite obvious that we are becoming a more specialized society. It is hard to imagine a situation where people are not specializing. Specialization does not dehumanize the learning process; it humanizes it. Instead of trying to be all things to all people, the teacher now becomes a specialist, free to contribute her greatest strengths to helping the student learn how to learn. Just as we have made progress in medical science, in biological science, and in the world of engineering through specialization — by allowing individuals to utilize their strengths — the middle school can progress, through specialization, by differentiated staffing.

Chapter 13

Teacher Aides,
Parent Volunteers,
and Student Teachers

A variety of titles — teacher aides, paraprofessionals, volunteers, teacher assistants — are appearing in middle schools throughout the country. These titles are usually descriptive of the work performed by the title holder. Auxiliary personnel are considered essential to the effective operation of the middle school.

One primary reason for an aide and volunteer program is to increase teacher effectiveness by freeing them from the necessity of devoting large amounts of time to nonprofessional functions. Teachers spend a large portion of their day doing tasks that could be performed just as well by a person with less training. Also, such a program helps to maintain a quality educational program while coping with rising costs and increasing enrollments.

We expect middle school teachers to humanize education; to expand their role to include diagnosing, prescribing, and evaluating; and, in short, to be professional educators, who are equipped to meet the needs of all students. If teachers are expected to accomplish these goal-oriented tasks, they must be permitted to spend most of their time performing the tasks that only they can perform. When they must type their learning activity packages, record all evaluations, operate all equipment, and do all sorts of other nonprofessional tasks, they cannot be expected to accomplish their goals or to meet the needs of their students. A middle school cannot afford to be without auxiliary personnel.

Teacher Aides

The major distinction between teacher aides and paraprofessionals is that teacher aides usually perform noninstructional tasks such as clerical work, and paraprofessionals usually work with instructional related duties, working directly with students. For our purposes, we will refer to anyone who assists the teacher as a teacher aide.

Teacher aides can make possible more flexible grouping patterns, can enhance the effectiveness of teachers, and can cause educational programs to become more innovative. They can permit the professional teachers to plan strategies to meet the needs of individual students. But these benefits do not accrue to a school by the mere acquisition of aides. To realize the full potential of auxiliary personnel, the following should be provided.

1. An Orientation Program

To develop skills and competencies that will foster the nonprofessional's upward mobility, an orientation session would be given before the beginning of school. Quite opportunely, certain professional standards which must be maintained could be explained at this time. Aides should comprehend what it is that teachers and educators are trying to accomplish and must understand their role in the overall programs. As the meetings progress, they become aware of the middle school philosophy and the special needs of middle school youth.

Many school practices may be completely new to aides. If they know of these practices prior to the beginning of school, and have an opportunity to perform their tasks with confidence, their effectiveness is enhanced. For example, if they are aware of behavioral objectives, the purpose of objectives, and what they are doing and why they are doing it, they will do a better job. Educational programs must be meaningful to them. If they are to type concepts, behavioral objectives, and other material in learning activity packages and do not understand the purpose of the learning activity package, frustration and possibly boredom can occur. A working knowledge of the what and the why of the educational program is vitally necessary.

Many times, for the sake of expediency, the orientation program consists of a lecture. The lecture method may be effective at times, but just as it is often ineffective for middle school use, it also becomes ineffective in this instance. There is a great need to insure maximum involvement of aides during the orientation program. Only through involvement can they begin to synthesize and fully understand the middle school philosophy, the special needs of middle school youth, and the need for humanizing education.

2. A Handbook for Aides

Many rules, regulations, and procedures can be clarified for teacher aides through a handbook. Some items in the handbook should be discussed during the orientation program; others just require reading. This reference could and should assist the teacher aides to understand their relationship to the professional teacher and their proposed contribution to the overall objectives of the middle school program. Through a clarified role for the aide, the printed reminder can contribute to the development of high morale throughout the school. Interest and enthusiasm generated in the aides will carry over to the professional teachers and will directly enhance the learning experiences of middle school youth.

L. W. Kindred refers to teacher aides as "front line" interpreters of the school (164:288). Their attitudes toward the school are just as important as those of the teachers in influencing the public. He views an employee handbook as a basic tool for establishing good internal and external relations.

3. In-Service Training

One goal for the teacher aide is to develop communication skills and basic understandings that are needed for success in the middle school. The first few months are especially critical, but the in-service program should be an ongoing process. Both middle school teachers and administrators must realize that there is a great need for in-service training of teacher aides. Their need for this process may be even greater than that of professional teachers since aides may have no formalized training.

Aides need to acquire information about basic psychology so that they can understand why a student "misbehaves" at times. For example, a student may do unacceptable things to gain the attention of the aide. The aide must realize that his "misbehavior" is not necessarily the problem but his way of expressing a problem.

Another topic for in-service training may be how to make and display certain visual materials. Communication, child psychology, and audio-visual materials are just a few of the many subjects that will require an in-service program.

4. Team Membership

Although aides do not engage in actual teaching or instruction, they can be used to reinforce a learning concept or skill. For example, they may supervise groups that are working on learning activity packages, or sit in on small reading groups. But if a desirable working relationship is to exist, the aides must feel that they are a part of the team. A sense of working with someone, rather than for someone, is much more conducive to an effective working relationship. The high morale that can occur as a result of a strong team effort by both teachers and aides should result in a much stronger educational program for middle school students. Positive attitudes and harmonious communications will breed friendliness, happiness, and a humanistic approach to education.

5. Personalized Attention to Students

All aides should have certain qualifications. Recommended qualities include: a genuine interest in students of middle school age, a desire to help and to contribute to a strong educational program, the willingness to assist in any way possible to make a stronger program for the students. Aides should also be employed on the basis of other qualities such as a neat appearance, past employment, a good attitude, discretion, and the ability to work effectively with students and adults. The overall motivation of teacher aides should be to either directly or indirectly contribute to a personalized education for middle school youths.

6. Working Space

Just as teachers need an area away from interruptions, aides, too, need privacy at times. Room where materials can be prepared properly in the least amount of time is essential. Improper space can result in shoddy and inefficient work. A lack of space and materials may cause a simple task to consume considerably more time than necessary; thereby wasting precious time. Proper space for aides is just as important as a good preparation area for teachers.

7. Adequate Budgeting Procedures

If teacher aides are used effectively, the middle school staff will realize their great advantages. Success of the program will foster additional requests for aides to do both noninstructional and instructional tasks. School administrators should foresee this possibility and plan for it with an adequate budget.

8. Instructional Related Tasks

Teacher aides may work directly with students by helping them to locate materials and information or by providing help on routine matters. They may assist in orientation and follow-up activities. Frequently aides perform the administration, scoring, and filing of routine student information. They may maintain diagnostic records so that teachers need only to glance at the records to determine where a student is and where he needs help. These and many other instructional related tasks can be performed by teacher aides.

When aides perform many of the clerical and routine tasks, the role of the middle school teacher is more likely to be that of a diagnostician, prescriber, and evaluator. Teachers must do a more effective job in team teaching, in organizing various sized groups, and in encouraging students to learn independently. For teachers to perform all of these functions and still have time for planning, creativity, and innovation, teacher aides must be used. With aides the teacher is free to accomplish the professional tasks.

Other examples of instructional related tasks might be:

> a. Correcting standardized tests and preparing student profiles.
> b. Interviewing students with specific learning difficulties.
> c. Observing child behavior and recording such information.
> d. Preparing instructional materials such as flash cards, charts, and transparencies.
> e. Collecting and arranging displays for teaching purposes.
> f. Preparing special learning materials to meet individual differences, such as taping reading assignments for less capable students.
> g. Listening to oral reading.
> h. Supervising pupil laboratory work.

9. Noninstructional Related Tasks

Most noninstructional tasks are the unending clerical jobs that need to be performed in the middle school. As teachers are constantly diagnosing, prescribing, and evaluating specific student needs, numerous records must be maintained.

Considerable typing of material for duplication and distribution is always needed. This is especially true when teachers are developing learning activity packages and writing pretests and posttests.

Checking objective tests is another effective use of an aide. The teacher then has only to look at incorrect responses to properly diagnose specific needs and to determine the proper learning sequence for a student. Listed below are other examples of non-instructional related tasks:

a. Filing correspondence and reports in students' records.
b. Sending for free classroom materials.
c. Keeping attendance records.
d. Keeping records of books that students have read.
e. Typing teachers' correspondence.
f. Filing resource materials for various teaching units.
g. Setting up appointments for parent-teacher conferences.
h. Setting up appointments for home visits.
i. Preparing public relations materials to explain the middle school program.
j. Keeping bulletin boards current and neat.
k. Arranging interesting and inviting areas for learning.
l. Supervising the loading and unloading of school buses.
m. Telephoning parents of absent students to show a genuine interest in the student and to offer assistance.

Volunteer Parents

Many school districts are experiencing the financial strain on budgets caused by inflation. Volunteer parents can make a significant contribution to middle school programs and also ease this financial burden. More important than financial advantage, though, is the active participation by those parents who serve. Many communities are fortunate to have people who are qualified and willing to offer their talents to the middle school program. This type of partnership between home and school serves as a positive force to provide the best possible educational environment for each student.

The attempts of middle school programs to individualize instruction for all students and the increased demands of such programs require that schools seek ways to include volunteer parents. Increased communication between the school and the home is definitely fostered through such joint ventures. A constructive impact takes place when the middle school program is espoused by enthusiastic volunteer mothers. Community support of the school is greatly influenced by the communication that takes place from parent to parent. New potentials can be realized through volunteer parents. Parents may see things that teachers miss. They may also assist students in innumerable ways.

Initial Venture

The parent-teacher organization is an excellent place to recruit parents. Many mothers are willing to give a day a week if they feel that their services are genuinely needed and wanted. As volunteers are rewarded by expressed appreciation from teachers and administrators and their own warm feelings of satisfaction, the number of volunteers will increase greatly.

Policies

Definite policies should exist for volunteer programs so that parents know what their responsibilities are and what limitations exist for them. Policies greatly reduce the possibility of awkward and embarrassing situations for both parents and school personnel. Organization is the key to acquiring and maintaining good volunteer parents. Policies that assure volunteers of adequate preparation and productive use of time enhance organization.

Specialized Talents

Routine and possibly boring tasks may be appropriate once in a while, but no capable volunteer will last long on a continuous diet of boredom. There is a need to identify and to use specialized tal-

ents in art, music, dramatics, cooking, sewing, woodworking, etc. By utilizing the special skills of volunteers, the educational program is enriched and the talents of teachers are enhanced. Being permitted to use their talents will result in a higher morale for volunteers, hence a chain reaction on the high morale of teachers and students, too!

Student Teachers

The traditional role of student teachers has been one of teaching under the close supervision of a cooperating teacher and an instructor from the university for a period of time sometime during the junior or senior year of college. The student teaching program was intended mainly to benefit the student. It was considered a training program only, and little consideration was given to the youth within the schools.

New programs that are emerging in a few of our institutions of higher learning show some promise for providing a stronger background for the student teacher and for improving the instructional program for the middle school student.

The new student teaching preparation program for future middle school teachers may consist of a four-year program. During the freshman academic year, students will be required to do one semester of low level tutorial work in nearby-schools. The students will not be paid for this service. They will be under close supervision by university personnel. After this first year they can possibly make a realistic decision about continuing in education or transferring into another area.

During their second year of college, students will serve as assistants to a teaching team in the middle school. They will probably receive pay for their work, which will include both instructional and noninstructional related tasks. They will work in half-day sessions in one school for the entire year. The remaining half-day will be spent at their university in regular course work. The course work will also be closely correlated with their particular needs. For example, they might be required to attend one seminar per week to discuss their perceptions and observations of the educational program.

During their third year of college, they will be classified as associate teachers and will gradually assume full responsibility for the classes in which they are placed. They will remain in the same school that they were in during their freshman and sophomore years so that they can begin to know students and their particular needs. The college student will also have the advantage of working with a teaching team so that he can begin to understand the middle school philosophy, to learn how teams function most effectively, and to gain other knowledge that usually takes a new teacher at least a year or so to acquire. Again, the remaining half-day will be spent at the university.

During the senior year, the student teachers will enter an intern program and will be appointed to a teaching team. They will be paid on a professional basis and will possibly be eligible for other professional benefits. This practical experience will be coupled with a seminar conducted by university personnel. The early practical experiences will enable college students to decide if they really do want to become teachers, if they can work closely with a team of teachers and with students for a period of time, and will give them many hours of on-the-job, in-service training to further prepare them for their future profession. A four-year program of this type should provide a more complete and effective program for all concerned — the student teachers, the professional people with whom they work, and certainly the students involved.

Effective use of teacher aides, parent volunteers, and student teachers can provide many benefits. These benefits include a better instructional program for the middle school, more opportunities for student-teacher interaction, more opportunities for humanizing education, more attention to individualized needs, and a wider variety of educational opportunities. The teacher also benefits by having more time to be professional, to do the goal-oriented jobs that teaching requires.

Teacher aides will contribute greatly to middle school educational programs of the future. Professional roles for teachers will become reality. New organizational patterns will likely occur. Teachers will eventually have the time and the opportunity to become more creative and innovative. In the meantime supporting personnel cannot be considered "the frosting on the cake"; they are an essential ingredient to the "recipe." Teacher aides are a *must* for quality education.

Chapter 14

Staff Development
for Facilitating Change

The pressures of our changing society have made approaches of the past obsolete. The motivation for change and innovation in education today might be considered identical with that for survival. This is clearly brought out by P. A. Ellis and D. V. Meyer's statement that the demands of an electronically oriented society and the temper of today's students dictate that we consider the opportunities inherent in those developments and use them imaginatively (101:24-25). Therefore, if new approaches to organization, instruction, and learning in middle schools are to be effective, some fundamental questions concerning new concepts of social change and human perceptions must be considered.

In discussing our society today and how transformations are continually taking place, J. W. Gardner states that the system which is in equilibrium today will be thrown off balance tomorrow (118:28). Change is continuously needed to cope with altered circumstances.

There are some, perhaps, who feel that a change process can be successfully accepted and implemented without the involvement of the entire staff. Some educators may argue that aggressive leadership by the middle school principal, central office personnel, or an outside change agent is the quickest and most feasible way to bring about desirable alterations in a middle school program.

Other educators would encourage, instead, an open system where modification is produced through experiences which develop new understandings, new perceptions, and new skills for all concerned. Teachers would participate on a voluntary basis in workshops focusing on such topics as how students learn. Other experiences might include viewing demonstrations by outstanding teachers and working with consultants.

Mark Chesler and Robert Fox would be prone to encourage the open system, too (75:25-26). They state that, in order to establish a healthy climate for innovation and change, we must first develop ways for individual teachers to share new ideas with other teachers and to gain support for worthwhile change. They believe that there is a need to make teachers feel that they have had some influence in developing change by adopting new administrative styles which decentralize decision-making.

In the past, most high schools have experienced changes that have been initiated at the superintendent's level. The alterations then have flowed from the top to the team of teachers that is expected to make the change effective. The middle school philosophy would encourage that rearrangements flow from the teaching team. Middle school teachers should look at their jobs creatively and should be receptive to new ways to do their work more effectively. Given support, staff members can develop creatively within a school that is consistent with the middle school philosophy. When transformations originate with teachers, they can make the alterations successful. The middle school that can involve its teachers and encourage them to initiate change is the middle school that will become and will continue to be dynamic and exciting.

It is suggested that every middle school have two committees to provide information for in-service training and staff development. The first of these committees would be a steering committee. A steering committee is composed of teachers from each discipline or team within the school, the building principal, two or three middle school students, and two or three parents. This committee serves as a direct communication link between parents and students and teachers and principal. The steering committee might ask the question, "How can we better meet the needs of middle school students?" A brainstorming session can take place weekly to arrive at various answers to this question. Proposed changes would then be suggested. The committee would communicate the recommended rearrangements to the school staff. By keying in on one particular need, the staff and principal combined can design a meaningful staff development program.

The second committee would be a curriculum advisory council at the district level. This council would be composed of teachers at all levels, from elementary and high schools as well as from other middle schools. The council would increase the flow of information between teachers and central office personnel. Communication lines both upward and downward would be improved. Members of the council would get constant feedback from their respective staffs concerning in-service needs.

Although many middle schools schedule the building level steering committee and curriculum advisory council meetings prior to or after school, the trend is to provide released time for meeting during the school day. This time can be covered by other teachers on the teaching team taking up the slack, thereby freeing the committee members. However, a more realistic practice is for school systems to provide paid substitutes on a regular basis to fill in for teachers who serve on these committees. Other school systems may provide additional pay with no released time for such teachers. Although the teachers appreciate the extra pay, it is doubtful that anyone can be as productive after interacting with students for a full day as they would be earlier in the day. Other solutions might see summer employment for committees to interact and to react, with professional growth credit.

To fully implement the ideas and changes advocated by the professional staff, students, and parents, considerable time may be required. The delay in bringing about change is not always due to a lack of information or a shortage of funds. Many times the delay is due to the necessity of changing attitudes and values of teachers. It is foolish to proceed with a change before the staff is receptive to it. One key to successful implementation of any innovation is staff commitment.

It should be kept in mind that in any school system staff development may take considerable time. Martha Dawson, in speaking about the movement to a nongraded or continuous progress program, states that a minimum of two years should be devoted to

orientation and study prior to the initiation of a nongraded program (87). She states that if there is to be an adjustment in time,
it should be extended rather than shortened. Her justification for
this is that the American educational scene is full of schools that
are nongraded in name but are in practice extremely rigid, perhaps more so than the many schools that do not wear a "nongraded" label. Dawson further states that there are many schools
that have launched premature nongraded programs and suddenly
have found themselves at an educational impasse, after which
the staffs revert back to their original patterns. Therefore, she
believes that there is strong evidence that the likelihood of having a highly successful program that allows for individual differences and continuous progress is much greater when ample
time is given to study and orientation prior to the initiation of a
nongraded program.

Certainly the two-year minimum time requirement for nongraded schools, as recommended by Dawson, would not pertain to
all changes. However, the importance of ample time to study a
program and to properly provide for staff development is well
taken. If a staff, the student body, and parents are not ready to

see a program initiated, that program stands a great chance of failure. Once failure has occurred the staff will probably be much less receptive to any change.

Many programs will not be as successful initially as one would hope. One should be receptive to changes, provide for proper staff development, and then realize that many *small* failures may occur along the way. Sometimes, failure is the best way to progress. It is the *complete* failures that develop into chaotic and highly undesirable situations that may stifle future creativity. Small mistakes are likely to occur and may be beneficial; big mistakes should be eliminated by proper staff development.

Staff Development For
Humanizing Education

One of the most valid reasons for in-service training and staff development is to work on practices and self-improvement techniques that will foster a more humanistic approach within the middle schools. The need for a more humanistic approach can be demonstrated through such practices as interaction analysis, where teachers listen to themselves and to their classes on an audio tape recorder; through video tape replay; and through students and teachers conferring openly. Whenever teachers can see themselves as they are with children, the need for further in-service training is evident.

If teachers should learn through audio/video tape replays that they are coercive or sarcastic in their responses to students, they will welcome a chance for staff development work. Many times teachers do not realize that they have behaved in a negative way. If teachers find that they are not as encouraging as they should be, that they are not as optimistic as they should be, if they are not as self-respecting and self-accepting as is desirable, if they are not in general making each child feel that he has personal value and worth — then in-service sessions to change staff attitudes are needed and vital.

One may look at a teacher who exhibits negative attitudes toward students and say, "That is her problem. It is her responsibility to see the changes that she should make and to make them herself." One might say, "If a teacher is more negative than positive, she should not be a middle school teacher." Both of these approaches are pessimistic. Such responses assume that teachers are always aware of how they relate to and are perceived by students and are able to change their own behavior. Self-improvement is difficult; self-analysis, without a specific technique, is impossible. The following techniques are suggested:

1. Consult with the principal and/or fellow teachers and ask the question, "What am I doing *to* children rather than for or with children?" This might expose what effect one actually has on students. Verbalizing helps one understand how he is perceived by others. An open and free climate where a teacher feels that she can talk about difficulties without being defensive is a great asset to staff development.

2. Sitting down with a team member and/or principal and listening and viewing one's actions via video tape may make one aware of certain changes in behavior that are needed. It is helpful if the teacher can identify needed changes herself rather than having another person call the weaknesses to her attention. Once the teacher is aware of incorrect behavior, the consultant, team members, and/or principal may be able to provide constructive suggestions.

3. Staff development through role playing may be very helpful. Role playing can be done without pointing a finger at any one individual. The purpose is to have a situation portrayed so vividly that teachers can see behavior that needs to be modified through their own efforts or through team efforts.

4. Commercially prepared case studies or those that teachers write themselves may be helpful. The situations may be very real and should help the teacher analyze the behavior of people in the case studies. After analyzing a case, teachers may be able to see themselves in similar situations. Self-awareness of difficulties must occur before any improvement can take place. If teachers do not see the need to change their be-

havior but are forced to change anyway, only superficial changes will occur.

5. Questionnaires designed to gather student opinion may assist in the identification of communication gaps between teachers and students. The questionnaire should be so constructed that the student can respond openly and honestly. For example, students and teachers often see things quite differently. A staff may perceive an open school environment while the students perceive a closed environment.

6. Some people may benefit from viewing and analyzing a film that presents problems that relate to humanizing education. Others might benefit by reading outstanding texts on humanizing education, viewing certain transparencies, listening to particular records, or hearing tapes of a dynamic speaker. In all cases it is profitable for teachers to discuss what they have read, seen, or head. Verbalizing will aid understanding.

Certainly staff development and in-service training are essential in all areas. A professional staff must be encouraged to search for innovative practices that will improve the learning program. Once innovations are identified, an in-service program should be designed to help the staff successfully implement them. A search for better ways of doing things necessitates a complete evaluation of what one is presently doing. A middle school that is exciting and stimulating will encourage a positive attitude toward change and will necessitate staff development. Only through staff development and a strong in-service program can successful changes be made.

If changes that are advocated in the middle school are to be lasting and worthwhile, all of the staff who will be affected by the change must be involved in the decision-making process. It is not required that a staff have 100 percent agreement before any change is initiated. However, any proposed change must be accepted by all those in leadership positions.

If changes are to occur, superintendents, central office personnel, and principals must be willing to delegate authority. The delegation of certain responsibilities will give teachers a better outlook on the change; they are more likely to view a proposed innovation as *their* change and work harder for its success. If an innovation is viewed as having originated at the superintendent's level, teachers will less likely share the discomforts of frustrations and anxieties that may occur when things do not go as smoothly as one would like. A sharing of responsibilities by administrators and teachers will lead to commitment. Teachers, in turn, will encourage other teachers to share their commitment. Consultant services, travel, and financial assistance for staff development must also be provided. If support is provided, rearrangements will more likely be accepted by the total staff.

Staff development during in-service sessions goes beyond the professional staff. Students and their parents must also view a change as being desirable and having merit. Therefore, it is best to have teachers, students, and parents informed at the very beginning of a planned innovation and to assist the successful implementation of the program if they are involved from the start. Parents can advise the professional staff on the proper timing of a change since they will not only know their own views and the views of their children, but many times the views of their neighbors and friends as well. Most individuals are more receptive to ideas if they have had the opportunity to express their views and feel that their opinions have been considered.

Some school systems involve parents only at a very superficial level. School personnel may have in the backs of their minds the need to involve students and their parents so that levies can be passed to fund certain programs within the middle school or so that bond issues can be approved. Although it is important to get support for levies and bond issues, it is wrong to "use" people for this reason only. Students and parents have a right to determine if certain programs are desirable and advisable since they will be directly affected. One may argue that a professional staff has been employed to investigate certain programs and to recommend changes. This is true; however, parents should certainly have the privilege of expressing their opinions. Educators should encourage involvement that will assist free and open communication. Total commitment by all — students, parents, and educators — will permit such a program.

Part 4

Student Outcomes

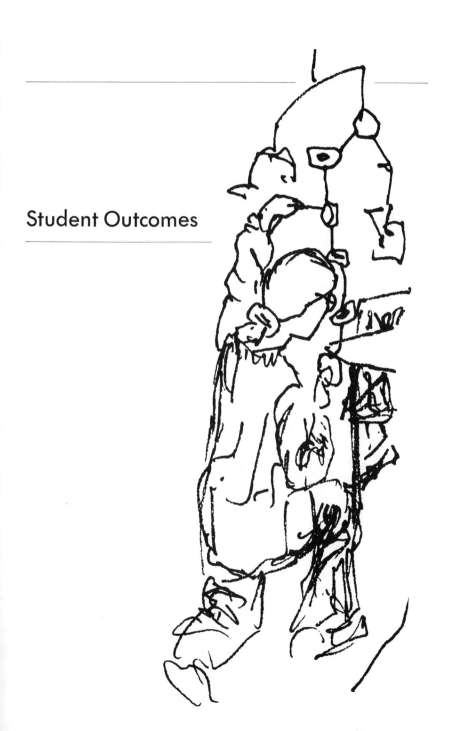

Chapter 15

Learning How to
Learn Independence
and Self-Reliance

Getting youth to think for themselves and to rely on their own judgment have long been goals of American education. In the middle schools of today and of tomorrow, it is imperative that we plan opportunities for students to learn how to learn and to become confident of their ability and judgment.

Attitudes play a very important part in determining whether a student develops the ability to learn on his own. Teachers and parents do influence attitudes toward learning. Robert Mager reacted to this by stating:

> One of the important goals of teaching is to prepare the student to use the skills and knowledge he has learned to prepare him to learn more about the subjects he has been taught. One way of reaching this goal is to send the student away from the learning experience with a tendency to approach, rather than avoid, a subject of study (191:5).

If we can get middle school students to approach learning eagerly, we will have come a long way in developing the confidence students must have to rely on themselves for the learning sequence.

Certainly we would be ridiculously optimistic to assume that all middle school youth can learn on their own, completely independent, with little assistance from the teachers. We are not suggesting that this even be a goal of the middle school. We are implying that every middle school student should be given the opportunity to become independent and should not have to rely on the professional staff to provide direction for every move.

Forces in Opposition to
Self-Reliance and Independence

Before any middle school staff can attack the problem of what must be changed to permit students to rely more on themselves and to gain independence, they must first ask the question, "What are we doing now that is in opposition to these needs?" An analysis might reveal that some of the approaches that are presently used would stifle any change that might be advocated by the staff. Some of the forces prohibiting middle school students from gaining independence and self-reliance are given here.

1. Traditional teacher roles of
lecturer or presenter.

If a teacher sees her role as possessor of all knowledge and primary generator of the learning process, students will not have the opportunity to become independent and to rely on their own volition to explore new and different areas of learning. Certainly there are times when a presentation is given by a teacher to stimulate the inquiry process and present information that is not accessible to students. A motivational presentation may get students excited about an area and inspire them to study the area in depth. Once a student becomes excited about a certain topic the teacher should guide and facilitate learning rather than dominate.

2. A threat to the traditional
image of the teacher.

Some teachers may feel that students do not possess the ability or maturity to determine their own needs or to know what is best for them. If the teacher's role is not to determine student needs, then teachers may feel a loss of prestige and importance. Teachers may look at the student determining some of his own needs as a threatening situation because student independence is translated to mean disregard of teacher opinion.

3. Students lack the maturity to
   make certain decisions.

Most educators would agree that students must make certain decisions about their education. There is considerable disagreement about what decisions students should make, at what age or at what level of maturity. Independence and self-reliance do not magically appear at age eighteen or twenty-one or on completion of high school. Independence and self-reliance are gained slowly through many years and are not realized at one point in time by all students. The argument that students of middle school age are not mature enough to help determine some of their own needs is in direct opposition to self-reliance and independence.

4. Time is too precious.

Many practices in schools are based on the clock. Some educators feel that there is not enough time for independent study activities. There is not enough time to diagnose the unique needs of a student. There is not enough time to sit down with students and explore the question, "What are the unique needs of this individual student, and how can our team best meet his needs?" The most important priority might be to assist the students in becoming independent and in gaining self-reliance. If students can learn how to learn and rely on their own intellectual powers, our jobs as teachers will be fulfilled.

5. Reliance on a single source.

If a single textbook is the primary instructional resource and if all test material comes from the textbook, students are not likely to gain independence, nor will they learn to look for other sources of information upon which to base their decisions. Education for the student must be more than simply reading the text, listening to the teacher, and answering test questions. Students have little to discuss in a small group when rewarded by grades or teacher approval based upon ability to repeat or memorize a single textbook or lecture.

6. Homogeneous grouping practices.

The practice of grouping students of like ability makes no more sense than grouping students based upon the color of their eyes. Many teachers feel homogeneous grouping enables them to have all the bright students in one class, all the average students in another class, and all the dull students in a third class. If we are looking for grouping patterns that foster self-reliance through the development of self-concept, homogeneous grouping does not often meet this need. Homogeneous grouping certainly does not enhance the self-concept or increase the confidence of students in the lower two groups. The practice of not permitting students to interact with students of various ability levels lacks the humaneness that the middle school should be striving to accomplish.

In addition to these six forces operating in opposition to self-reliance and independence, Mager has identified nine practices that not only oppose independence and self-reliance but also affect the humaneness of a school (191:53-54). The following procedures that Mager has identified lower student pride and self-respect by humiliation and embarrassment:

1. Publicly comparing a student unfavorably with others.
2. Laughing at a student's efforts.
3. Spotlighting a student's weaknesses by bringing them to the attention of the class.
4. Making a student wear a badge of his "stupidity" (putting him in a special seat or section, for example).
5. Belittling a student's attempt to approach a subject by such replies to his questions as "Stop trying to show off."

6. Insulting a student for his attempt to approach the subject by such comments as, "You couldn't possibly understand the answer to that question," or otherwise telling him by word or deed that his questions are considered stupid.
7. Repeated failure.
8. The "special class" set up for students the teacher is not competent enough to handle. Students are singled out and sent to another place for a variety of remedial treatment. They are branded as "different" and somehow inadequate.
9. A common elementary school practice leading to humiliation and embarrassment frequently occurs after a teacher has asked the class a question.

In this last case Mager is referring to the student who is eager to answer a question and, in his enthusiasm, lets the answer slip out of his mouth while frantically waving his hand. He states that the consequence is that the student is reprimanded because he did not wait until he was called upon. Certainly this approach along with the other eight possible conditions would do much to reduce the effort to learn independently and to rely on oneself.

Encouraging Self-Reliance

It is vital that a middle school staff identify the practices that lead to self-reliance and independence. What experiences can a middle school permit, provide, and construct that will increase a student's confidence, improve his self-image, stimulate him to work on his own, and generally provide the kinds of experiences that are greatly needed in any educational program?

Learning Rates and Style

Each middle school student differs from every other student. Each student has a different capacity, different needs, and different interests. These differences change, not only over a long period of time, but change on a day-to-day basis. Student concern at a particular time about peer relationships, erratic growth concerns, or body development might take precedent for a day or more over academic concerns. These different concerns provide sign posts for providing a student with some control over the rate of learning.

Students learn in many ways. Middle school students should have the opportunity and the freedom to make many of their own decisions. It is recognized that within freedom, responsibility must be accepted. When students are given freedom and responsibility to choose many of their own learning situations and to structure their own time, they must also accept responsibility for their own behavior and their own decisions. The middle school staff may continually guide and advise a student, but it need not make every decision for him.

Individualizing instruction is a way teachers work with students. Middle school staffs must take student differences into consideration and allow each student to develop specialized skills and competencies. Indeed, each student does hear a "different drummer," and we must consider individual differences as assets, not liabilities. A middle school student must be afforded every opportunity to continue learning at a rate that is appropriate for him. Continuous progress affects the behavior and motivational development of a student.

If students are permitted to learn at varying rates, a different role will exist for the innovative middle school teacher compared with the traditional teacher. Teachers themselves will function in a variety of roles. Considerably more emphasis will be placed on such activities as listening, asking questions, and advising. Less emphasis will be placed on telling and directing, the traditional role of the past. Teachers will be more cognizant of, and sensitive to, the factors that affect pupil motivation and learning rates.

Readiness plays a very important part in learning rates, and readiness necessitates frequent diagnostic evaluation procedures. The new role of the middle school teacher will make it mandatory that teachers know more about the students, that they may be able to identify the many concerns that influence the rate at which students are ready to learn and the degree to which they do learn.

Group Projects and Interaction

The learning situation must guide the student to collect data, to generalize, to try out solutions in problem solving, and to act on the facts. Learning situations must be so designed that they guide a student to work with others for a common good. The process of cooperating to achieve responsible, orderly change is a valuable experience.

Every person must learn to interact with others. Some people connected with education place great emphasis on the interaction process. Rudolf Dreikurs concurs with this when he states:

> Many teachers treat each child as individually responsible, assigning tasks according to his performance, viewing shortcomings as an individual matter. The child is thus systematically oriented to standing on his own feet, and rising and falling according to personal achievement only. He is not directed toward facing problems in a social context or developing plans for solving them with others. This emphasis on independent action has many harmful effects. The more a child succeeds in learning exclusively by and for himself, the greater is the loss to him as an individual (93:77).

Middle school students do learn effectively from one another. They can assist each other in developing understanding and mastery in many learning areas. The experienced students can assist the inexperienced students. One student helping another student facilitates and enriches the learning experiences of both students.

Having experienced students assist inexperienced students and having high performers assist students who are having difficulty may lead educators to ask such questions as, "Are we expecting middle school students to become teachers?" or, "Should we be concerned about the student taking another student's answers rather than working them out for himself?" Teaching is an excellent way of learning. One student helping another student is not immoral or wrong. Learning together and cooperating to accomplish an objective should be encouraged. If teachers require "busy work" then there is a temptation to "copy" just to have so many pages or problems completed. When students are rewarded for mastery and for quality not quantity, then one learner assisting another learner is most acceptable.

Many students will also assist others and in a sense become teachers. This is not just true of the glib, verbal students who understand a process but may include all students from time to time. This is particularly true if multiage grouping and variable sequencing of learning tasks is considerable. Students may learn better by working with other students, sharing work, and becoming teachers themselves. Certainly, students will learn how to express themselves better through the process of helping others.

The small group provides an excellent opportunity for students to interact with one another. For example, it is possible through the group process to magnify the chances for pupil-teacher interaction as well as pupil-pupil interation. Small group interaction also encourages pupil self-initiated action. Group activity permits the teacher to see the student as an individual learner and enables each student to contribute uniquely to the group activity.

Middle school students who are exposed to a variety of student contacts in a free-flowing environment may see a cultural backdrop against which they can form their own pattern of concepts. Students can greatly benefit from the interaction that takes place with other students. They can also benefit by the interaction that takes place with pupil and teacher or with teachers who represent a varied set of academic backgrounds and teaching styles.

The degree to which students work on group projects and converse with others depends on many factors such as the students' learning styles and the skills of teachers. The goal of small group work is to help the student develop a spirit of inquiry that will lead him away from dependence on the teacher and toward independent learning. As an essential part of his educational development, each student is involved in a personal decision-making process. Motivation and a commitment to encourage group projects and small group activities must frequently be provided by the professional middle school staff. Group interaction must be more than an incidental matter in the behavior of a student. Group projects must be encouraged and carefully planned.

Student Choice of
What and How to Learn

In the middle school, teachers must expect an individual standard, not a group standard. A predetermined sequence of assignment, lecture, recitation, and testing is no longer acceptable. A rigid sequence is inconsistent with what educators know about how students learn. The middle school staff strives for a different learning program for each learner. The learning program is determined by teacher evaluation and diagnosis and student involvement.

Some educators may question student involvement in determining the learning program. Teachers may interpret "involvement" as turning students loose to direct their own learning. Thorwald Esbensen would reject such an interpretation. He believes that structuring an educational program is not such a simple matter that can allow students to completely control their own learning. Instead, he indicates that teachers need to provide a variety of learning activities that are highly motivational, that provide enough self-instructional devices to ease the problem of classroom management, that accommodate a wide range of individual differences, and that encourage the accomplishment of worthy objectives. Esbensen also indicates that moving toward self-directed learning is ideal, but that this movement must be in stages, moving gradually from teacher-directed to self-directed activities (105:75).

Students learn from experience. It is through involvement that the student experiences, expresses, relates, learns, and develops his own potentialities. Learning is exploration and discovery for personal meaning. By individualizing instruction, each student can work on projects that hold some interest for him and perform on a level that is challenging without being overwhelming.

Teachers should carefully reflect on their own beliefs about individualizing instruction to see if they actually subscribe to individualizing instruction to the extent that their beliefs are operational in the school. Individualizing instruction for some means that everyone should do the same thing at different times. It should be questioned whether all students should learn the same thing, or if different students should learn some different things related to their interests and their needs.

An enjoyable but frustrating experience is listing all of the concepts and skills that one expects all students to master. Once this has been done, a teacher can carefully analyze the list to see if, indeed, all students do need to master all items on the list. The number of concepts and skills that are essential for all students is probably far less than we ever imagined in the past. The idea that students should design their own learning sequence is not a radical idea.

Giving the middle school student some choice in determining his learning program provides the very essential ingredient of involvement. Positive involvement is provided through choices. It should be the student's choice of reviewing a film that identifies a single concept, or listening to a tape that has been prepared by a teacher, or doing other activity that meets his personal learning needs at a particular time. Teachers must work closely with the students during the learning sequence so that students develop confidence. This does not mean that the teacher makes all the choices concerning sequence and subject matter. The teacher merely assists the student by helping him know where he has been and where he is going so that he can select the best sequence for himself.

A student develops his own study assignments with the teacher and uses the teacher as a resource person rather than the director of study. The middle school teacher becomes a sounding board for ideas. Teachers offer options and ask questions that will assist the student along his way. A student is encouraged to establish his own learning program and he helps to evaluate his own work.

Varied Sources for Learning

The middle school student must be able to learn and work with materials most appropriate for his learning style. A staff recognizes that not all students learn through reading and writing and listening. Various media should be available so that a student may avail himself of the media that is most appropriate for him.

If the student does not discover knowledge for himself day after day, if education does not come alive for him, then he is not truly gaining knowledge. Many students think knowledge already exists out there in the world somewhere, and the business of learning is just getting answers by looking in books or asking the teacher. This is an inadequate conclusion for today's world. It should be our goal to help the student discover how to keep on learning and growing. If the student learns to reason and solve problems, hopefully he will become a lifelong learner. After the student has explored a given subject, he will continue to learn and to explore other subjects long after leaving the direction of a teacher. At the end of middle school experiences, the staff should be able to say that students have found potentials, have learned concepts, and have discovered values and satisfactions that were closed to them before they entered the middle school.

Different sources for learning may include media such as film-strips, video tapes, or models. Other media might include reading materials at various levels of reading difficulty. Permitting students to use and select different sources will encourage independence and self-reliance. A contract might be established between the student and the teacher that is *student made* and *student assigned*. Such contracts would encourage a student to use various sources for learning those things that are of special interest to him.

Learning Through Mistakes

Learning experiences for middle school students should be characterized by continuity and a voluntary action to reassess, to re-examine, or to recycle concepts that have not been mastered to the degree that is desirable. The teacher assists the student in accomplishing certain tasks at certain levels whenever he is ready for them. Perhaps, a more important role for the teacher is to encourage the child and to convince him that everyone can and does learn by making mistakes. The purpose is not to encourage mistakes but to develop a self-realization that mistakes can and do occur.

Middle school teachers should not produce anxiety by traditional tactics such as lowering a student's grade when he makes mistakes or becoming overly concerned about his doing something only one way. Teacher techniques must not bring about insecurity in students. Student insecurity results in more and more reliance on a teacher's directions and less on his own ability. Independence and self-reliance cannot be fostered through anxiety-producing approaches. The student's self-concept must permit him to rely on his own judgment with the realization that small mistakes will be made and that he can profit from such mistakes.

Encouraging Creativity

The uniqueness of the middle school student is evidenced by what the student perceives and how he chooses to perceive. The middle school staff should establish an environment that would encourage freedom of choices. At times, a student should be permitted to go in a nonspecific direction. Students can be encouraged to think creatively with themes in language arts, in art while painting a picture or constructing a model, in industrial arts while deciding on a pattern for a woodworking project, and in every discipline in the school. Inductive or discovery approaches can enhance the creative approach within a middle school. Teachers must give students every opportunity to make choices.

If a teacher were to give a student choices and then veto the choices, creativity would be discouraged. Teachers should not ask a student to think critically and then reprimand him when his thinking does not agree with theirs. One must not speak of independence and then repress a student when his independence causes frustration for adults. Instead, we do encourage creativity within the middle school and accept the creative approach.

Dealing with Reality

A student must be guided in the learning process; he should be encouraged to ask questions and to learn how to organize information and to draw generalizations from his information. Emphasis must be placed upon inquiry and the process of learning. To exercise this process of learning, the middle school student should have the opportunity to select from a wide field ideas and concepts for study that are relevant and have meaning to him.

Encountering Daily Success

If the student is to achieve a high self-concept, success must be experienced regularly. All students do not need the same amount of time to learn a specific concept nor do all students come to school with equal backgrounds or talents. The students who take longer to learn a specific concept or those students who come to school with a background in which learning has not been important should not be penalized or meet with failure in school. All students must experience success.

Students must meet daily success. Many school practices in the past have not subscribed to this concept. Tests were frequently used to tell students what they did not know rather than what they did know. All students were compared with a class or a grade norm. It should be recognized that each student lives and learns differently. There should be no failure; little is accomplished by failing students. When success is experienced, performance increases. A student learns more effectively and more enthusiastically when attention is given to what he can do rather than what he cannot do.

It is difficult to keep from doing things for students that they can do for themselves. At times, it is very difficult to let students grow up and try out new experiences. But try them out they must — if they are going to develop into independent, responsible individuals who have confidence in their own abilities and who are pleased with themselves. The job of the parent is to assist the child in becoming independent so that the child can operate on his own and make correct decisions in new experiences. The same is true with the middle school staff. It is really the job of a teacher to guide the student to the point where he does not need a teacher.

Teachers sometimes find it difficult to let students do things for themselves even though they are quite capable. It is much easier to step in and do for the student. But the students must get on with the business of becoming independent learners and should not rely on a teacher for learning. The middle school staff must maintain confidence in students' ability to manage successfully much of their learning and to take an active part in the learning process.

Summary

Believing in individualizing instruction is not adequate. This is a general term that most can accept. The middle school staff must make individualizing instruction operational. With future research and additional knowledge about middle school students, beliefs about how students learn may change; but for now, the concepts discussed in this chapter should serve as a basis for the middle school staff to formulate its own list of beliefs about students and the learning process.

The total emphasis of the school should be upon developing the individual. The primary emphasis must not be solely on content and skill, though these are necessary. Certainly students must be able to read, to write, and to master certain mathematical skills. But equally important is an environment in which the student can develop a respect for his own worth and the unique qualities and rights of others.

There may be some idealism expressed in the statements about how middle school students learn independence and self-reliance. Assuming a personal responsibility for one's own learning is not an easy task and does not begin in the first year of middle school. The behavior transition from dependence and reliance to independence and self-reliance is a trying experience for any student. It is equally difficult for teachers to make the transition possible. This may be especially true when all ranges of pupil capabilities are considered in the total middle school context.

Chapter 16

Student Involvement

"Student power." "Freedom." "Dissent and disruption in schools." "Activism." "Relevant curriculum." "Stop the war." "My rights." "Dress codes." "Underground newspapers." These are no longer words or phrases heard just on the college campus or in the secondary schools; they have now filtered down into certain middle schools.

America has entered an era of individual rights, and it is evident that secondary schools are being seriously affected. It is also increasingly evident that middle schools are or soon will be affected. The new freedoms have been and probably will be debated for some time. The middle school administrator and the middle school staff cannot wait for final answers on what are correct actions and how we should adjust the school to this new era. The middle school must adapt now to the demands of society and reflect the social changes that take place.

A staff should encourage students to become concerned about their community and about their nation. Becoming concerned does not mean simply pointing out the faults. The focus should be on proposing constructive solutions to problems and outlining what students as individuals can do to improve the community or the nation.

Some students are so interested in boy friends or girl friends, sports, or their own interests, that they find little time for the issue of "student involvement." Noninvolvement in the decision-making process takes the form of boredom, or the idea that school is not a particularly exciting place to be. Many middle school students, however, want to be participants in education and not just recipients of it. Often students in their seventh and eighth years of school tell us they want to be involved in the decision-making process.

In some middle schools students have shown some of the same characteristics of student activism previously displayed by college or secondary school students. One author witnessed a student walkout in a middle school. When students were asked why they had disrupted classes and what point they were trying to make they replied, "Some high school students helped us plan it (the walkout) and we thought it would be fun." By thoughtful planning this example of student activism could have been channeled into a dynamic and positive outlet.

Legal Trends

On February 24, 1969, the Supreme Court delivered an opinion in the case of *Tinker v. Des Moines School District*. The Court's decision is that the First Amendment applies to students as well as to adults (90:5-7). The rights guaranteed by the First Amendment must apply to the school environment. In light of this decision it is now highly improbable that schools can enforce dress codes, limit the length of students' hair, or outlaw underground newspapers.

Even if a middle school staff could legally control students' dress, censor a school newspaper, or carry out reasonable locker searches, they would probably reject these methods. Such actions treat the middle school student as an irresponsible and completely immature adolescent, without the emotional or intellectual readiness to assume responsibility.

Before a staff can formulate any guidelines to student involvement the real question might be to first decide what kind of school it wants to operate. Perhaps it is inappropriate to ask "How do we deal with activism in the middle school?" "How do we deal with activism" implies that we want to coerce or to repress or to control student energy, student concern, and student involvement. The question that a middle school staff should consider is, "How can we, as a staff, help students to become more involved in school?" What sort of activities can be constructed to both educate and interest students? How can the student government be structured so that every student becomes committed to his school and his community?

The belief that we learn most by doing is not new. Let us consider student involvement as a desirable approach to learning. Involvement is a key. That which is heard is short lived, but that which is experienced is learned so that it becomes a part of a person. It is involvement, which is lasting, that the middle school must try to make available to the students.

It might be that viewing the involved student and how to channel his energies is not the appropriate focus. In many middle schools the number of students who are noticeably active is very small. Perhaps a middle school staff should consider itself fortunate if 5 or 10 percent of the students are concerned enough to become active in one form or another. Perhaps then the real question that we are concerned with is, "How do we assist students to become more concerned about their school, and how do we encourage concerned students to become involved?"

Any student involvement must, of course, conform to building regulations, school board regulations, and state laws. A middle school staff cannot change state rules and regulations overnight, but the staff can significantly alter building rules and regulations where they need changing. Hall passes, library passes, cafeteria rules, and dress codes are examples of building regulations that must be thoughtfully reviewed by the middle school staff. These restrictive regulations must be reviewed with the goal of humanizing education. A good yardstick to use in evaluating present rules is to think, "How would I like this rule if I were the student?"

The Delegation of
Responsibilities to Students

Perhaps delegating responsibilities to students does involve some risk, but this is to be expected. Whenever delegation is made there is some risk that the other person will not carry out his part of the job. Perhaps a student will not carry out his responsibilities in the same way a staff member would. Therefore, the middle school staff must give the student the right to be individual in his approach to goals. If the goal is clear, then acceptable methods of reaching the goal do not have to be static. Accepting different methods is always good in theory, but most difficult in practice.

The staff must be willing to delegate responsibility. For so long the acceptable role of the teacher has been to do things for students they could do for themselves that teachers are reluctant to surrender this practice in the classroom. Delegation of power makes the teacher insecure because delegation is interpreted to mean the teacher has less control of any situation. When teachers delegate they are not losing control. Helping a student gain independence by allowing him to exercise some control over his learning program is simply good educational practice.

Students are fearful to take the lead. The "teacher's pet" image has too long been the label of the active helper. It is not easy to convince students that they are ready to assume an active part in the classroom. Anytime role changes take place there can be a transition period when roles are not clear and confusion or disorder prevails. Some disorder and confusion may be natural until students adjust to a new learning environment.

Middle school personnel must not only permit but must also encourage students to work on social problems relevant to our present culture. Students should have more opportunity in school to discuss freely any topic that concerns them, no matter how controversial or innovative. Responsible participation within the ability of their age range, feeling that they have a place in and are a part of the community, provides students with sound preparation for life in a democratic society.

Student Government

The student council represents one of the best agencies in the school for putting into practice all the objectives for democratic citizenship. A creative middle school staff does not view the student council as an elected organization, controlled by the administration or by the student council sponsor. If there is to be a student council, then the middle school staff must honor its power so that the council can — within state laws, school board policy, and building regulations — affect school policy. One problem with student councils in the past has been that the organization never had a specific job to do. Rather than electing one student council to handle all problems, an alternative might be to have a number of ad hoc committees working on specific problems. Once a specific task has been identified, then a committee could be appointed to find creative solutions. As soon as a solution is found that committee is dissolved. New, different committees could be formed whenever another task needed to be done. If a school had a number of ad hoc committees working on specific tasks or specific problems, these committees could be coordinated by the student council. Many ad hoc committees would allow more students to participate.

A middle school staff must seriously consider the organization of student representation. Should the student council be elected from homerooms, or classes, or might there be other types of grouping patterns that would be more realistic? For example, neighborhood patterns might be more meaningful to the students than homerooms. The members of the student council would represent the neighborhoods in which they live rather than the homeroom or a given age level. Structuring student representation by neighborhood might encourage some carryover on projects after school hours in that the students who are assigned to work together are the ones who normally play together in nonschool hours. Whatever grouping pattern is selected for one committee does not have to be kept for all committees.

If a group of students or a student government organization, through a free exchange of ideas and viewpoints with the faculty and administration, does present a written recommendation to the school staff, then such a recommendation must receive serious attention. Assuming the students' request is legitimate, it should be granted. The point is that a middle school staff should honestly review and consider student opinions and not pass them off as part of a childish game. Moreover the middle school staff cannot assume that all is well if they do not hear any complaints from the student body. If there is no dialogue the students could feel that their position has become one of token participation with no real influence. The staff must be sensitive to student needs and should constantly check the pulse of student opinion.

Responsibility and Involvement in the Instructional Process

All instructional activities must be examined for meaning and relevance in the real world of the middle school student. The effective middle school should be committed to student participation and involvement in school life. Involvement implies that the students become active and concerned about life.

Students must be concerned about their community and feel a responsibility toward it. This concern will require students to make suggestions about what they want to study, the kinds of problems they want to consider, and the methods they desire to use in studying the chosen problem. Once students become concerned about their community during school they become involved in their community after school. As students become involved and active, the modes of learning need to be different from what exists in many schools today. If students are to become involved in community problems, perhaps some of their time could best be spent outside of the school on learning activities.

The temptation is always great for middle school staff members to say that they know what is best for students or that students are making poor or wrong choices. When the temptation to make such value judgments occurs, the staff must go back and examine what they believe about school, about the learning process, and what it is they are trying to accomplish in the middle school. Is acquiring facts of paramount concern; or is it the process of education, the involvement of students, and the attitudes of students toward learning that are the real goals? The temptation to reject student opinion and student involvement is just as great for a middle school staff as it is for a parent of a 10 year old. It is temporarily easier to have the student inactive. But when children or students 12 and 13 are active, the parent and staff are forced to work long and hard to channel their energy.

Middle school students have requested independent study programs dealing with problems such as student rebellion, "X" rated movies, race relations, dissent, pros and cons of the Vietnam war, or how a local public official is doing his job. Such topics must be considered by the social studies and language arts teams if the school is going to have a curriculum relevant to student needs. Perhaps both the social studies and English teams will want to conduct seminars on these issues. Individual rights, protest, and dissent are controversial topics, but topics which are of interest to students. Similar concerns in other teaching teams must be dealt with if, indeed, we are to appeal to our students to think and to do.

Communication of Student Opinion and Ideas

Freedom of speech should be encouraged along with responsibility for one's actions. If students can express their ideas to someone who will listen, then the ideas are not nearly as inflammatory as they might first appear. The middle school staff must take time to listen to what students are saying and should allow students to talk out their ideas without automatically condemning or judging.

Listening enhances two-way communication between the students and the middle school staff.

High school students have requested the right to express opinions on issues such as dress codes, the elimination of all forms of physical punishment, student controlled newspapers, greater responsibility and authority for student organizations. They have also questioned the traditional grading policies. Middle school students are becoming increasingly active in many of these areas. There are several reasons for their new found concern for school policy and involvement. The involvement of high school students in determining school policy and certainly the television coverage of college students as they strive to dictate policy on college campuses give middle school students encouragement to be vocal on issues that they are concerned about. Also, many parents feel that their children should begin to take an active part in our school by involvement in student organizations. Many parents encourage their students to question longstanding traditions.

Access to School Personnel

There should be a procedure established for consideration of student problems. If a student feels he has a problem that needs the attention of the principal, he must feel free to contact the principal. Each student should feel that he can make an impact on the school or at least that someone is listening and understands how he feels.

As a two-way communication system becomes operational, students become more knowledgeable and thus more sympathetic to the issues and problems of the school staff. By the same token, as the staff becomes more aware of the students' point of view they have more empathy and can more effectively meet their needs.

Student Activities

Involvement requires that some activities be planned for the benefit of all. Other activities might be elected by those students interested in a particular area. Activities must meet two criteria: first, the special abilities and interests of middle school youth must be considered; second, the activities should be generated by students and teachers working together.

Activities should be provided that will enable middle school students to organize and to make decisions. Many activities are continuations of classroom procedures to develop responsibility, group interaction, and cooperation. Students will naturally be permitted to engage in activities that are meaningful to them. Although an activity may seem stimulating and appropriate by adult standards, it must also seem appropriate to each student. Otherwise, the activity may be wasted time for everyone.

Many hours may be consumed by a team or teams of middle school teachers sitting around and discussing activities that might be appropriate and meaningful to middle school students. They should consider the special needs of students experiencing a period of rapid growth, such as peer adjustment difficulties. Many youth are just beginning to find themselves and to realize their potentials. With the needs of students foremost in mind, many activities could be considered and identified that would be appropriate. The final test before adoption of an activity should be to involve students to determine whether they feel the activity meets their needs. Some activities may be selected entirely by the students with only guidance provided by the staff.

The suggested activities that follow may take place either inside or outside of the school setting. Normal activities such as basketball, football, or other games will not be mentioned.

Activities Out of School

One activity that is very adaptable to the middle school is the "life science center." This activity may vary according to available money and suitable sites.

All students are scheduled for a one week period during their first year of middle school. Groups are heterogeneous with no more than twenty-five boys and girls in each group. Students spend five days and four nights in a learning activity with parents acting as chaperons at night. This is an excellent opportunity to involve parents in the middle school.

Part of the week's activity is the study of relationships between plants and animals and their environments. Students deal with concepts of nature by examining animals and plants in their natural environment. "What happens when you cut down a forest?" and "What is the result of killing off all of an animal's predators?" are typical of the questions that the students will attempt to answer. Hopefully, they will discover that ecology is a useful aid in interpreting the world of life around them.

The director of the center and a teacher act as activity group observers in answering the above questions. The staff may also assist students in debating questions related to establishing a value system. A question of this type might be, "Should the United States government spend more money on pollution control or space travel?" The students have an opportunity to interact with others of varying interests and abilities in an atmosphere of relaxation. Questions debated in such an environment help the student establish his own value system and at the same time develop his personality.

Many middle school students are undergoing a social development challenge. The life science center enhances middle school efforts toward social development. Many of the activities at the life science center require the cooperation of all students. The students must work together and assume responsibility for making their own beds every morning. The challenge of having the neatest dorms develops a strong esprit de corps among students. A student is encouraged to assume the responsibility for the group as well as for himself.

Cooperation and responsibility are emphasized by having students take turns setting the table, clearing up after meals, and acting as host and hostess for the group. Students do learning activity packages on ecology and environment. They take nature hikes to identify trees, to examine rocks and fossils in the area, and to observe animal life. There is also time to participate in sports and games and, in general, to enjoy a relaxed atmosphere conducive to the development of strong peer relationships.

Activities in School

An activity that may be included during the school day is a "great book seminar." Usually a seminar is thought of as an activity that is appropriate at the senior high level, but this one may be incorporated in the middle school with considerable success.

The seminar can be structured in many ways. One way begins with the teacher and students selecting appropriate literature. These books are not included in any of the regular curriculum. Students who are interested in joining the group read the books on a time schedule. At intervals each book is discussed with either a teacher, a parent, or a student leader. Each student is encouraged to express the ideas and impressions he received from the book. Students can benefit from the great book seminar by learning how to interpret feelings, impressions, and ideas as presented in a book. They may also gain good listening and speaking skills through group interaction.

Another activity that can easily be included during school hours is the career day. Students are introduced to many careers and are encouraged to seek information about those career areas in which they are most interested.

Activities in the middle school are varied and each activity has many purposes. Activities assist a student to better understand himself, his peers, and the world around him. Through this understanding and the interrelationships of all people, the middle school student becomes a more complete individual.

The following student clubs are enjoyed by the students in the middle school of Independent School District No. 413, Marshall, Minnesota, Norman G. Olsen, principal (219). The clubs are scheduled four times during the year and each club meets a total of five times.

1. Girls' Shop Club
   Students in this club work with wood and metal in building a project.
2. Boys' Chef Club
   Students in this club learn to make popcorn balls, bacon and pancakes, sloppy joes, cookies, bacon and eggs, cheesedogs, cocoa, brownies, and pizza.
3. Arts and Crafts
   Students in this club work on art projects that include tissue paper mobiles; bleach-out designs on cloth; wall hangings of burlap, yarn, and felt; psychedelic designs, using magic marker; tie dyeing, using facial tissue; and string-starch-balloon shapes.

4. Extended Physical Education

   Open to boys only. Activities include volley-
   ball; crab soccer; ping pong; dodgeball; bad-
   minton; box hockey; hiking; sledding and
   tobogganing, if possible; and other activities
   in which there is an interest by the boys and
   for which facilities and equipment are available. Boys decide with the club leaders which
   activities should be available each time.

5. Girls' Gymnastics

   Open to girls only. Girls in this club learn
   basic tumbling skills and new techniques as
   one's skill increases. Routines based upon
   skills are planned and developed by each girl.
   These routines are presented to the other
   girls in the class.

6. Hockey

   Open to boys only. Boys in this club must
   have skates and, if possible, a hockey stick.
   Members learn the basic rules and positions
   for ice hockey. Most of the time is spent in
   playing hockey games. Six teams are formed
   into a league. Each team plays one game every session.

7. Journalism

   Students in this club learn about the parts
   of newspapers and how to write for a newspaper. To do this, club members take field
   trips to local newspaper offices and one
   printing shop. They are involved in writing
   newspaper articles for their own newspaper.

8. Story Telling

   Students in this club learn to tell a story in
   an effective and entertaining way. This skill
   is put to use by telling stories and by reading to elderly people in the rest home at the
   hospital.

9. Art Club

   This club is designed to develop creative expression in an art program to fit individual
   needs. Activities include tempera painting;
   water color; printing stations, including veg-
   etable printing, eraser, wood block, and card-
   board printing; carving of soap, wax, and
   combination of soap and wax; use of natural, man-made, and commercial materials
   in making a mural; making a collage; sand
   casting, and casting of lead.

10. Dramatic Arts
   Students in this club learn the basic techniques of play production. One or more plays are produced.

11. Photography
   This club is designed to assist students who are interested in photography. They learn to take pictures and develop pictures and prints. The function of a camera is studied along with various types of cameras.

12. Archery
   This club is designed to help students who are interested in archery learn the techniques of handling a bow and arrow. Demonstrations on technique and safety are provided. There is practice on a regulation archery range in team competition.

13. Radio Club
   The purpose of the radio club is to develop interests of students in areas related to audio-visual aid equipment, ham radio, radio, and TV. Club members operate various types of audio-visual equipment and visit areas of interest such as the high school station, middle school radio shack, and possibly the college facility. Radio club members all take turns operating the radio room. Members have the exclusive privilege of operating this radio room each recreation period.

14. Science Projects Club
   Members in this club are involved in planning, developing, and building projects for the science fair each year. Field trips are taken to science related areas to assist in planning the science projects.

15. Math, Statistics, and Probability Club
   Students who are interested in further exploring the mysteries, puzzles, and structure of statistics and numbers are given an opportunity to do so in an entertaining way. Probability odds in such things as coin flipping are explored.

16. Chess Club
   Students interested in matching wits on the chess board have an opportunity to form a weekly chess league. Ten games are played each week.

17. Tutoring Club
    The students in this club work with younger
    students in elementary schools on a one to
    one basis helping them with reading, math,
    or other areas of school work.

18. Consumer's Club
    This club is designed to help students be-
    come aware of advertising gimmicks, prices
    of different necessary items, and how to uti-
    lize the skills of comparative shopping. An
    attempt is made to involve local merchants
    as resource people and to arrange guided
    comparative shopping trips to local stores.

19. Bowling Club
    Students in this club bowl each week. Teams
    are formed and records kept for high indi-
    vidual games, team games, etc., each week.

By proper planning now a middle school staff can assure themselves that student involvement in the school will be through
evolutionary rather than revolutionary means.

Student governments should be given a significant place in
school affairs. In the past many schools have allowed student governments to participate in insignificant activities which taught
little about assuming responsibility and the democratic process.
Curriculum should be made more meaningful and relevant to students. It is the right of students to expect the best education
possible. Students should be involved in planning activities, suggesting interest areas, and appraising the courses offered by their
school.

The middle school principal should be open to student opinion
and ideas. Students should be free to organize groups within the
school for social, athletic, or other lawful purposes. Discussion of
controversial matters should, in fact, be encouraged. If a school
newspaper exists, it should be an avenue for communication of
student ideas and opinions. Students should realize that freedom
to express one's opinion also carries the responsibility for published statements.

Students should have access to school personnel. The middle
school staff should be available to help students directly with their
problems or concerns. The middle school staff can set up special
student committees through which students can criticize the

establishment or can offer suggestions for improving school life. The school atmosphere must allow a student to take his criticism to the teacher involved.

Student involvement can lead to school improvement when the middle school staff is perceptive and uses insight and understanding in the development of school programs and practices.

Summary

The value of student involvement can be realized only if this involvement is channeled into constructive activities. Students today want their "rights," and they want to have a larger share in the decision-making of the institution that shapes their lives. This *share in decision-making* is frequently translated to mean a desire to study or inquire into areas that might be different from the areas the teacher had in mind. A middle school staff must find ways to develop and guide student concern and desire for inquiry.

Part 5

Facilities

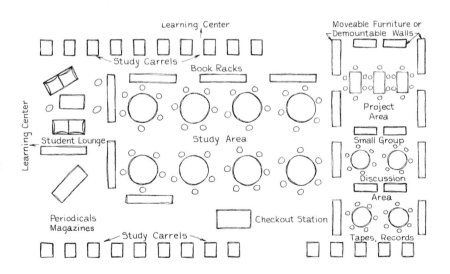

Chapter 17

Procedures for
Initiating Change
in School Facility Design

The new demands for humanizing educational facilities for middle school students mandate the involvement of the teaching staff, administration, board of education, and citizens in the planning process. This chapter will discuss the important aspects of this involvement and will suggest the roles of the participants in planning the facility.

Gathering of Data to Indicate
the Need for a New Facility

Initially the superintendent or administrative team of the school district must do a thorough job of developing a rationale indicating the need for the new middle school facility. The rationale should include enrollment projections for the future, an evaluation of the existing school facilities, the financial situation of the school district, and a recommended plan of action for construction of the building.

Projecting accurate school enrollments over a period of years is very important in planning school building programs. For this reason, many school districts have used the services of consultant experts to compile school population projections for the administration. Consultants will use projection techniques which will consider the preschool census, the average survival ratio which compares birth and school enrollment five or six years later and predicts future enrollments from pupil survival from grade to grade, and saturation studies which include ultimate use of land for homes, probable density per home, and the rate at which homes are being completed.

By applying the data received from the school population projections, the administration of the school may evaluate the existing school facilities to determine their adequacy for housing students. This evaluation should include the number of pupils the facilities can accommodate and the ability of the existing buildings to provide a proper learning environment. For example, are the existing buildings because of their age a hazard to the health and safety of students, are they properly heated and ventilated, and is lighting adequate?

When it is determined that the existing school facilities will not adequately house the school population, the school administration must make a thorough study of the financial situation to determine alternative solutions to the problem. For example, such questions that must be answered are: How much local money must be raised to support the proposed building program? Will it be difficult to convince the average family they can afford the tax increase? What federal funds are available? What state support might be made available? How well has the community supported financial proposals in the past? Are there legal debt limitations?

After the preceding data are assimilated and weighed, the administration will be ready to present a recommended plan of action to the board of education. The plan should provide affirmative answers to the following questions:

1. Does the plan facilitate a desired program?
2. Does the plan provide possible community services?
3. Is the plan a long-range plan?
4. Does the plan utilize existing school facilities to the fullest extent?

5. Does the plan outline in detail the immediate action to be taken?
6. Does the plan provide for adequate and healthful housing of youngsters?
7. Does the plan include possible alternatives?
8. Does the plan consider the financial ability of the district?
9. Will the plan be easily understood by the board of education and the community?

Selecting the Architect, the Educational Specifications Committee, and the Citizens' Committee

The selection of an architect is a task which should not be taken lightly. The best architect ordinarily charges no higher fee than the rest. Obviously, a thorough selection effort should be made in choosing him.

After a preliminary screening process of architects, the board of education will want to conduct interviews with them, view their completed projects, and consult with former clients. Suggested guidelines for evaluating an architect are shown in Figure 9.

Name of Firm _____

Check one:

Good	*Average*	*Weak*	
[ ]	[ ]	[ ]	1. Adequacy of staff.
[ ]	[ ]	[ ]	2. Competent talent to perform on all phases of project.
[ ]	[ ]	[ ]	3. Flexibility of design staff — ability to design for individual program requirements of each client; avoids stereotyped buildings; exhibits fresh ideas.
[ ]	[ ]	[ ]	4. Experience in school design.

Check one:

Good	Average	Weak	
[ ]	[ ]	[ ]	5. Evidence of originality in designing for education program.
[ ]	[ ]	[ ]	6. Understanding of educational process, problems, and changes.
[ ]	[ ]	[ ]	7. Interest in related aspects of the project which are not specifically architectural.
[ ]	[ ]	[ ]	8. Experience in meeting deadlines and time schedules.
[ ]	[ ]	[ ]	9. Integrity and ethics.
[ ]	[ ]	[ ]	10. Exhibits client-oriented business procedures.
[ ]	[ ]	[ ]	11. Sensitivity to "boardmanship," administrative problems, and school-public relations.
[ ]	[ ]	[ ]	12. Evidence of cooperation and compatibility between architect and boards of education.
[ ]	[ ]	[ ]	13. Percentage of clients rehiring architect.
[ ]	[ ]	[ ]	14. Experience and history of working within budget and cost estimates.
[ ]	[ ]	[ ]	15. Sense of economy, knows how and where to effect economy.
[ ]	[ ]	[ ]	16. Concern for maintenance costs expressed in design.
[ ]	[ ]	[ ]	17. Site planning, orientation of building to site, parking to entrance, etc.
[ ]	[ ]	[ ]	18. Attention to detail: student flow within building, relationship of areas, concern for problems of weather (wind, sunlight, outdoor maintenance, etc.).
[ ]	[ ]	[ ]	19. Complete, thorough, and clear drawings and specifications.
[ ]	[ ]	[ ]	20. Procedures during bidding period.
[ ]	[ ]	[ ]	21. Amount, quality, and effectiveness of inspection during construction.
[ ]	[ ]	[ ]	22. Follow-up procedures after completion of construction.

Fig. 9. Guideline for evaluating architect*

When the data pertaining to each item is assimilated and evaluated, the board of education will be ready to select the architect.

*Evaluation criteria developed by Norman McLean for Houston Associates, Architects, Cleveland, Ohio. Reprinted by permission.

The good architectural firm will provide services beyond the designing and the administration of the building project. These services will include evaluation and selection of sites for the buildings, detailed construction cost estimates, appraisals of the existing school facilities, advice on school population projections, and educational consultants or the cost of educational consultants to work with the administration and the teaching staff.

After the architect has been selected, the superintendent, the architects, and the board of education should visit an innovative successful middle school. Proper preplanning should take place prior to the visit. The persons visiting the innovative school should be briefed by the administration on aspects of the school they should consider during the visitation. Aspects to consider would include:

1. Interest Shown by Students in Their School and Program.

Nothing is so convincing as an enthusiastic group of teachers and students. In the successful middle school, visitors have the opportunity to see for themselves the benefits of team teaching and acoustically treated flexible space. They will notice that students appear to be learning and are interested, are not visually distracted in flexible space, and noise factors are not a particular problem.

2. Reaction to a Lack of Windows.

The aesthetic qualities of the building's interior make the lack of windows unnoticeable. Excellent lighting and proper air circulation contribute to a positive reaction by both the students and staff.

3. Freedom of Movement.

Students can flow from one area of the building to another without crowding, shoving, or jolting accompanying the movement. The openness of the building enhances the movement of grouping and regrouping with a minimum of confusion and noise.

4. Wiser Use of Space.

Space normally used for halls in traditional buildings comprises from 20 to 30 percent of the total building square footage. In the compact acoustically treated structure, this space may be eliminated.

Before visiting the innovative school, the school principal can summarize how the program of the school depends upon flexible space to carry out models of instruction which break the content and pace lockstep so familiar to traditional schools. When the representatives visit the school make sure this summarization is explained to their board and citizens. If the person guiding the tour does not emphasize the use of flexible space, one of the group may bring up the subject by directing questions to him such as, "How does the flexible space enhance your program? Could you operate this type of program in a cubicle structure? If not, why not?" The fact is, the school in all likelihood will be meeting the special needs of all its students by utilizing instructional models which would be impossible to employ in the standard inflexible classroom.

When the group has established the need for a new school, selected an architect, and visited one or more innovative middle schools, it will be ready to employ the services of a consultant, to select a "citizens' committee," and appoint an "educational specifications committee."

The citizens' committee's major function should be to communicate occurring changes to the parents of the middle school students and the community. Important points for the citizens' committee include:

1. All segments of the school district should be represented. Power structure, geographic and ethnic groups, and sociological classes must be considered when appointments are made.
2. As many middle school parents as possible should be in the representative group selection.
3. The purpose of the group is to communicate the middle school concept to the community. It should not be a part of the decision-making process for new programs. This function should remain with the professional staff and the board of education.

4. The initial meeting should be called by the board of education. At this time, the superintendent or president of the board of education should chair the meeting, explain the purpose and function of the committee, and provide the committee with information in narrative and written form explaining what the school board is attempting to accomplish by the new approach.
5. A regular meeting time for subsequent citizens' committee meetings is established at their staff meeting.
6. The administration and the staff should give progress reports to the citizens, pass out information, and answer questions as requested by the citizens' committee.
7. The major goal of the citizens' committee should be to disseminate information relative to the change which is taking place or is to take place.

The following suggestions should be considered in selecting the educational specifications committee.

Members of the committee should include (a) the superintendent, (b) the principal, (c) one seventh and one eighth grade teacher from each program area to be offered in the new middle school, (d) two teachers from the sixth grade, and (e) two teachers from the fifth grade if fifth graders are to be housed in the new school.

Selecting the teachers for the educational specifications committee may be done by administrative appointment or by the teaching staff electing representatives. The use of the latter method has the advantage of a greater probability of total staff acceptance of the new middle school concept since they are involved in selecting representatives.

The Role of the Consultant

The consultant's role may be categorized into three phases. *Phase one* will consist of an initial visit to the school system for a two-day period. During this time, the consultant will gather background information for the school district, plan the schedule of meetings to be held with the groups involved in the planning, and meet and present details to the board of education on how the program will be carried out.

The *second phase* of the consultant's role will consist of scheduled meetings with the following groups:

> Group A. One or more meetings with the total school district staff.
>
> Group B. One or more meetings with the selected citizens' committee.
>
> Group C. Scheduled meetings with the administration and board of education.
>
> Group D. Meetings with the educational specifications committee.

The consultant should meet with Groups A, B, and C above to explain to them exactly what is being planned for their school system, why it is being planned, who is going to be involved in programming the change, and how he will be involved in working with the community and staff.

The consultant should meet with the total educational specifications committee and subgroups of the committee on a scheduled basis. The number of meetings held will depend upon the total progress of the group. The meetings of the educational specifications committee must be structured in a manner which allows the committee members to provide the major input into program planning for the new school.

At the conclusion of the initial meeting with the educational specifications committee, the committee should be divided into curricular area subgroups. The consultant should pass out a form to each subgroup which asks their subcommittees to provide the following information:

> 1. What are the goals and objectives of their department, subject, or grade level?
>
> 2. What changes in program or organizing for instruction would their department like to implement?
>
> 3. What kind of activities do they believe should be carried out in teaching their subject?
>
> 4. What are the furniture and equipment needs, types, sizes, and amount of furniture required for each teaching station?

5. What special equipment is required, such as special plumbing facilities, lighting treatment, electrical equipment or ventilation?
6. What are the space requirements (approximate number of square feet) needed to house their curricular programs per teacher station?
7. What should be the special relationships of various activities in their teacher station?
8. Where should their department or teaching station be located in the school?
9. Should any spaces in your curricular area have movable walls?

After the educational specifications committee has received its work assignments, periodic meetings should be scheduled with each subcommittee to discuss various innovative techniques that could be applied in each curricular area, the type of equipment needed in special areas, space requirements for each area, and benefits the students and staff will derive from using a new and different approach to instruction. When the committee has completed several work sessions with the consultant, it is not unusual for the educational specifications committee to be very enthusiastic about the new approaches proposed.

Phase three of the consultant's role involves the consultant assimilating the materials formulated by working with the educational specifications committee and presenting these materials in written form to the architect and the board of education. The educational specifications should contain the following information in this numerical order:

1. The goals and philosophy of the new middle school.
2. The specific goals and objectives of each curricular area and activity in the new middle school.
3. A description of the activities that will occur within the school building and on the school site.
4. The amount of square footage requirements for each activity and the type of physical spaces needed.
5. The spatial relationships of each activity to one another.
6. The kinds of fixed and movable equipment necessary in each activity space.

7. The kinds and amounts of furniture required in each activity area.
8. A conclusion or summary of the project.

The Role of
the Educational
Specifications Committee

The educational specifications committee will meet with the consultant on a regularly scheduled basis over a period of time as a total group and as subgroups to assess the present curricular programs and design programs and activities which will be offered in the new middle school. Specific investigation and discussion on the following items should be covered thoroughly in the series of meetings:

1. Specific team teaching models and their ability to aid in the individualization of instruction.
2. The inability of the traditional lockstep program to humanize education.
3. The need for using the multimedia approach to prepare curricular activities for students.
4. The necessity of flexible spaces to provide for the use of team teaching models in instruction.
5. How programs might be scheduled in a new middle school.
6. How the teachers' professional stature will be enhanced as they become prescribers, diagnosticians, and evaluators of their instructional programs.
7. How an acoustically treated air-conditioned building enhances the learning environment for students and staff.
8. The amount of square foot space requirements for each activity of the middle school.
9. The type and amount of movable and fixed equipment for the school.
10. The type and amount of furniture and other equipment needed for the new school such as desks, chairs, tables, chalkboards, and audiovisual equipment.

11. Discussing with the architect, at a minimum
of two different meetings, preliminary sketches
and spatial arrangements of the new school.

After the educational specifications committee has gone
through the process of thoroughly discussing and perusing the
preceding items, the architect will be ready to receive the educational specifications in written form and commence preliminary
drawings for presentation to the board of education.

The Role of the Administration

The administrative staff of the school system should guard
against taking the dominant role in the meetings scheduled with
the educational specifications committee. The role played by the
administration can certainly be an active one; however, if it is
overdominant, there is a definite danger of the teachers on the
staff feeling they are being used as a rubber stamp committee for
the school administration. Severe differences should never occur
between the administration and the teaching staff over different
aspects of the program. If a devil's advocate is needed, the role
should be filled by the consultant. The school administration
should function in the following manner during the planning
process:

1. The superintendent should arrange schedules
for the consultant, architect, and educational
specifications committee meetings.

These meetings should be so arranged that
members of the educational specifications committee have released time from their regular
teaching duties for the entire day when the consultant is working in the school district. If staff
involvement is given high priority, it is most
necessary to allow the involved staff members
this released time. The released time will be
used by the consultant to schedule work sessions
for the committee.

2. The administration should provide a liaison function to the citizens' committee and board of education.

Regularly scheduled meetings should be held with the citizens' committee for the purpose of questions, helping members with news releases, and information dissemination to the public. A method of communication with the public which has worked successfully in some school districts is for the citizens' committee to mail a printed progress report to all residents of the community. Another method often used is for the school officials and the citizens' committee to schedule block "house" meetings throughout the school district. The program at the house meetings might include a slide presentation by a speaker of the citizens' committee after which the citizens have the opportunity to ask questions concerning the building, the program, and the new approach to instruction that is being proposed.

3. The superintendent should arrange a schedule of periodic meetings for the administrative staff and consultant.

These meetings are necessary for the administration and the consultant to plan, evaluate, and coordinate work sessions of the groups and to offer suggestions from the administrative staff to the consultant.

4. The superintendent should arrange for a visitation to innovative middle schools by the educational specifications committee.

These visitations should be scheduled when the educational specifications committee has had the proper background and readiness for such a visitation.

5. The administration should arrange its schedule so that it will be possible for the members to participate actively in the planning process with the educational specifications committee.

In the final analysis, the role of the administration is one of service, leadership, coordination, and support to the planning process. Its members should guard against domineering members of the educational specifications committee, but at the same time, actively participate in the total planning process.

The Role of the Architect

The architect should be present at as many of the meetings of the educational specifications committee as possible in order to understand clearly the school program design. The school's program of activities has a direct bearing on the interior design of the building. The architect must design the building to provide optimum functional capabilities. General guidelines and procedures for the architect to follow are:

1. He should visit and observe the innovative middle schools with the board of education and the educational specifications committee. During the visits, he should be especially cognizant of the building design as it relates to the functioning of the school program. In addition to observation, he should question the teaching staff and the principal of the school on the strong and weak points of the facility as it relates to school program.

2. The architect should be present or have a representative present during each general meeting of the educational specifications committee for the purpose of summarizing the results of the meetings.

3. The architect should meet periodically with the consultant for assimilation and interpretation of the information provided as a result of the work of the educational specifications committee.

4. He should prepare sketches of the building and be scheduled for at least three individual meetings with the subgroups of the educational specifications committee for their critique of the floor plan of the building.

5. The architect should meet individually with the administrative staff on at least three different occasions to receive their critique of the floor plan of the building.

6. After he has met with these different groups and received their input, he may then prepare a preliminary drawing for approval by the board of education.

7. Upon the board of education's approval, the architect will proceed to complete the working

drawings, prepare for the letting of bids of the building, and follow through with supervision and completion of the building.

8. During the planning and construction period of the project, he should be presenting periodical progress reports to the board of education and the administration. These same progress reports should be distributed to the educational specifications committee and the citizens' committee in order to keep the group thoroughly informed.

In the final analysis, the success of the planning process for the new middle school will be largely dependent upon how effectively each individual or groups of individuals fulfill their role. The effort must be a team effort if the best possible facility for students of the district is to be assured.

Summary

Planning new school facilities that are designed for humanistic programs of the future are currently receiving widespread attention at all levels of education. Educators and architects are discovering that the repetition of the traditional, inflexible school building design is rapidly outliving its usefulness. The closed room is being replaced by compact, acoustically treated, air-conditioned flexible spaces. The advent of this new approach in school design has necessitated a change for many school systems in their philosophical approach to planning schools.

It is not possible for the educator to simply meet with the architect and redraft an old blueprint to handle the same old problems. The designing of buildings for our new approaches mandates the involvement of the total school community. The teaching staff must be retooled and involved in the planning process. The community must be thoroughly informed of the impending change, and procedures for implementing change must be carried out and planned properly if the venture is to culminate in success.

The architect, the administration, the teaching staff, and the consultant must each fulfill an important role in planning the new facility. The architect must design the building for the changing programs envisioned by the teaching staff. The administration must provide leadership but not dominate the planning process. The consultant must provide the necessary catalytic leadership for change. If planning is culminated properly, the results will be reflected in the design and spatial provisions of the school.

Chapter 18

The Middle
School Site Selection

The selection of the proper site for a new middle school is of eminent importance. Factors relevant to the choice of a particular site should be researched and rationalized thoroughly prior to a commitment. These factors may be categorized into two broad areas.

First and foremost, a site should be selected which will enhance the middle school philosophy and program. The second factor to consider relates to a cost analysis pertaining to the location of the school on a particular site. The board of education should develop a priority system encompassing both of these areas and make the final decision whenever factual data have been evaluated.

Location of the
Middle School Site — Its
Effect on Philosophy and Program

The middle school should be located away from the existing high school since the philosophy of the middle school calls for a unique environment which will provide for a transcending experience from the elementary to the high school years. This location measurably diminishes the possibility of the middle school becoming a stepchild of the high school with its highly socialized and departmentalized atmosphere. If the school is constructed for 600 students, the amount of acreage needed for these activities is approximately twelve acres.

The well-functioning middle school will be involved with parents during open house and other special school events; consequently, it is quite important that adequate parking space be made available. Parking spaces and roadways located on the school site will take a considerable amount of acreage. The school with an enrollment of 600 students will need at least 350 parking spaces—fifty for school employees and 300 for parent and visitor parking. If the school is built for 600 students, three and one-half acres must be allotted for parking purposes.

In addition to the above allowances, acreage should be allotted for a wooded area to serve as a nature park for use in the school science program. The minimum amount should be at least five acres.

When we add the sum of acreage required for a school of 600 students, it amounts to twenty-three and one-half acres.

Size of the Middle School Site

National and state associations for the development of school sites recommend minimum acreage standards for elementary, junior high, and high school sites. With the advent of the middle school, most school systems have concluded that the appropriate middle school minimum acreage site standards should approximate the amount recommended for junior high schools. The required standards for junior high school usually stipulate a minimum of twenty acres plus one acre for each one hundred students who will be housed in the building. The acreage required for a middle school depends on the size of the building, walkways and roadways, parking, and the educational program.

The middle school program of activities will include physical education for both boys and girls and a strong intramural program. These activities require a considerable amount of acreage in close proximity to the building. Space will be required for a ball diamond, football and soccer field, a special area for archery, a special area for tennis, an outside basketball court, and additional space for play area for physical education classes.

It is possible that for various reasons a school district may find it necessary to place their middle school on a smaller site. If this is the case, it will be necessary to plan multiple-use areas. For example, the parking area may be limited and overflow crowds might use the intramural-physical education area. The nature park may be eliminated or the intramural-physical education area may be decreased in size so that separate areas are not provided for each activity. If the size of the site is reduced and a multiple-use plan is followed, maintenance of the school site will be difficult at best. In addition, multiple use of various areas of the school site presents the probability of scheduling problems for school activity programs.

Table 1 is a summary of minimum and desirable acreage for a middle school site. The table indicates that the least amount of acreage required for a middle school of 600 students is fifteen acres and the desirable amount for that number of students is twenty-three and one-half acres. Various factors must be considered when deciding the minimum and desirable site size of the middle school. Each school district contemplating acquisition of a site should consider carefully the program and activities planned.

TABLE 1

Minimum and Desirable Acreage for a Middle School Site

| | 600 Students | |
	Minimum Acreage	Maximum Desirable Acreage
Placing Building	3	3
Physical Education and Intramurals	8½	12
Parking	3½*	3½
Nature Park	0	5
Total Acreage	15	23½

*Multiple use parking and physical education activities

The Desirable Shape
of the School Site

The site selected for the middle school should be a compact square area if possible. Each activity area should be in close proximity to the building to achieve maximum utilitarian use of the acreage. The compact arrangement will also provide for optimum flow of individuals and vehicles using the acreage.

Figure 10 depicts the ideal compact school site. Each area is located in close proximity to the building and is situated on the site so that individuals using the various areas can move to and from the building into any area without circulation interference.

Figure 11 is an illustration of the same acreage with the space depicted as an oblong rectangular area. The diagram clearly illustrates problems of utilization of the space and problems related to circulation of individuals in the various areas.

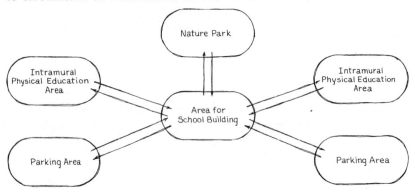

Fig. 10. School Site—Building Activity Relationships—Compact Square Area

These two illustrations in all probability are examples of extremes in school site shapes; however, they do illustrate rather clearly that a school site should be selected which will provide the possibility of balanced spatial relationships.

The Cost Analysis
of the School Site

The board of education should have at its disposal all data relating to the initial cost, developmental cost, and operational cost of the school site before making the final decision on site acquisition. It is advisable for the school district to employ an outside consultant service to gather and assimilate this information prior to the board's final decision on school site selection. This approach offers these advantages:

1. Most school districts purchase only one or two school sites in a period of fifty years. Obviously, board of education members and administrators are not trained site selectors.

2. Outside experts will assure an objective evaluation and recommendation of alternate sites, thereby eliminating the possibility of community-vested interest charges in the purchasing of the new school site.

3. An outside agency can make an anonymous approach to the sellers of the property thereby eliminating the possibility of the seller knowing the school is interested. In most instances when

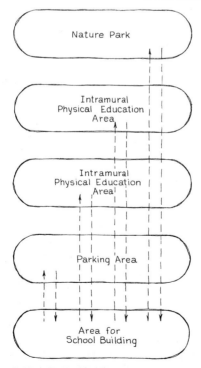

Fig. 11. School Site—Building Activity Relationships—
Oblong Rectangular Area

the administration of the school approaches a landholder, prices of property suddenly become dear simply because the seller immediately assumes that his land has been selected for the new school, and for some reason, he believes the school system will be willing to pay an exorbitant price.

4. The necessary time for a thorough site selection process may be very time consuming. The administration of the school in most instances is assigned maximum duties. If they are to assume added responsibilities of site selection, it is apparent that other areas in the realm of their duties will suffer.

Initial Cost

The initial cost of a school site is usually related to the proximity of the land to developed areas. As we move away from a population center, the per-acre cost of land decreases. The initial purchase price of the school site at a lower per-acre cost further from a population center is often very attractive to schools; however, it is not always the most economical. Other important factors must be considered if we are to eliminate the possibility of error.

Operational Costs

Most school districts do not provide transportation service for youngsters who live within reasonable walking distance to their attendance school. This could very well mean that a school site located properly in an attendance area, even though it may be considerably costlier initially, might be most economical when calculating the transportation cost over the life expectancy of the building. For example, if Site A consisting of twenty acres near the population center was purchased for $200,000 and 400 students would not need transportation service at $40 per student, $16,000 per year in operational costs would be realized. Over a period of twenty years, the savings to the school district in transportation costs would be $320,000. If Site B, which is located farther from the population center necessitating the transporting of all students in the school, were purchased for $20,000, it would be a wise choice to purchase Site A even though the initial cost is considerably more .

Another factor relating to operational costs is the availability of public utilities such as sewage, water, and gas. Septic tank systems, oil heat, and drilled wells are generally much more expensive to maintain over a period of years than city service systems.

Developmental Costs

When calculating the cost of building on a school site, it will be necessary to have expert estimates for landscaping the school site, excavation of the school site, and costs of footers and foundations of the building. These costs may vary considerably depending upon the topography of the area and the texture of the subsoil. For example, it may be necessary to relocate an unusual amount of earth in order to provide a suitable site or it may be necessary to provide an unusual amount of fill for proper drainage of the site. To determine the texture of the soil, it will be necessary to have boring analysis of the site soil. If the subsoil is not substantially firm, it may be necessary to spend several thousand dollars to assure substantial footings and foundations for the building.

A cost analysis of site development should also include the cost of extending services of public utilities to the building. If the services must be extended a considerable distance to the building, costs for these services will naturally increase.

Finally, school site selection is not a task that should be taken lightly. Accurate data should be assimilated and evaluated relative to the site size, shape, initial cost, operational costs, and developmental costs prior to the purchase of the site.

Chapter 19

Design and
Spatial Requirements
for the Middle School

If we are to humanize education for students, the physical design for the middle school should be significantly different from the school of yesteryear. The standard, traditional structures which have perpetuated a graded curriculum with graded teachers and graded standards are simply not appropriate for the approach to learning this text proposes. The changing approaches to learning which will occur in the 1980's and '90's and the present innovative programs and those envisioned for the future are mandating new approaches to the design of school buildings.

The key features in new middle school designs include the following:

1. Compact physical shapes of the buildings.

The exterior design of the building which allows for minimum length of exterior walls in proportion to interior space is normally the most economical to build. Exterior walls are expensive. For this reason, architects and school planners are designing buildings with a minimum number of irregular exterior walls. The compact new buildings are either circular, square, or hexagonal in shape.

2. Air-conditioning, optimum lighting in the interior of the building, carpeted floors, acoustically treated ceilings, and no windows.

The practice of building new school facilities without windows is becoming rather common for several reasons:

> *First,* the heating and air-conditioning equipment of the windowless school provides more efficient and effective year-round climate control. Windows invariably are a source of heat loss or gain.
>
> *Second,* windows take up considerable wall space which can be used for chalkboards, tackboards, or permanent video screens.
>
> *Third,* it is more economical to build plain masonry walls than to build a wall with windows.
>
> *Fourth,* windows often cause uneven diffusion and distribution of the sun's rays. While there is no evidence that this may result in eye damage, there is a strong possibility that this uneven distribution and diffusion of light might have a negative psychological effect on the learning environment.
>
> *Fifth,* school systems that have pioneered the windowless school movement have found that windows have not been considered important by students or teachers when a suitable learning environment is provided in the interior of the building.

The acoustical treatment of floors and ceilings provides for a minimum of sound transmission. In addition, the carpet increases the warmth and aesthetic qualities of the learning environment. The carpeting is more expensive to install initially; however, it is considerably more economical.

Air-conditioning equipment is usually provided in newer structures for the purpose of providing desirable year-round temperatures and proper circulation of fresh air. Research has generally concluded that uneven temperature in the learning environment is detrimental to student learning and teacher efficiency.

3. Minimum number of stationary walls and no traditional halls.

Many of the new schools have no stationary interior walls. When partitions are provided, they are usually the demountable or folding type. The openness of the building provides maximum flexibility for the teaching team to organize for learning. Various size groups of students may be grouped or regrouped as the program requires. In addition, the open space makes possible the elimination of space requirements for traditional hallways. Most architects and school planners conclude that hallways and walls comprise 25 to 30 percent of the square footage in traditional school buildings. The space requirements for the hallways and the walls generally cost as much per square foot as does the remainder of the building. The savings accrued by the exclusion of hallways and walls in the open-plan buildings normally offset the additional funds needed for acoustical ceiling, carpeting, and air-conditioning the building.

4. Noisy activities isolated from quiet areas.

The new middle school designs must isolate the spatial areas for noisy activities such as home economics, typing, industrial arts, physical education, foreign languages, music, and art by placing these activities in separate learning centers or by using folding walls or demountable partitions.

5. Colorful interior designs inviting to the students.

Middle school interior designs should reflect results of experts working in color schemes which present a warm inviting atmosphere to students. Rich colors of carpeting, wall design on the interior of the building, and equipment used in the building, if blended properly, can have a positive effect on the attitude of students toward learning.

---

6. **Relationship of spaces to one another and square footage of various areas determined after the program of activities ascertained.**

Each spatial area is designed to meet the particular needs of the activities which will take place in the area. The areas of the well-planned middle schools should include the following:

a. Instructional materials center.
b. Learning centers for the basic curricular disciplines, such as social science, language arts, science, and math.
c. Areas for typing, foreign language, music, art, industrial arts, and home economics.
d. Area for physical education.
e. Teacher planning area.
f. Area for counseling and guidance.
g. Administrative area.

Following is a discussion of these areas including square footage requirements, spatial relationships of each area to other areas of the building, and fixed and movable equipment necessary for each area.

The Instructional Materials Center

The humanistic middle school program necessitates a new approach to the functional aspects of the traditional school library. Historically, school libraries have served as an area for storing several hundred books or as a substitute for the traditional study hall. The librarian's role has been to guard the books and keep the library areas quiet for student study.

The new approach envisions the library as an activity area or instructional materials center and the librarian as an instructional materials specialist. To understand the necessity of the spa-

tail requirements and the equipment needed for the instructional materials center, it is perhaps pertinent to list the kinds of activities students and the school staff will pursue in this area.

I.M.C. Student Activities

1. Groups of students studying specific assignments or receiving instruction from the instructional materials specialist on how to use the library key to locate periodicals, books, filmstrips, tapes, records, etc.
2. Groups of two to fifteen students working on projects, listening to tapes and records with headsets, or engaged in small group discussions.
3. Individual students obtaining materials for a written report or project, viewing films or filmstrips, listening to phonograph records or tapes, studying via a teaching machine, talking with other students, browsing through magazines or newspapers, reading for fun and checking out books for reading at home.

I.M.C. Librarian Activities

1. Holding regular conferences with teaching teams of the school to advise them of available materials for their curricular area.
2. Cataloging materials, checking out materials to students, and selecting multimedia materials for the classroom teams to use in the instructional setting.
3. Working with individual students and groups of students to counsel and help them in finding materials.

I.M.C. Teacher Activities

1. Previewing films and filmstrips.
2. Working with various size groups of students on projects or research.

3. Conferring with the instructional materials specialist in the purchasing of media.

A study of the activities carried out in the middle school instructional materials center and observance of innovative middle
schools by the authors indicate that the various student activities
for the instructional materials center require a minimum of ten
square feet per youngster using the area and that space should be
provided for at least twenty percent of the student body at one
particular time. Using this criteria, approximately 6,000 square
feet would be required for student instructional materials center
activities in a school with a capacity of 600 students.

Within this 6,000 square foot area, the space might be appor-
tioned as illustrated in Diagram 2. In this diagram, an area twenty
feet by twenty feet is utilized as a student project area. Two areas
fifteen by twenty feet are used for all small group discussions or
group listening. Study carrels are aligned on the perimeter of the
instructional materials center. An area approximately ten by
twenty-five feet is utilized for a student lounge, and the remainder is used as a study area.

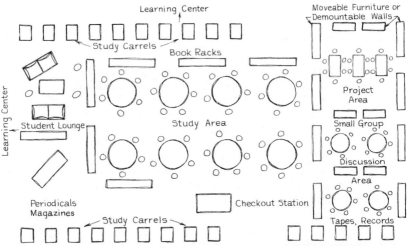

Diagram 2. Instructional Materials Center

In addition to the areas just described, rooms must be provided
for the librarian's office, audio-visual equipment and materials
storage, media preparation and workroom, room for processing

books and library materials, and a library staff-teacher conference room.

The middle school serving 600 students with a staff consisting of thirty teachers, one librarian, and a library aide would need a minimum of 1,000 square feet for these areas. Diagram 3 illustrates how three rooms directly adjacent to the instructional materials center could be utilized for these functional purposes of the center. The combined square foot area of the three rooms amounts to 1,000 square feet and is the minimum amount of space that is needed to properly serve a middle school of 600 students, thirty teachers, one instructional materials specialist, and one instructional materials aide. The total amount of square footage required to provide for all the functional aspects of the middle school instructional materials center serving 600 students amounts to approximately 7,000 square feet.

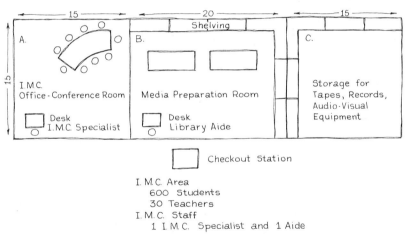

I. M.C. Area
    600 Students
    30 Teachers
I. M.C. Staff
    1 I.M.C. Specialist and 1 Aide

Diagram 3. I.M.C. Auxiliary Space

**Furniture and Equipment for the
Instructional Materials Center**

The instructional materials center will need tables and chairs in the small group areas, study areas, project areas, and the student lounge. The types of tables purchased for these areas vary with the activity conducted. Circular tables should be provided in the small group areas and student lounge while large square tables will be more appropriately used in the project and study areas. The school serving 600 students will need approximately ten large square tables and five circular tables.

Individual study carrels equipped with electrical power should be provided for student use in independent study, listening to tapes and records, viewing films, filmstrips, or filmclips, and using the teaching machine. Special care should be taken in the type of study carrel purchased to assure that the carrel provides adequate seclusion for the student since the idea of the study carrel is to provide an area for the student to work alone without interference. A minimum of thirty individual study carrels should be provided for the instructional materials center serving 600 students.

Library carts should be provided for the library books used in the instructional materials center. Several of these carts currently marketed which work well on tiled floors are not appropriate for the carpeted surface proposed in the middle school instructional materials center. The carts purchased should be the type which have a low center of gravity and are equipped with large casters. The school serving 600 middle school students will need approximately twelve library carts.

The typical middle school has special rooms provided for project and small group discussion areas, the rationale being that the rooms provide a quiet environment for the activities carried on in these areas. Following our observations, we would suggest movable storage carts be utilized for these areas; they can be rearranged at any given time with little effort as the activities dictate.

The student lounge area will be used for scholastic games and informal chatting. This area should be equipped with several lounge chairs, a circular table with four chairs, and one or two couches.

The checkout station should be a facsimile to a counter top large enough to accommodate two or more stations. The stations should be mounted on casters so they may be moved to different areas of the instructional materials center.

The instructional materials center specialist's office-conference area should be provided with a desk and chair, filing cabinet, shelving for the instructional material specialist's special literature, and a conference table and chairs for meeting with teams of teachers.

The media preparation room will need two work tables, a desk for the instructional materials center aide, shelving for the storage of materials, and special equipment for preparing multimedia materials.

The room utilized for storing tapes, records, and audio-visual equipment will need special files and shelving provided for storage of these items. The heavy equipment such as 16mm projectors and opaque projectors may be stored in the open areas of the room on rolling carts.

In addition to the movable furniture, a vast amount of equipment and materials should be provided for the middle school instructional materials center.

In purchasing equipment and materials, we suggest funds be held in escrow for a wide variety of materials and equipment as needs are identified and requested by the staff of the school. If the middle school is to humanize education for its students, the instructional materials center must have a multitude of materials and equipment to meet the diverse needs of the student body.

Spatial Relationships of the Instructional Materials Center to Other Areas of the Building

Due to the nature of the middle school program, the instructional materials center must be the focal point of the building. To accomplish this, it is most necessary to have the area located near the center of the building in as close proximity to other activity areas as possible. Diagram 4 illustrates the appropriate spatial relationship of the instructional materials center to the other activity areas.

Learning Centers

Technically, the middle school learning center may be defined as any area of the building which students and teachers use in the learning process. In addition to the instructional materials center,

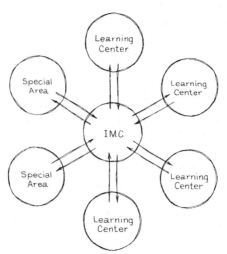

Diagram 4.   Spatial Relationship of Instructional Materials Center to
Other Activity Areas

other centers for learning in the middle school include the centers
for the basic curricular areas and the centers for the special curricular areas. The basic curricular areas include science, math,
social science, and the language arts curriculum. The special areas
include unified arts, home economics, industrial arts, art, typing,
foreign language, music, physical education, and special education. We may appropriately make these two classifications of
learning centers in the middle school because the curricular areas
in each classification conduct activities which require similar spatial needs.

The characteristics of the activities in the basic curricular learning centers are:

> 1. The activities are taught by teams of teachers
>   using various instructional models.
> 2. The activities are usually low-level noise activ-
>   ities.
> 3. The activities of the subject areas are presented
>   to all children attending the school on a daily
>   basis.

The characteristics of the activities conducted in the special
curricular learning centers include:

1. The activities may or may not be carried out by a team of teachers.
2. The activities are usually high-level noise activities.
3. The activities of these particular curricular areas are normally considered supplementary to the basic curricular areas and may or may not be presented to all children attending the school on a daily basis.

The characteristics of the activities of the learning center classifications require that the building design provide these features:

1. The special curricular learning centers are isolated from the basic learning centers either by their location in the building or by acoustical walls.
2. The combined basic curricular learning centers must be large enough to handle the entire student body for a block of time on a daily basis.
3. The special curricular learning centers size for each curricular area will vary depending upon the number of times the activity is offered and the number of students involved in each activity. Normally, each learning center is considerably smaller than the basic curricular learning centers.

Keeping in mind the characteristics of the middle school learning centers, we will discuss the specific spatial and equipment needs for each classification.

Spatial Requirements and Equipment Needs for the Basic Curricular Learning Centers

Spatial requirements and equipment for the basic curricular learning centers include four learning centers located in close proximity to the instructional materials center so that students may go to and from this center with a minimum amount of difficulty. The total spatial requirement for the four learning centers may be divided by using demountable walls, permanent walls, or portable cabinets. The majority of the open-plan middle schools currently operating have divided the learning centers by using permanent or demountable walls. While this feature in middle school design is rather common, no evidence exists to indicate that the portable cabinets would not be as appropriate for separating the learning centers.

The amount of square footage required for each learning center will depend upon the number of students the school will serve at maximum capacity. For optimum functional operations of the curricular programs in the middle school, thirty square feet per student should be allotted for the total square footage requirements of the basic curricular learning centers. Using this formula, the middle school designed for 600 students would have four learning centers 4,500 square feet in size and a total of 18,000 square feet in the four learning centers.

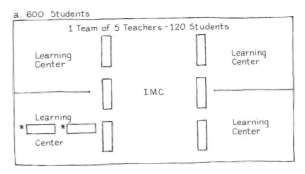

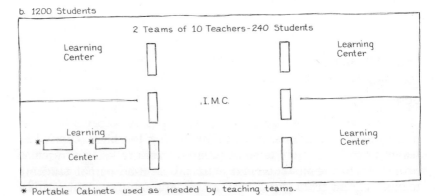

* Portable Cabinets used as needed by teaching teams.

Diagram 5. Basic Curricular Learning Centers

Diagram 5 illustrates how four learning centers in the basic curricular areas would be used to serve 600 students or 1,200 students.

Fixed and Movable Equipment for the Basic Curricular Learning Centers

Fixed equipment for the basic curricular learning centers includes laboratory equipment, sinks, water fountains, permanent video screens, electrical power, and gas. Movable equipment includes such items as chalkboards, tackboards, fold-down video screens, portable cabinets, tables and chairs, student desks, and portable lab equipment.

1. Laboratory Equipment Fixed laboratory equipment should be available in at least one of the learning centers. A minimum of one permanent science lab station per twenty students enrolled in the middle school should be provided for the middle school student to pursue a wide variety of experiments in various fields of science. The lab stations should be equipped with gas, water, and electrical power. The middle school of 600 students would have a minimum of thirty permanent lab stations.

2. Sinks Each of the basic curricular learning centers should have one large deep sink and a drain area for various experimental activities. If possible, the sinks should be located so that each learning center will have access to two sinks at a given time. A most appropriate place for their location in the middle school which has a learning center divided by permanent or demountable walls would be at the front of the learning center as depicted in Diagram 6. If the learning centers are divided by movable cabinets, the sinks may be located in the rear as shown in Diagram 7.

3. Water Fountains Each learning center should have at least one and preferably two water fountains available to the students using the area. The water fountains should be located near the sinks for plumbing economy and student accessibility.

4. Video Screens At least four permanent video screens, three by five feet, should be made available in each learning center. The screens may be either placed or painted on the interior or on each side of the learning center. Screens will be used by the teaching teams to show films, filmstrips, or to give demonstrations using the overhead projector.

5. Electric Power   Each learning center should have wire loops under the carpeting in all areas of the learning center and two electrical receptacles for every 900 square feet in each learning center. The receptacles should be placed as follows: one-half of the receptacles evenly spaced on the exterior walls of the learning center and one-half either depressed in the carpeting or ceiling

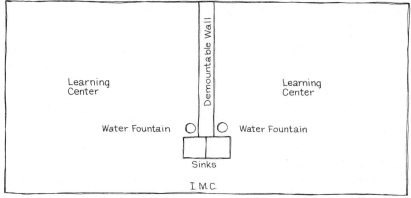

Diagram 6.   Learning Center — Demountable Wall Arrangement

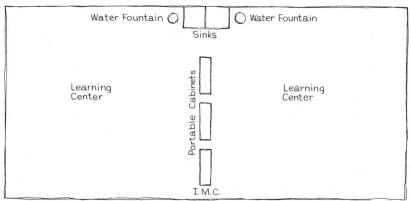

Diagram 7.   Learning Center — Movable Cabinet Arrangement

pull-down receptacles. The wire loops and the electrical outlets will allow the teaching staff and the students to utilize electrical equipment and establish listening stations in any area of the learning center.

6. Gas   Natural or butane gas should be provided for the fixed laboratory equipment in the science learning center so that students may utilize Bunsen burners for experiments.

7. Chalkboards   Chalkboards are expensive items and too often are not effectively used by the teaching teams. One four-by-ten foot permanent chalkboard is more expensive than the best over-head projector and is a considerably less effective tool for instruction. Consequently, we recommend a maximum of no more than four portable chalkboards for each learning center. The chalkboards may be mounted on the back of portable cabinets or be purchased already mounted on a light aluminum frame.

8. Tackboards Each team of teachers using the learning center should have available a large tackboard for posting articles, notices, and student work. Each learning center should also have one large pull-down video screen made available for large group demonstrations and films. The screen may be placed in one corner of the learning center.

9. Portable Cabinets One portable storage cabinet should be made available for use in the learning centers for each thirty students enrolled in the middle school. The school serving 600 students would need twenty portable storage cabinets, five for each learning center. In addition to the portable storage cabinets which are used for general supplies for students and teachers, enough cabinets for the storage of tote trays should be provided to allow for each student of the school to store a tote tray containing his personal supplies.

10. Tables and Chairs Enough table and chair combinations or tablet-arm chairs should be purchased so that each student who uses the basic learning centers at any given time will have a station where he may sit and pursue learning. This type of furniture will most appropriately meet the needs of the teaming activities which occur in each learning center. The middle school with an enrollment of 600 students will need 300 tablet-arm chairs, 300 chairs for use at rectangular or oval tables, and enough oval or rectangular tables to accommodate 300 students.

Spatial Requirements
for the Special Learning Centers

Unified Arts Learning Center —
Home Economics, Industrial Arts, Art

The unified arts learning center should be an open learning center acoustically isolated from other areas of the building as the unified arts activities are high-level noise activities. The open learning center will make possible an interdisciplinary approach on unified projects. The middle school serving 600 students should have one teacher station in home economics, one in industrial arts, and one in art. The total square footage required for this learning center would be 4,050 square feet: one-third of the area to be used for industrial arts, one-third for art, and one-third for home economics.

The entire unified arts learning center should have acoustically treated floors and ceilings. School planners sometimes err by eliminating carpeting in certain areas of the learning center on the assumption that the activities conducted make it impossible to maintain the carpet adequately. If the activities are properly conducted, the activity residue in this learning center will consist of water color paint, sawdust, and food. This kind of residue is not harmful to commercial carpeting. The carpet may be maintained more economically and efficiently than other types of floor coverings.

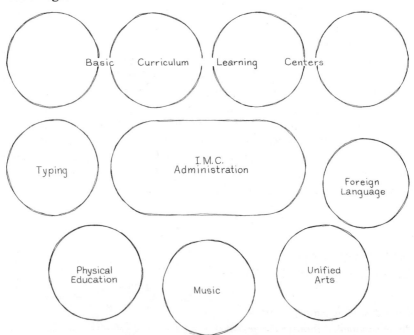

Diagram 8a. Spatial Relationships of the Unified Arts Area

In addition to the square footage required for the learning center area, the three-teacher station unified arts area should have two additional rooms of approximately 400 square feet each. One room would be utilized as a supply center for receiving and storing materials and one room would house power equipment for the industrial arts area. Each of these rooms should be located preferably on the perimeter of the building for easy outside access. Diagrams 8a, 8b, 8c, and 8d depict the spatial relationship of the unified arts learning center to other areas of the building and the arrangement of the furniture and equipment within the learning center.

1. Fixed Equipment for the Home Economics Station The home economics station should have a cooking center, a sewing center, and a family living center. The cooking center will need a minimum of two stoves, two refrigerators, two sinks, four base cabinet units, and four overhead cabinet units. This equipment may be attached to the wall of the learning center or arranged as an island in one area of the learning center.

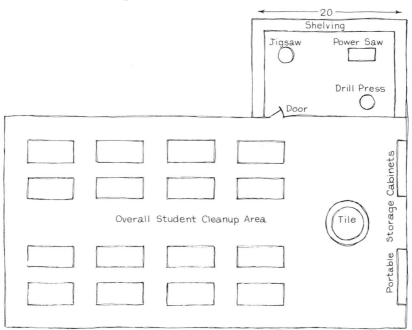

Diagram 8b. Industrial Arts Area

2. Movable Equipment for the Home Economics Station   Movable equipment for the home economics area for the school serving 600 students would include two combination tables and chairs for the cooking area, six sewing machines, four three-by-five foot tables and chairs for the sewing area, and one living room furniture arrangement for the home and family living area.

3. Fixed Equipment for the Art Area   The fixed equipment for the art area teacher station will require one large deep sink located on the wall of the learning center flanked on either side by cabinet units for storage of materials used in the art activities, one high temperature kiln, and one potter's wheel.

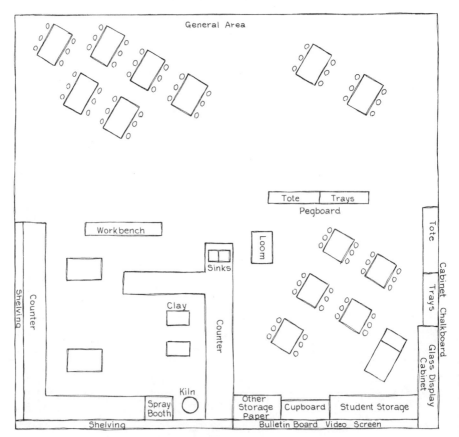

Diagram 8c.   Art Area

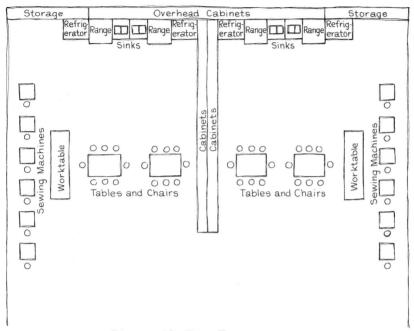

Diagram 8d.   Home Economics Area

4. Movable Equipment for the Art Area   The movable equipment required for the art center will consist of a minimum of five three-by-five feet rectangular tables, thirty to thirty-five chairs, a storage cabinet for the teacher, and cabinetry for storing student tote trays.

5. Fixed Equipment for the Industrial Arts Area   The industrial arts area should have provided in a separate room a power saw, a jig saw, a hand saw, a wood lathe, and a metal lathe. This equipment should only be used by students under close supervision of an instructor or by the instructor in aiding a student with particular projects. Additional fixed equipment in this area includes storage cabinets for the various hand tools used by the students and a large oval wash basin for student use.

6. Movable Equipment for the Industrial Arts Area   Movable equipment in the industrial arts area includes a minimum of eight four-by-five foot rectangular tables mounted on casters and such items as hand sanders, hand saws, hammers, various types of wrenches, soldering irons, etc.

The spatial requirements and equipment needs which have just been discussed assume that a 600 unit middle school unified arts program would operate at a maximum of thirty students for one and one-half periods three times per week at each teacher station. The school serving less students or more students would need to consider this factor.

Spatial Requirements and Equipment Needs for the Typing Center

The typing learning center preferably should be isolated away from other learning centers by enclosing the learning center with permanent or demountable walls; typing is a high-level noise activity.

Because typing activities are limited in the middle school, one typing teacher station for each 600 middle school students will be sufficient. The teacher's station should contain approximately 900 square feet. The equipment needed will be thirty manual typewriters, thirty chairs, thirty typing desks, and a portable storage cabinet for the typing instructor.

Spatial Requirements and Equipment Needs for the Foreign Language Learning Center

The foreign language learning center must support high-level noise activity as the middle school will, in all probability, be teaching conversational language; consequently, this area must also be acoustically isolated. Square footage requirements, using the middle school philosophical guidelines which stipulate student exposure to a minimum of two foreign languages on a limited basis for some and on an extended basis for others, necessitates two teacher stations of approximately 900 square feet each.

Equipment for the foreign language area may be entirely movable equipment. Movable equipment in the form of a portable lab console, and headsets for each teacher, is considerably less expensive and more practical for the instructional activities which will be conducted in this learning center. The equipment needs for the two teacher stations will include two portable lab stations, sixty headsets, two record players, two tape recorders, sixty student chairs, and two portable storage cabinets for instructional materials.

Spatial and Equipment Requirements
for the Music Learning Center

The middle school music learning center's spatial and equipment requirements should provide for vocal and instrumental student activities, both of which are extremely high-level noise producing programs. These activities must be acoustically isolated from the remainder of the school building. The middle school serving 600 students will require one teaching station for instrumental music, containing 1,300 square feet of which 900 square feet will be used for the classroom instructional area and 400 square feet will be used for four ten-by-ten foot individual practice rooms and instrument storage.

The vocal music area's spatial requirement necessitates 1,100 square feet. This area should be separated from the instrumental learning area with an acoustically treated, electrically operated folding wall so that it can be opened for unified projects or large rehearsal groups. The area should be divided into one area for classroom instructional purposes encompassing 900 square feet and two small areas encompassing 100 square feet each for small group student project pursuits.

The only necessary fixed equipment for the vocal and instrumental learning center is built-in storage cabinets for instrument storage and the ten-by-ten-foot instrumental and vocal practice rooms. The remainder of the equipment may consist of movable equipment including sixty folding chairs, sixty music stands, and two teacher storage cabinets.

Spatial and Equipment Requirements
for the Physical Education Center

The middle school physical education activities will require one teacher station for each 300 students. The requirements for conducting the activity necessitate a playing activity area of approximately 3,000 square feet for each station.

In addition to the playing surface, spaces should be provided for the storage of gym equipment and dressing and shower facilities for students. The gym equipment storage area may serve both teacher stations and should be approximately twenty-by-twenty feet.

Two separate areas 1,600 square feet each should be provided for student dressing, basket storage, and shower facilities. It will not be necessary to supply spectator seating space as the low-keyed middle school program does not feature interscholastic athletics.

The equipment for the physical education center should include all types of equipment for assorted games, gymnastics, tumbling, and two mounted basketball baskets.

Spatial and Equipment Requirements for the Teacher Planning Area

Important considerations in the designing of this area should include the following:

1. It should be an enclosed area; this will insure privacy for the teaching staff and will provide them with the opportunity to "let their hair down" during teacher planning time.
2. The area should be centrally located as nearly as possible to all other areas of the school building to provide equal access by the total teaching staff.
3. The area should be large enough in size to accommodate the total teaching staff. This will assure the total staff the opportunity to communicate effectively on items and issues relating to the school.
4. Sixty square feet per school staff member should be allotted for the basic teacher planning area.

A middle school serving 600 students should provide a teacher planning area to accommodate a minimum of thirty teachers. Using this guideline, 1,800 square feet would be designed as teacher planning area.

5. In addition to the basic area, a storage-workroom area and conference room should be provided directly adjacent to the teacher planning area. The storage-workroom area will be used for storing various supplies and making instructional aids, i.e., transparencies, mimeograph, ditto copies, etc. The conference room will be used for individual conferences with parents or students.

A storage workroom of approximately 400 square feet and conference room of 120 square feet will be required for the school employing thirty teaching staff members.

6. It is also most desirable to have a men's and women's lavatory located directly adjacent to the teacher planning area. Diagrams 9a and 9b illustrate how the teacher planning area and surrounding areas might be designed.

Furniture and Equipment for the
Teacher Planning Area, Storage
Area, and Conference Room

The teacher planning area should have circular team tables with built-in filing cabinets as illustrated in Diagram 9a or desks arranged back-to-back for teams as illustrated in Diagram 9b. This type of furniture arrangement is necessary so each individual team member can confer easily with other members of his team. Diagram 9b illustrates the planning area with six team planning stations. The members of each team include five teachers and a teacher aide. Individual filing cabinets for the teaching teams may be a part of the table or arranged as separate units in close proximity to each teaching station.

In addition to the individual team stations, the planning area should include shelving for professional literature at eye-level height and occasional furniture for the teacher lounge area. The

conference area should be equipped with shelving for storage of
instructional supplies, two large tables, a ditto machine, a paper
cutter, and a copy machine.

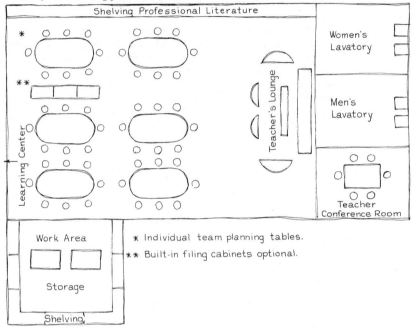

Diagram 9a. Teaching Planning Area

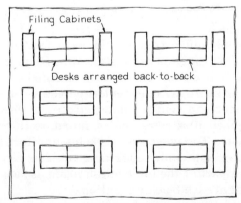

Diagram 9b. Teacher Planning Area — Optional Desk Arrangement
for Team Planning

Spatial Requirements and Equipment for the Middle School Guidance Offices

The middle school guidance counselor's role will be student-centered rather than administrative-centered. He will be counseling individual students, groups of students, and meeting with parents.

The guidance offices should be located so students have easy access without passing near the principal's office. One guidance office containing approximately 100 square feet should be provided for each 300 middle school students. The school of 600 students would require two counseling offices of approximately 100 square feet each and a secretarial-waiting area consisting of 150 square feet.

Furniture and equipment for this area includes standard office furniture and lounging furniture for the waiting area.

Administrative Complex Spatial Requirements and Equipment

The administrative complex includes the principal's office, waiting area, secretary's area, small storage area for administrative supplies, and the health clinic. These areas should be centrally located in the building directly adjacent to the teacher planning area to provide for effective communication with the teaching staff.

The principal's office should be large enough to be used as an office conference room which will accommodate small group conferences of eight to ten persons. To facilitate this function, approximately 300 square feet should be allotted for the principal's office. An area of approximately 120 square feet directly adjacent to the principal's office should be designed as space for the principal's secretary.

The health clinic should be located in close proximity to the principal's office and the secretary's area and should be approximately twenty-by-twenty feet for a total of 400 square feet. Included in the clinic area or directly adjacent to the area should be an area of approximately 30 square feet for toilet facilities.

The equipment for these three areas will include the principal's desk, conference table and chairs, secretarial desk, toilet facilities, cots for the clinic room, medicine cabinets, etc.

Summary

The ideal middle school design will feature a compact, air-conditioned, acoustically treated structure. The interior and spatial areas of the building will be flexible with large open areas being the rule rather than the exception.

The instructional materials center will be the focal point of the building. It will be large enough and designed in such a fashion that a broad variety of learning activities can take place.

The basic curricular learning centers will be utilized by teachers serving as diagnosticians, prescribers, and evaluators.

Spatial relationships of the various learning centers are very important in planning the building. The administrative complex, the instructional materials center, and the teacher planning area will be situated near the center of the building. The learning centers of the building will be so arranged in their spatial relationships that the high-noise level activities will be isolated in areas of the building either by location or demountable walls so that noise interference is not a problem.

When the building is completed, flexibility will be provided so that humanizing education is a reality for youngsters. New models for learning activities that take into account what we know about the needs of students and how they learn will emerge.

References

1. Abbenhouse, Lester. "Nongraded Schools — An Approach to Children." Letter Number Six, © 1968, SRA, Chicago. By permission of the publisher.
2. Abbott, M. G. and J. T. Lowell. *Change Perspectives in Administration.* School of Education, Auburn Univ., 1965.
3. Adams, James F., ed. *Understanding Adolescence.* Boston: Allyn & Bacon, 1968.
4. Alexander, William M., ed. *The High School of the Future: A Memorial to Kimball Wiles.* Columbus, Ohio: Charles E. Merrill, 1969.
5. Alexander, William M. "What Educational Plan for the In-Between-Ager?" *NEA Journal* 55 (March 1966) : 30-32.
6. Alexander, William M. and Vynce A. Hines. *Independent Study in Secondary Schools.* New York: Holt, 1967.
7. Alexander, William M. and E. L. Williams. "Schools for the Middle Years." *Educational Leadership* 23 (December 1965) : 217-223.
8. Allen, Dwight W. *A Differentiated Staff: Putting Teaching Talent to Work.* Washington, D. C.: NEA, 1967.
9. Allen, Dwight W. and Robert Bush. *A New Design for High School Education.* New York: McGraw-Hill, 1964. Used with permission of McGraw-Hill.
10. Allen, Paul M.; William D. Barnes; Jerald L. Reece; and E. Wayne Roberson. *Teacher Self-Appraisal: A Way of Looking Over Your Own Shoulder.* Worthington, Ohio: Charles A. Jones, 1970.
11. American Association of School Administrators. *Planning America's School Buildings.* Washington, D.C.: A.A.S.A., 1960.
12. American Library Association. *Standards for School Media Programming.* Washington, D.C.: NEA, 1969.
13. Ammerman, H. L. and W. H. Melching. *The Derivation, Analysis, and Classification of Instructional Objectives.* Alexandria, Va.: George Washington Univ., 1966.
14. Anderson, Robert H. "Organizing Groups for Instruction." *Individualizing Instruction.* Sixty-first Yearbook. Part I. NSSE. Chicago: Univ. of Chicago Press, 1962.
15. Anderson, Robert H. *Teaching in a World of Change.* New York: Harcourt, 1966. Chap. 6, "The People Who Work With Teachers."
16. _____. "Team Teaching." *NEA Journal* 50 (March 1961) : 52-54.
17. Anderson, Robert H.; E. A. Hagstrom; and W. M. Robinson. "Team Teaching in an Elementary School." *School Review* 68 (Spring 1960) : 71-84.
18. Anderson, Robert H. and Donald P. Mitchell. "School Plant Design." *Nations' Schools,* 65 (June 1960) : 75-82.
19. Armstrong, Robert J.; Terry D. Cornell; Robert E. Kraner; and E. Wayne Roberson. *The Development and Evaluation of Behavioral Objectives.* Worthington, Ohio: Charles A. Jones, 1970.
20. ASCD. *Evaluation as Feedback and Guide.* Washington, D.C., 1967.
21. _____. *Individualizing Instruction.* 1964 Yearbook. Washington, D.C.: NEA, 1964.
22. _____. *To Nurture Humaneness.* Washington, D.C.: NEA, 1970.
23. _____. *Perceiving, Behaving, Becoming.* Washington, D.C., 1961.
24. Ausubel, David P. "The Influence of Experience on the Development of the Intelligence." *Productive Thinking in Education.* Ed. by Mary Jane Aschner and Charles E. Bish. Washington, D.C.: NEA, 1965.
25. Aylesworth, Thomas G. and Gerald M. Reagan. *Teaching for Thinking.* Garden City, N.Y.: Doubleday, 1969.
26. Bahner, John M. "Grouping Within a School." *Childhood Education* 36 (April 1960) : 354-356.
27. Bair, Medill and Richard Woodward. *Team Teaching in Action.* Boston: Houghton Mifflin, 1964.
28. Baker, Robert L. and Roy P. Doyle. "Teacher Knowledge of Pupil Data and Marking Practices at the Elementary School Level." *Personnel and Guidance Journal* 37 (May 1959) : 644-647.
29. Battrick, Delmer H. "How Do Team Teaching and Other Staff Utilization Practices Fit Into the Instructional Program of a Junior High School?" *NASSP Bulletin* 46 (October 1962) : 13-15.

30. Baughman, M. Dale; Wendell G. Anderson; Mark Smith; and Earle W. Wiltse. *Administration and Supervision of the Modern Secondary School.* West Nyack, N.Y.: Parker Publishing.
31. Baynham, Dorsey. "School of the Future in Operation." *Phi Delta Kappan* 42 (May 1961) : 350-354.
32. Beatty, Walcott H., ed. *Improving Educational Assessments.* Washington, D.C.: ASCD, 1969.
33. Beggs, David W., III. *Decatur Lakeview High School: A Practical Application of the Trump Plan.* New York: Prentice-Hall, 1964.
34. _____, ed. *Team Teaching — Bold New Venture.* Indianapolis: Unified College Press, 1964.
35. Beggs, David W., III and Edward G. Buffie, eds. *Independent Study: Bold New Venture.* Bloomington: Indiana Univ. Press. Copyright © 1965. Reprinted by permission of the publisher.
36. _____. *Nongraded Schools in Action.* Bloomington: Indiana Univ. Press, 1966.
37. Beggs, David W., III and James L. Olivero. "Place Out of Space ... The Independent Study Carrel ... and a Variety of Studies in Lakeview High School, Decatur, Illinois." *NASSP Bulletin* 46 (January 1962) : 192-202.
38. Bell, Daniel. *Toward the Year 2000.* Daedalus Library. New York: Houghton Mifflin, 1968.
39. Bennis, Warren G.; K. Benne; and R. Chin. *The Planning of Change.* New York: Holt, 1961.
40. Berman, Sidney. "As a Psychiatrist Sees Pressures on Middle Class Teenagers." *Historical Education Association Journal* 54 (February 1965) : 217-240.
41. Bloom, Benjamin S. *Stability and Change in Human Characteristics.* New York: Wiley, 1964.
42. _____, ed. *Taxonomy of Educational Objectives — The Classification of Educational Goals, Handbook I: Cognitive Domain.* New York: McKay, 1956. Adapted by permission of the publisher.
43. Boles, Harold W. *Step by Step to Better School Facilities.* New York: Holt, 1965.
44. Borg, Walter R. *Ability Grouping in the Public Schools.* Madison, Wis.: Dembar Educational Research Service, 1966.
45. Baugh, Max. "Theoretical and Practical Aspects of the Middle School." *NASSP Bulletin* (March 1969).
46. Bowles, S. and H. M. Levin. "The Determinants of Scholastic Achievement: An Appraisal of Some Recent Evidence." *Journal of Human Resources,* 1968. (In press)
47. Bowman, Garda W. and Gordon J. Klopf. *New Careers and Roles in the American School.* New York: Bank Street College of Education, 1968.
48. _____. *Teacher Aide Program: A Research Report.* Minneapolis: Minnesota Public School District No. 1, Minneapolis Public Schools, 1966.
49. _____. *Teacher Aides at Work.* National Commission on Teacher Education and Professional Standards. Washington, D.C.: NEA, 1967.
50. Braithwaite, E. R. *To Sir, With Love.* Englewood Cliffs, N.J.: Prentice-Hall, 1959.
51. Breckenridge, Marian E. and Vincent E. Lee. *Child Development, Physical and Psychological Growth Through Adolescence.* Philadelphia: W. B. Saunders, 1965.
52. Brenton, Myron. *What's Happened to Teacher?* New York: Coward-McCann, 1970.
53. Brickell, Henry M. "Dynamics of Change." *NASSP Bulletin* 47 (May 1963) : 21-28.
54. Brighton, Stayner F. *Increasing Your Accuracy in Teacher Evaluation.* Englewood Cliffs, N.J.: Prentice-Hall, 1965.
55. Brod, Pearl. "The Middle School: Trends Toward Its Adoption." *The Clearing House* 40 (February 1966) : 331-333.
56. Brodwrick, Mary. "Creativity in Children." *National Elementary Principal* 46 (November 1966) : 18-24.
57. Brown, B. Frank. *The Appropriate Placement School: A Sophisticated Nongraded Curriculum.* West Nyack, N.Y.: Parker Publishing, 1966.

58. _____. *Education by Appointment.* West Nyack, N.Y.: Parker Publishing, 1968.
59. _____. *The Non-Graded High School.* Englewood Cliffs, N.J.: Prentice-Hall, 1963.
60. _____. *Profiles of Significant Schools — Schools Without Walls.* New York: Educational Facilities Laboratories, 1965.
61. Brown, James W.; Richard B. Lewis; and Fred F. Harcleroad. *Audio Visual Instruction: Materials and Methods.* Copyright 1964. Used with permission of McGraw-Hill.
62. _____. *Audio Visual Market Place, A Multimedia Guide.* New York: R. R. Bowker, 1969.
63. Burner, Jerome. *The Process of Education.* Cambridge, Mass.: Harvard Univ. Press, 1960.
64. Bush, Robert N. *A New Design for High School Education.* New York: McGraw-Hill, 1964.
65. Bushnell, Don and Dwight W. Allen, eds. *The Computer in American Education.* New York: Wiley, 1967. (Includes a chapter by Robert H. Anderson on "Sustaining Individualized Instruction Through Flexible Administration.")
66. Butts, R. Freeman. "Search for Freedom — the Story of American Education." *NEA Journal* (March 1960) : 33-48.
67. Byler, Ruth V., ed. *Teach Us What We Want To Know.* New York: Mental Health Materials Center, 1969.
68. Calvin, Allen D. *Programmed Instruction.* Bloomington: Indiana Univ. Press, 1969.
69. Carbone, Robert F. "A Comparison of Graded and Nongraded Elementary Schools." *The Elementary School Journal* 62 (November 1961) : 82-88.
70. Carlton, Patrick W. and Harold T. Goodwin. *The Collective Dilemma: Negotiations in Education.* Worthington, Ohio: Charles A. Jones, 1970.
71. Carswell, Evelyn. "Teacher-Determined Variable Scheduling." *Innovations for Time to Teach.* Washington, D.C.: Association of Classroom Teachers, NEA, 1966.
72. Central Michigan College. *A Cooperative Study for the Utilization of Teacher Competencies.* Second printed report. Mount Pleasant, Mich., 1955.
73. Chamberlin, Leslie J. *Team Teaching: Organization and Administration.* Columbus, Ohio: Charles E. Merrill, 1969.
74. Chase, Dave. "The School Library as an Instructional Materials Center." *Peabody Journal of Education* 41 (1963) : 15-18.
75. Chesler, Mark and Robert Fox. "Teacher-Peer Relations and Educational Change." *NEA Journal* 56 (May 1967) : 25-26.
76. Cloward, Robert D. "The Nonprofessional in Education." *Educational Leadership* 24 (April 1967).
77. Coleman, James S. *The Adolescent Society.* New York: Macmillan, 1961.
78. Committee for Economic Development. *Innovation in Education: New Directions for the American School.* New York, 477 Madison Avenue, 1968.
79. Compton, Mary F. "The Middle School: Alternative to the Status Quo." *Theory into Practice* VII (June 1968) : 108-110.
80. *The Cost of A School House.* New York: Educational Facilities Laboratory, 1960.
81. Crary, Ryland W. *Humanizing the School: Curriculum Development and Theory.* New York: Knopf, 1970.
82. Cunningham, Luvern L. "Keys to Team Teaching." *Overview* 1 (October 1960) : 54-55.
83. _____. "The Teacher and Change." *Elementary School Journal* 62 (December 1961) : 119-29.
84. Davis, Harold S. *How to Organize an Effective Team Teaching Program.* Englewood Cliffs, N.J.: Prentice-Hall, 1966.
85. Davis, Joe. *Public Relations for Schools.* Worthington, Ohio: Charles A. Jones, forthcoming.
86. Dawson, Martha. "The Nongraded School and Concomitant Factors." Letter Number 18, © 1968, SRA, Chicago. By permission of the publisher.

87. _____. "Teacher Education — Pre-service and In-service Training for Nongraded Schools." Letter Number 17, © 1968, SRA, Chicago. By permission of the publisher.

88. Dennison, George. *The Lives of Children.* New York: Random House, 1969.

89. Dispasquale, Vincent C. "Dropouts and the Graded School." *Phi Delta Kappan* 46 (November 1964) : 129-133.

90. "Dissent and Disruption in the Schools, A Handbook for School Administrators." Institute for Development of Educational Activities, Inc., /I/D/E/A/, an affiliate of the Charles F. Kettering Foundation, Dayton, Ohio, 1969, p. 5-7.

91. Dole, Edgar. *Audio Visual Methods in Teaching.* Holt, 1969.

92. Doll, Ronald C. *Leadership to Improve Education.* Worthington, Ohio: Charles A. Jones, 1972.

93. Dreikurs, Rudolf. *Psychology in the Classroom.* New York: Harper, 1968.

94. Dufay, F. R. "When Nongrading Fails." *School Management* 11 (February 1967) : 110-113.

95. Durrell, Donald D. "Implementing and Evaluating Pupil-Team Learning Plans." *Journal of Educational Sociology* 39 (April 1961) : 360-365.

96. Durrell, Donald D. and Harvey B. Scribner. "Problems and Possibilities in Differentiating Instruction in the Elementary School." *Journal of Education* 152 (December 1959) : 72-78.

97. Ebel, R. L. *Measuring Education Achievement.* Englewood Cliffs, N.J.: Prentice-Hall, 1965.

98. Eichhorn, Donald H. *The Middle School.* New York: The Center for Applied Research in Education, 1966.

99. _____. "Middle School Organization: A New Dimension." *Theory into Practice* VII (June 1968) : 111-113.

100. Eldred, Donald M. and Maurie Hillson. "The Nongraded School and Mental Health." *Elementary School Journal* 63 (January 1963) : 218-222.

101. Ellis, P. A. and D. V. Meyer. "The Teacher's Quest for Quality." *NEA Journal* 56 (December 1967) : 24-25.

102. Ellsworth, Ralph E. and Hobart D. Wagener. *The School Library — Facilities for Independent Study in the Secondary School.* New York: Educational Facilities Laboratories, 1963.

103. Emerling, Frank C. and Kanawha A. Chavis. "The Teacher Aide." *Educational Leadership* 24 (November 1966) : 175-183.

104. Englehardt, Nichalous L. *Complete Guide for Planning New Schools.* West Nyack, N.Y.: Parker Publishing, 1970.

105. Esbensen, Thorwald. *Working With Individualized Instruction.* Palo Alto, Calif.: Copyrighted 1968 by Fearon Publishers/Lear Siegler, Education Division. All rights reserved. Reprinted by permission.

106. Espich, James E. and Bill Williams. *Developing Programmed Instructional Materials.* Palo Alto, Calif.: Copyrighted 1967 by Fearon Publishers/Lear Siegler, Education Division. All rights reserved. Reprinted by permission.

107. Featherstone, Joseph. "How Children Learn." *New Republic* 157 (September 2, 1967) : 17-21.

108. _____. "Schools for Children." *New Republic* 157 (August 19, 1967) : 17-21.

109. Fitzroy, Dariel and John L. Reid. *Acoustical Environment of School Buildings.* New York: Educational Facilities Laboratories, 1963.

110. Florida State Department of Education. *Differentiated Staffing — Giving Teaching A Change to Improve Learning.* Tallahassee, Fla., 1968.

111. Foster, R. L. "The Search for Change." *Educational Leadership* 25 (January 1968) : 288-291.

112. Franseth, Jane and Rose Koury. *Survey of Research on Grouping as Related to Pupil Learning.* HEW, Office of Education, Bureau of Elementary and Secondary Education, Document No. FS 5.220:20089. Washington, D.C.: Government Printing Office, 1964.

113. Frymier, Jack R. and Horace C. Hawn. *Curriculum Improvement for Better Schools.* Worthington, Ohio: Charles A. Jones, 1970.

114. Full, Harold, *Controversy in American Education: An Anthology of Current Issues.* New York: Macmillan, 1967.

115. Gagné, R. M. "Educational Objectives and Human Performances." Ed. by J. D. Krumoltz. *Learning and the Educational Process*. Chicago: Rand McNally, 1965.
116. _____, ed. *Learning and Individual Differences*. A Symposium of the Learning Research and Development Center, University of Pittsburgh. Columbus, Ohio: Charles E. Merrill, 1967.
117. Galloway, Charles and Jack Frymier. *Personalized Teaching and Individualized Learning*. Worthington, Ohio: Charles A. Jones, forthcoming.
118. Gardner, J. W. *Self Renewal — The Individual and the Innovative Society*. New York: Harper, 1964.
119. Gesell, Arnold; Frances L. Ilg; and Louise Bates Ames. *Youth: the Years from Ten to Sixteen*. New York: Harper, 1965.
120. Gladstein, Gerald A. "A New Approach for Identifying Appropriate Individual Study Behavior." *The School Review* 71 (Summer 1963): 168-169.
121. Glasser, William. *School Without Failure*. New York: Harper, 1969.
122. Glatthorn, Allan A. *Learning in a Small Group*. Dayton, Ohio: In a publication distributed by the Institute for Development of Educational Activities, /I/D/E/A/.
123. Gleen, Edward E. "Plan Ahead for Team Teaching." *American School Board Journal* 154 (June 1967): 33-36.
124. Goldberg, Miriam L. "Studies in Underachievement Among the Academically Talented." *Freeing the Capacity to Learn*. Papers and reports from the Fourth ASCD Research Institute. Ed. by Alexander Frazier. Washington, D.C.: ASCD, 1960, pp. 56-73.
125. Good, H. G. A. *History of American Education*. New York: Macmillan, © by Macmillan, 1956, 1962.
126. Goodlad, John I. *The Future of Learning and Teaching*. Washington, D.C.: NEA, 1968.
127. _____. "Individual Differences and Vertical Organization of the School." *Individualizing Instruction*. Sixty-first Yearbook. Part I. NSSE. Chicago: Univ. of Chicago Press, 1962.
128. _____. "Nongraded Schools: Meeting Children Where They Are." *Saturday Review* 48 (March 20, 1965): 57-59, 72-74.
129. Goodlad, John and Robert Anderson. *The Nongraded Elementary School*. New York: Harcourt, 1963.
130. Goodlad, John I. and M. Frances Klein. *Behind the Classroom Door*. Worthington, Ohio: Charles A. Jones, 1970.
131. Gores, Harold B. "What Principals Should Know About New Developments in School Design." *NASSP Bulletin* 47 (April 1963): 190-200.
132. Gorman, Alfred H. *Teachers and Learners; the Interactive Process of Education*. Boston: Allyn & Bacon, 1969.
133. Goulet, Richard R., ed. *Educational Change — The Reality and the Promise*. New York: Citation Press, 1968.
134. Griffin, William M. "The Wayland, Massachusetts High School Program for Individual Differences." *NASSP Bulletin* 47 (March 1963): 118-127.
135. Grooms, M. Ann. *Perspectives on the Middle School*. Columbus, Ohio: Charles E. Merrill, 1967.
136. Gross, Ronald and Judith Murphy. *Educational Change and Architectual Consequences*. New York: Educational Facilities Laboratory, 1968.
137. Hamilton, Norman K. and J. Galen Saylor, eds. *Humanizing the Secondary School*. Washington, D.C.: NEA, 1969.
138. Hanslovsky, Glenda; Sue Meyer; and Helen Wagner. *Why Team Teaching*? Columbus, Ohio: Charles E. Merrill, 1969.
139. Hanson, Earl H. "What is Success and How Should We Report to Parents?" *Education* 82 (October 1961): 126.
140. Harris, Ben M. and Woiland Bessent. *In-Service Education: A Guide to Better Practices*, 1969.
141. Hauenstein, A. Dean. *Curriculum Planning for Behavioral Development*. Worthington, Ohio: Charles A. Jones, 1972.
142. Heather, Glen. "Team Teaching and the Educational Reform Movement." *Team Teaching*. Ed. by Judson T. Shaplin and Henry F. Olds, Jr. New York: Harper, 1964, pp. 345-375.

143. Hedges, William D. "Differentiated Teaching Responsibilities in the Elementary School." *National Elementary Principal* 47(September 1967) : 48-54.
144. Henry, Nelson B., ed. *The Dynamics of Instructional Groups.* Fifty-ninth Yearbook. Part II. NSSE. Chicago: Univ. of Chicago Press, 1960.
145. _____, ed. *Individualizing Instruction.* Sixty-first Yearbook. Part I. NSSE. Chicago: Univ. of Chicago Press, 1962.
146. Hillson, Maurie. "The Nongraded School." *New Frontiers in Education.* Ed. by Fred Guggenheim and Corinne L. Guggenheim. New York: Grune and Stratton, 1966, chap. 13.
147. _____. "The Nongraded School: Record Keeping, Evaluation, and Reporting Individual Progress." *Hillson Letter No. 13.* Chicago: SRA, March 27, 1967.
148. Hillson, Maurie, ed., et al. *Change and Innovation in Elementary School Organization: Selected Readings.* New York: Holt, 1965.
149. Hillson, Maurie and Harvey B. Scribner, eds. Readings in *Collaborative and Team Approaches to Teaching and Learning.* New York: Selected Academic Readings, 1965.
150. Holt, John C. *How Children Learn.* New York: Pitman Publishing, 1967.
151. Horrocks, John E. *Assessment of Behavior.* Columbus, Ohio: Charles E. Merrill, 1964.
152. Howard, Eugene R.; Robert W. Bardwell; and Calvin E. Gross. *How to Organize A Nongraded School.* Successful School Management Series. Englewood Cliffs, N.J.: Prentice-Hall, 1966.
153. Howe, Harold. "The Curriculum, the Team, and the School: An Examination of Relationship." *California Journal of Secondary Education* 37(October 1962) : 353-361.
154. Huffmire, Donald W. "Analysis of Independent Study Projects." *Science Teacher* 29(April 1963) : 31-39.
155. Hull, J. H. "Are Junior High Schools the Answer?" *Educational Leadership* 23(December 1965) : 213-226.
156. Hunter, Madeline. "The Dimensions of Nongrading." *Elementary School Journal* 65(October 1964) : 20-25.
157. Jarvis, Galen M. and Roy C. Fleming. "Team Teaching as Sixth Graders See It." *Elementary School Journal* 66(October 1965) : 35-39.
158. Joyce, Bruce R. "Staff Utilization." *Review of Educational Research* 37(June 1967) : 323-336.
159. _____. "The Teacher and His Staff: Man, Media, and Machines." Washington, D.C.: NEA, 1967.
160. Kabler, Robert J.; Larry L. Barker; and David T. Miles. *Behavioral Objectives and Instruction.* Boston: Allyn & Bacon, 1970.
161. Kapfer, Philip G. "An Instructional Management Strategy for Individualized Learning." *Phi Delta Kappan* (January 1968).
162. Keppel, Francis. *The Necessary Revolution in American Education.* New York: Harper, 1966.
163. Kiell, Norman. *The Universal Experience of Adolescence.* New York: International Universities Press, 1964.
164. Kindred, Leslie W. *School Public Relations.* Englewood Cliffs, N.J.: Prentice-Hall, 1957.
165. Kneller, George F., ed. *Foundations of Education.* New York: Wiley, 1967.
166. Knirk, Frederick G. and John W. Childs, eds. *Instructional Technology, A Book of Readings.* New York: Holt, 1968.
167. Kohl, Herbert R. *The Open Classroom: A Practical Guide to a New Way of Teaching.* New York: Review/Vintage, 1969.
168. Kohl, John W.; William E. Caldwell; and Donald H. Eichhorn. *Self-Appraisal and Development of the Middle School — An Inservice Approach.* Univ. Park: The Pennsylvania School Study Council, Inc., July, 1970.
169. Korwitz, Gerald T. "The Management of Motivation." *Phi Delta Kappan* 49(October 1967) : 77-80.
170. Krathwohl, David R.; Benjamin S. Bloom; and Bertram B. Masia. *Taxonomy of Educational Objectives — The Classification of Educational Goals, Handbook II: Affective Domain.* New York: McKay, 1956, 1964. Adapted by permission of the publisher.
171. Krech, David. "The Chemistry of Learning." *Saturday Review* 51(January 20, 1968) : 48-50.

172. Krohn, Mildred L. "Learning and the Learning Center." *Educational Leadership* 21 (January 1964) : 217-222.
173. Lambert, Philip. "Team Teaching for Today's World." *Teachers College Record* 64 (March 1963) : 480-486.
174. Larmee, Roy A. and Robert Ohm. "University of Chicago Lab School Freshman Project Involves Team Teaching, New Faculty Position, and Regrouping of Students." *NASSP Bulletin* 44 (January 1960) : 275-289.
175. Lavin, David E. *The Prediction of Academic Performance.* New York: Russell Sage Foundation, 1965.
176. Leeper, Robert R., ed. *Changing Supervision For Changing Times.* Washington, D.C.: ASCD, 1969.
177. _____, ed. *Supervision: Emerging Profession.* Washington, D.C.: ASCD, 1969.
178. Leggatt, Timothy William. "The Use of Nonprofessionals in Public Education: A Study in Innovation." Ph.D. thesis. Chicago: Univ. of Chicago, 1966.
179. Leuba, Clarence. "Using Groups in Independent Study." *Improving College and University Teaching* 12 (Winter 1964) : 26-30.
180. Lewis, James, Jr. *A Contemporary Approach to Nongraded Education.* West Nyack, N.Y.: Parker Publishing, 1969.
181. Lieberman, Myron. *The Future of Public Education.* Chicago: University of Chicago Press, 1960, p. 77.
182. Lindvall, C. M., ed. *Defining Educational Objectives.* Pittsburgh, Pa.: Univ. of Pittsburgh Press, 1964.
183. Lobb, M. Delbert. *Practical Aspects of Team Teaching.* Palo Alto, Calif.: Copyrighted 1964 by Fearon Publishers/Lear Siegler, Education Division. All rights reserved. Reprinted by permission.
184. Lounsbury, John and Jean Marani. *The Junior High School We Saw: One Day in the Eighth Grade.* Washington, D.C.: ASCD, 1964.
185. Lutz, Frank W. *Toward Improved Urban Education.* Worthington, Ohio: Charles A. Jones, 1970.
186. McCandless, B. R. *Children: Behavior and Development,* 2nd ed. New York: Holt, 1967.
187. McClurkin, W. D. *School Building Planning.* New York: Macmillan, 1964.
188. McLaughlin, William P. "The Nongraded School — A Critical Assessment." The University of the State of New York, the State Education Department, Associate Director-Research Training Program, September, 1967.
189. McNeil, J. R. "Concomitants of Using Behavioral Objectives in Assessment of Teacher Effectiveness." Chicago: Paper read at the AERA Convention, 1966.
190. Madon, Constance A. "The Middle School: Its Philosophy and Purpose." *The Clearing House* 40 (February 1966) : 329-330.
191. Mager, Robert F. *Developing Attitudes Toward Learning.* Palo Alto, Calif.: Copyrighted 1968 by Fearon Publishers/Lear Siegler, Education Division. All rights reserved. Reprinted by permission.
192. _____.*Preparing Instructional Objectives.* Palo Alto, Calif.: Copyrighted 1962 by Fearon Publishers/Lear Siegler, Education Division. All rights reserved. Reprinted by permission.
193. Manlove, Donald C. and David W. Beggs, III. *Flexible Scheduling — Bold New Venture.* Bloomington: Indiana Univ. Press, 1965.
194. Marsh, R. "Team Teaching: New Concept." *Clearing House* 35 (April 1961) : 296-499.
195. Mead, Margaret. "Early Adolescence in the United States." *NASSP Bulletin* 49 (April 1965) : 5-10.
196. _____. *School in American Culture.* Inglis Lecture Series. Cambridge, Mass.: Harvard Univ. Press, 1951.
197. _____. "We're Robbing Our Children of Childhood." *Rochester Democrat and Chronicle* (May 21, 1961).
198. Meierhenry, Wesley C. *Media and Educational Innovation.* Lincoln: Univ. of Nebraska, 1964.
199. Mendenhall, C. B. and K. J. Arisman. *Secondary Education.* New York: William Sloane, 1951.
200. Miles, Mather. *Innovation in Education.* Teachers College Press. New York: Columbia Univ., 1964.

201. Miller, Richard I., ed. *The Nongraded School: Analysis and Study*. New York: Harper, 1966.
202. _____. *Perspective on Educational Change*. New York: Appleton-Century-Crofts, 1967.
203. Moore, Arnold J. "An Approach to Flexibility." *Educational Leadership* 24 (May 1967) : 691-695.
204. Morphet, Edgar L. and Charles O. Ryan, eds. *Designing Education for the Future, No. 3: Planning and Effecting Needed Changes in Education*. New York: Citation Press, 1967.
205. _____. *Designing Education for the Future: Perspective Changes in Society by 1980*. New York: Citation Press, 1966.
206. Morphet, Edgar L. et al. *Educational Organization and Administration*, 2nd ed. Englewood Cliffs, N.J.: Prentice-Hall, 1967.
207. Murphy, Judith. *Middle Schools*. New York: Educational Facilities Laboratories, 1965.
208. NEA "Auxiliary Personnel in the Elementary School." *National Elementary Principal* 46 (May 1967) : 1-100.
209. _____. "How the Profession Feels About Teacher Aides." *NEA Journal* 56 (November 1967) : 16-19.
210. _____. "Individualizing Instruction." *NEA Journal* 54 (November 1966) : 31-40.
211. _____. *Remaking the World of the Career Teacher*. Washington, D.C.: Teacher Education and Professional Standards Conferences, 1966.
212. _____. *The Teacher and His Staff: Differentiating Teacher Roles*. Washington, D.C., 1969.
213. National Society for the Study of Education. *The Changing American Schools*. Sixty-fifth Yearbook. NSSE. Chicago: Univ. of Chicago Press, 1966.
214. Neagley, Ross L. and Dean N. Evans. *Handbook for Effective Curriculum Development*. Englewood Cliffs, N.J.: Prentice-Hall, 1967.
215. Nerbovig, Marcella H. *Unit Planning: A Model for Curriculum Development*. Worthington, Ohio: Charles A. Jones, 1970.
216. Noar, Gertrude. *New Partners in the American School: A Study of Auxiliary Personnel in Education*. New York: Bank Street College of Education, 1967.
217. _____. *Teacher Aides at Work*. Washington, D.C.: NEA, 1967.
218. Nunnally, J. C. *Educational Measurement and Evaluation*. New York: McGraw-Hill, 1964.
219. Olson, Norman G. "Student Clubs Interest Sheet." In literature dissemination to Middle School Students, Independent School District No. 413, Marshall, Minn.
220. Oregon State Department of Education. *A Computer-Developed Modular Flexible Schedule*. A progress report on an Oregon program activity at Marshall High School, Portland, Oregon. Salem: Division of Education Development, Oregon State Department of Education, 1964.
221. Parker, Floyd G. and Richard L. Featherstone. "How to Specify Educational Needs for a New School." *Nation's Schools* LXXIII, No. 1 (1964) : 49-54.
222. Payne, D. A. *The Specification and Measurement of Learning Outcomes*. Waltham, Mass: Blaisdell, 1968.
223. Perkins, Bryce. "Factors Which Have Influenced the Development of the Role of the Paraprofessional in the Public Elementary Schools of Norwalk, Connecticut." Ph.D. thesis. New York: New York Univ., 1961.
224. _____. *Getting Better Results from Substitutes, Teacher Aides, and Volunteers*. Successful School Management Series. Englewood Cliffs, N.J.: Prentice-Hall, 1966.
225. Peterson, Carl H. *Effective Team Teaching*. West Nyack, N.Y.: Parker Publishing, 1966.
226. Petrequin, Gaynor. *Individualizing Learning Through Modular Flexible Programming*. New York: McGraw-Hill, 1968.
227. Polos, Nicholas C. *The Dynamics of Team Teaching*. Dubuque, Iowa: William C. Brown, 1965.
228. Popham, W. J. *Instructional Objectives*. Chicago: Rand McNally, 1969.
229. Popham, W. J. and Eva L. Baker. *Establishing Instructional Goals*. Englewood Cliffs, N.J.: Prentice-Hall, 1969.

230. Postman, Neil and Charles Weingartner. *Teaching As a Subversive Activity*. New York: Delacorte Press, 1969.
231. Pula, Fred John and Charles Fagone. *Multi-Media Processes for Education*. Worthington, Ohio: Charles A. Jones, 1972.
232. Pula, Fred John and Robert J. Goff. *Technology in Education: Challenge and Change*. Worthington, Ohio: Charles A. Jones, 1972.
233. Rand, M. John and Fenwick English. "Toward a Differentiated Teaching Staff." *Phi Delta Kappan* 49 (January 1968) : 265-268.
234. Randolph, Norma and William Howe. *Self-Enhancing Education*. Palo Alto, Calif.: Sanford Press, 1966.
235. Rich, John Martin. *Humanistic Foundations of Education*. Worthington, Ohio: Charles A. Jones, 1971.
236. Robb, Mel H. *Teacher Assistants*. Columbus, Ohio: Charles E. Merrill, 1969.
237. Rollins, Sidney P. *Developing Nongraded Schools*. Itasea, Ill.: F. E. Peacock, 1968.
238. Rosenthal, Robert and Lenore Jacobson. *Pygmalion in the Classroom: Teacher Expectation and Pupil's Intellectual Ability*. New York: Holt, 1968.
239. Schmitthausler, Carl Marvin. "Analysis of Programs Using Nonprofessional Teacher Helpers in Public School Systems." Ph.D. thesis. Berkeley: Univ. of California, 1966.
240. Schmuch, Richard "Concerns of Contemporary Adolescents." *NASSP Bulletin* 49 (April 1965) : 19-28.
241. Shane, Harold G. "The School and Individual Differences." *Individualizing Instruction*. Sixty-first Yearbook. Part I. NSSE. Chicago: Univ. of Chicago Press, 1962.
242. Shane, June Grant; Harold G. Shane; Robert Gibson; and Paul Munger. *Guiding Human Development: The Counselor and the Teacher in the Elementary School*. Worthington, Ohio: Charles A. Jones, 1971.
243. Shaplin, Judson T. and Henry F. Olds, Jr., eds. *Team Teaching*. New York: Harper, 1964.
244. Shaw, Archibald B. et al. "Space for Individual Learning." *Overview* 4 (March 1963) : 30-40.
245. Shideler, Ernest H. "An Individualization Program." *Journal of Higher Education* 5 (February 1964) : 91-98.
246. Shostrom, Everett L. *Man, The Manipulator*. Nashville: Abington Press, 1967.
247. Shulman, L. and E. Keislar, eds. *Learning by Discovery: A Critical Appraisal*. Chicago: Rand McNally, 1966.
248. Simpson, Elizabeth Jane. *Scheme for Classification of Educational Objectives, Psychomotor Domain*. Illinois Teachers of Home Economics, X, No. 4 (Winter 1966-67) : 110-112, 113-144. This material will be published in the *Taxonomy of Educational Objectives, The Classification of Educational Goals: Psychomotor Domain*. Worthington, Ohio: Charles A. Jones, forthcoming.
249. Skinner, B. F. *The Technology of Teaching*. New York: Appleton-Century-Crofts, 1968.
250. Smith, B. Othanel; Saul B. Cohen; and Arthur Pearl. *Teachers for the Real World*. Washington, D.C.: AACTE, 1969.
251. Smith, Lee L. *A Practical Approach to the Nongraded Elementary School*. West Nyack, N.Y.: Parker Publishing, 1968.
252. State Department of Education. *Flexible Staff Organization Feasibility Study-Interim Report*. Tallahassee, Fla., 1969.
253. Sunderlin, Sylvia, ed. *Aides to Teachers and Children*. Association for Childhood Education. Washington, D.C.: Education International, 1968.
254. Swenson, Gardner. *Flexible Scheduling*. Englewood Cliffs, N.J.: Prentice-Hall, 1966.
255. Tewksbury, John L. *Nongrading in the Elementary School*. Columbus, Ohio: Charles E. Merrill, 1967.
256. Thelen, Herbert A. *Classroom Grouping for Teachability*. New York: Wiley, 1967.
257. _____. *Education and the Human Quest*. New York: Harper, 1960.
258. Thiagarajan, Sivasailam. *The Programing Process: A Practical Guide*. Worthington, Ohio: Charles A. Jones, 1971.

311

259. Thomas, R. Murray and Shirley M. Thomas. *Individual Differences in the Classroom.* New York: McKay, 1965.
260. Tobias, Milton. "Disordered Development Is the Key to Unlawful Behavior." *Loyola Digest* (May, 1963) : 5.
261. Torrance, E. Paul. *Education and the Creative Potential.* Modern School Practices Series, No. 5. Minneapolis, Minn.: Univ. of Minnesota Press, 1967.
262. _____. *Guiding Creative Talent.* Englewood Cliffs, N.J.: Prentice-Hall, 1962.
263. _____. *Rewarding Creative Behavior: Experiments in Classroom Creativity.* Englewood Cliffs, N.J.: Prentice-Hall, 1965.
264. Trow, William Clark. *Teachers and Technology, New Design for Learning.* New York: Appleton-Century-Crofts, 1963.
265. Trump, J. Lloyd. "Basic Changes Needed to Serve Individuals Better." *Educational Forum* 26 (November 1961) : 93-101.
266. _____. "Images of the Future II — How the Principal Organizes the Secondary School to Expedite Instructional Improvements." Multilithed paper, n. d.
267. _____. "Images of the Future: A New Approach to Secondary Education." Urbana Commission on Experimental Study of the Utilization of Staff in Secondary School, *NASSP Bulletin* (January 1959).
268. Trump, J. Lloyd and Dorsey Baynham. *Focus on Change: Guide to Better Schools.* Chicago: Rand McNally, 1961.
269. Turney, David T. *Secretaries for Teachers.* Nashville: George Peabody College for Teachers, 1962.
270. Varner, Glenn F. "Team Teaching in Johnson High School, St. Paul, Minn." *NASSP Bulletin* 46 (January 1962) : 161-166.
271. Von Haden, Herbert I. and Jean Marie King. *Innovations in Education: Their Pros and Cons.* Worthington, Ohio: Charles A. Jones, 1971.
272. Vorobev, G. "Developing Independence and Creativity in Students." *Soviet Education* 4 (September 1963) : 41-48.
273. Waite, L. L. "Educational Specifications — Key to Good Buildings." *American School and University* XXXVIII, No. 7 (March 1966), 32.
274. Walbesser, H. H. *Constructing Behavioral Objectives.* College Park, Md.: Bureau of Educational Research, Univ. of Maryland, 1966.
275. Weber, Evelyn. *Early Childhood Education: Perspectives on Change.* Worthington, Ohio: Charles A. Jones, 1970.
276. Wilson, Russell E. "A Study of Educational Specifications for Planning School Buildings, Their Evolution, Preparation, and Contents." Ph.D. dissertation. Univ. of Michigan, 1955.
277. Wiman, Raymond V. *Instructional Materials.* Worthington, Ohio: Charles A. Jones, 1972.
278. Wolfson, Bernice. "The Promise of Multi-Age Grouping for Individualizing Instruction." *Elementary School Journal* 67 (April 1967) : 354-362.
279. Woodring, Paul. "The New Intermediate School." *Saturday Review* 48 (October 16, 1965) : 77-78.
280. Yale-Fairfield Study of Elementary Teaching. *Teacher Assistants.* New Haven, Conn., 1959.
281. Young, Virgil M. "Inquiry Teaching in Perspective." *Educational Technology* 9 (August 1969) : 36-39.

Index

314